THE MEANING OF HOUSING

A pathways approach

David Clapham

First published in Great Britain in July 2005 by

The Policy Press
University of Bristol
Fourth Floor
Beacon House
Queen's Road
Bristol BS8 1QU
UK

Tel +44 (0)117 331 4054
Fax +44 (0)117 331 4093
e-mail tpp-info@bristol.ac.uk
www.policypress.org.uk

British Library Cataloguing in Publication Data
A catalogue record for this book is available from the British Library.

Library of Congress Cataloging-in-Publication Data
A catalog record for this book has been requested.

ISBN 1 86134 637 9 paperback

A hardcover version of this book is available

David Clapham is Professor of Housing at Cardiff University, Wales.

Cover design by Qube Design Associates, Bristol.
Front cover: photograph supplied by kind permission of www.third-avenue.co.uk
Printed and bound in Great Britain by MPG Books, Bodmin.

Preface and acknowledgements

The ideas on which the book is based have been formulated over a number of years with colleagues in the housing research community. A particularly important stimulus has been the work of Jim Kemeny in applying concepts of social constructionism to the field of housing. My early attempts at devising an analytical framework for housing based on social constructionism were first rehearsed in a paper at the European Network for Housing Research conference in Cardiff in 1998. This was developed into an article which was published in the journal *Housing, Theory and Society* in 2002. The commentaries on this article were very helpful in refining the approach on which this book is based. Material in individual chapters in the book has been presented at Housing Studies Association and European Network for Housing Research conferences and I am very grateful for the discussions at these events which have contributed greatly to my thinking. I would particularly like to thank Bo Bengtsson and Chris Allen for very constructive criticisms of particular chapters. Bridget Franklin helped considerably in early studies of the social constructionist approach in our work together on housing management. I am also grateful for her useful comments on the draft typescript.

I have used the approach outlined here as a means of structuring a module in housing for Planning and Geography undergraduate students. Their reactions have helped in decisions about how to present material and what to include or leave out. My confidence in the usefulness of the book to students is based on the success of this module over the years in presenting material in an interesting and accessible format which is seen to be relevant to the lives and future careers of the students.

The author and publishers are grateful to the following for permission to reproduce copyright material: Taylor and Francis for material from Clapham, D. (2002) 'Housing pathways: a post modern analytical framework', *Housing Theory and Society*, vol 19, pp 57-68; Ashgate Publishing for material from Clapham, D. (2004) 'Housing pathways: a social constructionist research framework', in K. Jacobs, J. Kemeny and A. Manzi (eds) *Social constructionism in housing research*, Aldershot: Ashgate; and John Wiley & Sons for material from Clapham, D. (2003) 'Pathways approaches to homelessness research', *Journal of Community and Applied Social Psychology*, vol 13, pp 119-27. We are also grateful to Craig Gurney for permission to use material in Table 5.1 from his unpublished 1996 PhD thesis entitled 'Meanings of home and home ownership: myths, histories and experiences'.

On a personal level I would like to thank Ravi, Lizzie and Hannah for keeping me sane and happy during the long process of writing this book.

Introduction

The main aim of this book is to establish and elaborate a framework for analysing the housing field based on the concept of a housing pathway. This framework casts a different light on housing and opens up a new and potentially important research agenda. The book explores the insights to be derived from the pathways framework by reviewing existing research and drawing attention to the many important gaps in our knowledge of housing. The book is aimed primarily at researchers active in the field of housing, but the review of literature in each chapter may be of interest to students and others interested in particular topics.

The geographical focus of the book is Britain, largely because it would be impossible to include the meaning of housing in other countries within the space available. However, readers not specifically interested in British housing may nonetheless find the book useful in illustrating an interesting and illuminating approach that can be applied in any national context.

The main inspiration for the book has been dissatisfaction with the major ways of analysing the housing field. Most current approaches tend to be positivist in orientation and to ignore or downplay the perceptions and attitudes of individuals and households. Where individuals and households are considered, they are often assumed to have simple, universal and rationalistic aims. Some approaches focus on the choices that households make; others concentrate on the factors that constrain choice. There is little analysis of the interaction between choice and constraint, that is, between action and structure.

The framework developed in this book takes individuals and households as its primary foci and makes their perceptions and attitudes, and the meanings that housing has for them, the centre of analysis. Therefore, the approach adopted here is subjectivist, based as it is on the tradition of social constructionism. This approach is an important complement to the main positivist tradition of housing studies, but it is also justified by the increasing importance of 'lifestyle choice'. Following the work of Giddens and others it is argued that housing has increasingly become a means to an end rather than an end in itself. The end is personal fulfilment and the main task of housing research is to elucidate the links between housing and this overall aim. In this pursuit the concepts of identity and lifestyle are key. The achievement of self-esteem and a positive identity through a chosen lifestyle are said to be an important element of households' housing choices. The book assesses the relevance of this approach.

The framework is built around the concept of a housing pathway, which refers to the household forms in which individuals participate and the routes they take over time in their experience of housing. A housing pathway is linked to many other areas of life and runs alongside an employment pathway. The housing pathway is influenced by changes in household structure relating to marriage, the birth of children, or divorce. Along the housing pathway individuals and households make choices among the opportunities open to them. Some individuals and households have more opportunities than others, depending on decisions they have already made, as well as many other factors including their employment situation and income. The framework also focuses on the factors that structure these opportunities and influence the way individuals and households think about them and react to them.

Chapter One briefly reviews current ways of looking at housing and makes the case for a new approach. It examines some trends in what have been labelled 'postmodern' societies and stresses the importance of individualism and the growing capacity of people to 'make their own lives' with the lessening importance of traditional collective social structures. It is argued that these trends strengthen the value of an approach that places individual and household perceptions, and the meaning they attach to housing, at the centre of analysis. The basis for a new approach is the tradition of social constructionism, which is critically reviewed. It is argued that this approach is not adequate on its own and it is integrated with insights from the work of Giddens and work on the nature of power. The chapter then introduces the concept of a housing pathway and examines ways in which the concept can be used to structure the analysis of housing. The chapter is intended to provide a framework for the rest of the book that is based around the pathways approach and attempts to illustrate and further define the approach.

The book is meant to be read as a whole and each chapter adds to an appreciation of the varied and complex nature of housing and its connections to other aspects of life. The value of the pathways approach in providing a holistic framework of analysis becomes apparent when all of the aspects of housing are considered. However, if readers are primarily interested in particular topics, the chapters can be read independently. Each chapter focuses on individuals and households and the decisions they take in pursuing their housing pathway. But the factors that shape these decisions are also examined. These primarily take the form of discourses that shape not only the perceptions and attitudes of households but the actions of other agencies involved in the production and consumption of housing. One of the most important of these agencies is the state, and discourses are intimately related to public policy mechanisms that influence the type and extent of opportunities open to households.

Chapter Two focuses on the household, which is at the heart of the pathways approach. Demographic trends in the number and make-up of households are reviewed and linked to the changing nature of the family. The trends are made up of individual actions and choices, but these are influenced by discourses that shape popular perceptions and political debate and, therefore, influence policy in areas such as housing. The main discourses of the family are described and their impact on policy assessed. Finally, it is recognised that many households are made up of more than one person. Therefore, to understand the perceptions and actions of households it is necessary to understand how the household functions in terms of the dynamics of interpersonal relationships that create and sustain the routines and actions of the household. For example, how is the decision made about whether to move house? What factors are taken into account, and how are different views within the household reconciled? The chapter points to the need for more research to increase our knowledge of the way that different types of households function and the factors that influence their decisions.

The important interconnections between housing and employment that shape many aspects of housing pathways are explored in Chapters Two and Three. Housing and employment decisions are often inextricably linked for many individual households, and the employment experience can influence the opportunities available to households. At a broader level, government housing policies will be influenced by the current employment situation, which influences housing demand and need, as well as desired future employment policy outcomes, which may depend for their success on appropriate housing being available. Therefore, Chapter Three focuses on work, an important influence on household opportunity. It reviews trends in the labour market and assesses their impact on housing opportunities. An important theme is the impact on housing of what has been termed the 'flexible labour market'. It is argued that housing policy is increasingly seen as an instrument of employment policy as it is dominated by labour market goals. At the same time, employment patterns are leading to different needs and demands from households in the way housing is consumed and paid for. The chapter reviews our meagre knowledge of household decisions on housing and work, and argues for more research in this area to understand the way that different households relate these two important aspects of their lives.

Chapter Four continues this theme by examining the way that households pay for their housing. The chapter highlights our lack of knowledge of how and why households choose to spend very different amounts on housing. It also examines the institutional structures involved in the finance of housing, including government subsidies, and looks at some of their impacts. A particular focus is the structures of the financing of owner occupation and the way that they can lead to affordability problems for some households. Another focus is the present system of Housing Benefit for renters, which can lead to strong disincentive effects associated with poverty and unemployment traps.

Chapters Five and Six focus on the nature of the 'product' that households are consuming and making decisions about. Chapter Five looks at the concepts of house and home. This involves examining the relationship between the physical attributes of the house and its use and meaning. It is argued that the concept of quality in housing is a subjective one and hence defies easy definition or measurement. The meaning of home is discussed at length and its relationship to factors such as tenure assessed. Despite much research in this area in recent years, it is argued that research needs to focus more on the differences between households in their conception of home and its links with issues of identity and lifestyle.

One of the most important features of a house is its location. Chapter Six looks at the concepts of neighbourhood and community. It discusses the design of spaces around houses and the social interactions that take place there. The discourse of community is examined and its impact on design and social relations assessed. A key theme is the existence of different kinds of neighbourhoods that are linked to lifestyle choice. The applicability of the term 'community' to different kinds of neighbourhoods and efforts to create 'communities' are considered.

The next two chapters look at particular points in a housing pathway and examine the way in which the factors considered above interact. The aim is to give a flavour of the pathways approach as it is applied to two common areas of housing experience that have been the focus of much recent research. The chapters present new insights from the pathways approach and indicate the direction for future research on these topics. Chapter Seven examines the process of leaving home and establishing a 'new' household. It discusses how the discourses of labour market flexibility and 'the family' interact with a discourse of 'youth' to influence the actions of young people and their parents as well as government policy towards leaving home. It also examines the factors that shape the success or otherwise of the process. Particular emphasis is placed on the young people who endure some period of homelessness. The chapter then critically examines some attempts to apply a pathways framework to homelessness among young people and uses the shortcomings of this work to suggest directions for future research.

Chapter Eight furthers our understanding of the pathways approach by focusing on the later part of the housing pathway and examining the experience of housing in later life. The primary focus is on the discourses that shape the categorical identity of old age and structure government policy towards the provision of housing and support for older people. It is argued that the current discourse of 'community care' is based on negative views of old age and on professional judgements of need that bear little relationship to the preferences and desires of older people. The chapter argues for a new approach to policy that is based on a discourse which highlights issues of lifestyle, identity and self-esteem and which makes the control that households can exert over their pathway the key criterion. The chapter shows the value of the pathways approach in providing an analytical framework that highlights the relationship between discourses and the perceptions, identity, and lifestyles of individuals and households.

Chapter Nine points towards the future direction of research on housing using the pathways framework. This alternative approach needs a form of research that differs from the traditional positivist approach and highlights particular research methods. Therefore, the chapter looks at the research methods appropriate to a pathways approach and argues for techniques that place the meaning of housing at the forefront of the analysis. The chapter continues by outlining a research agenda for filling the gaps in our current knowledge of housing which have been identified in the book and which the pathways approach highlights. Such a direction for research on housing pathways will deepen our understanding of the meaning of housing.

ONE

Housing pathways

Many frameworks can be used to describe and understand the set of relationships involved in the production, consumption and distribution of housing. This chapter puts forward one way of looking at what will be termed the 'housing field'. This is not to deny the validity or usefulness of other frameworks or to put forward a housing theory that explains all there is to know about the nature and meaning of housing. Any framework offers only a partial insight into any social phenomenon and may obscure as much as it clarifies. Frameworks can be judged on the basis of their internal consistency and of the value of the insights that they provide, which by their very nature will be contested. This chapter reviews very briefly some common ways of looking at the housing field and puts forward a framework, based on social constructionism, that aims to be internally consistent and relatively comprehensive in its coverage. This framework forms the cornerstone of the book and succeeding chapters explore and elucidate the approach outlined here.

Characterising the housing field

Much research into housing is often criticised, either for being atheoretical, or for not making explicit the framework adopted (see Kemeny, 1992). This criticism is undoubtedly correct. Since most housing research in Britain is commissioned by government departments concerned to evaluate the impact of specific government policies, it is oriented to practical and policy issues and adopts an atheoretical, empiricist approach. Its contribution to furthering an understanding of the housing field has been questioned (Kemeny, 1992). In response there has been an upsurge in theoretically aware approaches to the study of housing, which are briefly described here.

A common approach, particularly in introductory textbooks, is to describe and analyse government policy towards housing. It strongly emphasises the legislative and institutional structure of the housing field. Much of the work in this tradition assumes that government policy is an important determinant of housing outcomes. Usually the state is viewed as a neutral arbiter between different interests reacting to 'housing problems' as they emerge. Political ideology is given some prominence as a mediating factor between housing problems and government action to solve them. In the British context political attitudes towards housing tenure and issues such as privatisation are much discussed. The emphasis in discussion of different national housing systems is on the varying definitions of the welfare state and on the construction of typologies of the contrasting relationships between the state and the market (see Esping-Andersen, 1990).

This approach, which is usually identified with the academic study of social policy, has yielded many important insights, but its major drawback is its overemphasis on the state and a corresponding lack of focus on, and understanding of, other actors in the field. Government policies can have many unintended as well as intended effects, which can be understood only in the context of the attitudes, perceptions and behaviour of other actors. An example of this is research into the outcomes of council housing allocation policies (Clapham and Kintrea, 1986). The impact of policies can be gauged only through an understanding of the complex interplay between organisational policies and their implementation on the one hand, and the way that applicants for housing react in the light of their perceptions and attitudes on the other. As Williams and Popay (1999, p 164) point out, welfare recipients are "creative agents, acting upon, negotiating and developing their own strategies of welfare". As a consequence, "They are not passive receivers of policy enactment, instead they help reconstitute the outcomes of formal and informal policy provision".

A further problem with the state policy approach is the withdrawal of many governments (particularly in Europe) from the housing field in recent decades in response to the financial pressures of globalisation and the widespread growth of owner occupation and the market, partly stimulated by privatisation policies. Governments are less important players in housing than in the past, and so concentration on their policies alone does not give a full picture of the housing field. There is a strong argument that their influence has never been as great as sometimes assumed. For example, the 1980 Housing Act in the UK, which introduced the 'right to buy' council houses as a national policy, is often quoted as a landmark in the privatisation of housing and the residualisation of the public sector in Britain. However, local authority sales of housing to tenants existed in some areas before the Act, and the trend of residualisation can be traced back at least to the 1950s (Robinson and O'Sullivan, 1983). Much government policy is following and reinforcing established trends rather than setting new directions.

A contrasting approach to the study of housing is the focus of neo-classical economics on housing markets. Unlike in the previous approach, the emphasis is on the relationships between different actors, which are viewed through the framework of a market. This approach tends to marginalise state involvement, usually characterising it as 'intervention', which can be justified only on certain very specific grounds (for example, for public goods or where there is market failure). The neo-classical tradition tends to be built on simplistic and universal assumptions of human behaviour. Examples are the assumed profit maximisation of companies or the utility maximisation of consumers. Not surprisingly, the approach provides most insights when applied to economic issues such as the determination of house prices or rent levels and when the focus is on housing production or consumption sectors in which private sector agencies play a major role and public 'intervention' is minimal. The approach has less to say about sectors, such as British council housing, that do not fit closely into the market framework because of the dominance of state decision making and the suppression of market processes in aspects such as the distribution of housing, which is undertaken through bureaucratic allocation procedures. Because of the assumption of universal motivation and the lack of focus on the context within which markets operate, neo-classical economists tend to put forward models and conclusions based on them which are said to be applicable in all contexts in which market processes are present. Therefore, the impact of, say, rent control in the private sector can be examined using the same tools and with the same basic conclusions in different countries if the policy instruments are similar.

The geographical approach has many similarities to the neo-classical one and is sometimes combined with it (for an example of the approach, see Clark and Dieleman, 1996). This approach focuses on understanding the factors that influence the spatial distribution of housing. As with the neo-classical approach, the emphasis is on the choices made by households and so common subjects of analysis include the processes of mobility, tenure choice and housing search. In examining these topics, which are also a common focus in the neo-classical approach, more complex assumptions about human behaviour are made. For example, it is assumed that housing preferences will vary over the household life cycle and according to other demographic and economic variables. As we shall argue later, this is a very valuable approach that begins to recognise the complexity of human behaviour, but it still attempts to generate universal propositions, for example, concerning housing careers, without a detailed and appropriate understanding of attitudes and behaviour. There are also problems in the treatment of the constraints on choice. Although it is recognised that the nature and size of the stock of housing available limit choice, there is little focus on how these constraints came about and only a limited understanding of their interrelationship with preferences and attitudes.

The final approach reviewed here is that associated with the sociological tradition. This approach has consisted mainly of applying general sociological thought to the field of housing. Thus, studies of housing using Marxist or Weberian traditions have, in their different ways, drawn attention to the structured inequalities in the distribution of housing (for example, Rex and Moore, 1967; Dickens et al, 1985). Thus, sociological approaches have tended to focus on the constraints on choice rather than on the choice process itself, as in the previous two traditions. This has provided valuable insights into the relationship between housing and the wider society and has drawn attention to the outcomes of the housing system. It has also introduced the concept of power to the study of housing with the realisation that not all households have the same capacity for choice.

Clearly this has been a very brief overview of the main theoretical approaches to the study of housing, which cannot hope to do justice to the rich material that has become available in the search to improve our knowledge of the housing field. The categorisation used here is crude and does not include the often interesting work that has been undertaken at the boundaries of the different approaches. However, current approaches are limited in their focus and there is substantial scope to develop alternative approaches. This does not mean that any theory of housing could ever cover all aspects and have a monopoly on insight. There is value in a diversity of approaches that can offer different kinds of insights. Nevertheless, current approaches are severely limited.

Despite their many differences, the existing approaches share many similarities and problems that have determined the nature of housing research. For example, all of the approaches lack a convincing focus on the behaviour of the actors in the housing system, particularly households. In some approaches they are merely the ciphers of structural forces but, even where households are at the centre of the analysis, as in the geographical and economic perspectives, they are assumed to have simple and universal attitudes and motives. In general it is assumed that households are rational and instrumental in their approach to housing decisions, and there is little empirical work that investigates and attempts to understand how different households perceive and react to the housing context facing them.

Also, all of the approaches are positivist in that they assume the existence of a world of social facts to be uncovered by researchers using quantitative and empirical research methods. The housing field is portrayed as an objective reality that is uncontentious and perceived in uniform ways by the participants in it. A growing body of research in the subjectivist traditions, such as ethnography or symbolic interactionism, would question this approach and provide an alternative way of looking at housing, but this work has rarely been integrated into the mainstream of housing research.

The focus of the different approaches is either on the actions of individual actors, such as households, or on the constraints that are said to limit actions. There is little focus on the relationship between the attitudes and behaviour of the actors on the one hand and the constraints and opportunities which they face on the other. In other words, approaches to the analysis of the housing field have failed to keep up with recent developments in sociology that have taken this agency-structure interface as the focus of their attention.

The common limitations highlighted here would be important to transcend at any time, but a strong argument can be made that the dominant approaches described are increasingly inadequate in the context of current postmodern society. It is to the nature of this context that we now turn.

Postmodernity

The dominant approaches to the study of housing outlined here were derived from paradigms formulated in a societal context very different from today's. Therefore, their foci and implicit assumptions about the nature of the social world are increasingly irrelevant. 'Postmodernity' is a common label given to current society, although it has its critics and some authors use alternatives such as 'late modernity'. There is not the space to enter this debate here, and the term 'postmodernity' will be used in this book. The aim of this section is to give an overview of the main trends that will be considered in more depth in the following chapters.

A common theme in the analysis of current Western societies is globalisation (for reviews, see Waters, 1995; Steger, 2003). Although the volume of world trade has not increased substantially, it is being increasingly dominated by large corporations that operate in many countries. Examples are the multinational car and oil companies that manufacture and sell across the world. Globalisation has many dimensions but two are particularly important to our discussion here. The first is the increasingly global reach of financial markets and the existence of what Waters (1995) calls 'floating finance', whereby money moves freely and rapidly between countries and uses. The housing finance system in Britain has become more integrated into these global flows. Associated with this change has been a discourse that has endowed the concept of globalisation with neo-liberal values and meanings of a consumerist free market world (Steger, 2003). The discourse has emphasised the inevitability of the free flows of capital, seeing globalisation as a natural force that governments are ill-advised to attempt to resist. Globalisation has become what Steger (2003) calls a 'strong discourse' that is "notoriously difficult to resist and repel because it has on its side powerful social forces that have already pre-selected what counts as 'real' and, therefore, shape the world accordingly" (Steger, 2003, p 96).

Globalisation has a number of consequences for housing. The first is caused by the reorientation of national governments that are associated with the globalisation discourse. Regulation and control of a global economy is thought to be increasingly difficult at the national level. The activities of multinational companies and of financial markets are difficult for national governments to influence, and the economic policy of an individual country has to be determined in the light of a possible flight of finance and jobs if conditions are considered to be more conducive elsewhere. This has led to the growth in multinational levels of governance such as the European Union (EU), but it has also left many governments with substantial constraints on their room for manoeuvre in taxation or public expenditure policies. One result has been a widespread reduction in state involvement and expenditure on housing, often including the privatisation of state-owned housing stock. Another has been the withdrawal of state intervention in the regulation of finance for home ownership in the light of the deregulation of general finance markets. One impact of the perceived need to prevent outflows of jobs and capital has been to enhance the flexibility of labour markets, with more job insecurity and greater geographical mobility. Each of these has major implications for housing and will be reviewed later in the book.

Giddens (1990) has argued that globalisation, associated with the rise in information technology, has resulted in a quickening of the pace of change in people's lives and an increasing feeling of alienation and lack of control over the forces that shape their life. Risk is perceived to have increased, whether of global catastrophe such as a nuclear accident or of personal misfortune through unemployment (Beck, 1992).

At the same time there has been a move towards individualism and a decline in traditional institutions that have framed people's life experiences. For example, the nature of the family is changing. It is estimated that by 2010 almost 40% of households in Britain will be made up of a single adult (Scase, 1999). Traditional collective institutions, such as the churches or trades unions, have experienced a decline in involvement and influence. There is a generally felt concern that local communities are in decline as information technology and mobility enable geographical constraints on social networks to be transcended. Traditional class ties are also loosening as new forms of occupational structure emerge with the flexible labour market, and class-based politics is eroded by new sources of fragmentation around gender, race and single issues such as the environment.

Giddens (1991) argues that all these factors constitute an 'opening out' of social life in which individuals are more able to make their own lives by actively making choices. This is encapsulated by the concern with 'lifestyle', by which is meant the desire to choose an individual identity that leads to self fulfilment.

> In modern social life, the notion of lifestyles takes on a particular significance. The more tradition loses its hold, and the more daily life is reconstituted in terms of the dialectical interplay of the local and the global, the more individuals are forced to negotiate lifestyle choices among a diversity of options. (Giddens, 1991, p 5)

Identity can be defined as a sense of who we are as individuals – a sense of self. It is also the way that we project ourselves to others – the way that we want others to see us. Social constructionists argue that identity is forged through social interaction with others. Jenkins (1996) terms this 'the internal – external dialectic of identification'. We constantly judge who we are by how we act towards others and their reaction to us.

> Individual identity – embodied in selfhood – is not meaningful in isolation from the social world of other people. Individuals are unique and variable, but selfhood is thoroughly socially constructed, a product of the processes of primary and subsequent socialisation, and in the ongoing processes of social interaction within which individuals

> define and redefine themselves and others throughout their
> lives.... An understanding emerges of the 'self' as an
> ongoing and, in practice simultaneous, synthesis of (internal)
> self-definition and the (external) definitions of oneself
> offered by others. (Jenkins, 1996, p 20)

Jenkins also sees identity as never settled. Rather, it should be seen as
a process of 'becoming'. Giddens (1991) sees identity as a life project,
which involves both continuity and change as we reflexively adapt to
changing circumstances in order to create a coherent and durable
individual social identity.

Identity is both singular and plural. We have a sense of different
identities that we may adopt in different situations or towards different
people. For example, we may be at the same time a son and a father
and see ourselves differently in our interaction with our mother and
our daughter. At the same time we attempt to forge an overall view of
who we are. This point is well made by Craib (1998, p 4):

> If I suffered a major tragedy in my family life, ceasing to be
> a husband and becoming a divorced man or widower, my
> identity would have changed in an excruciatingly painful
> way but I would still have an identity. Social identities can
> come and go but my identity goes on as something which
> unites all the social identities I ever had or will have. My
> identity always overflows, adds to, transforms the social
> identities that are attached to me.

Identity is about differentiating ourselves from others by forging a
sense of our own individuality. However, it is also about sharing
distinctive features with others – a sense of belonging to a category
defined by similarity. Taylor (1998) makes the important distinction
between categorical and ontological identity. Categorical identity is
concerned with the labels ascribed to us by ourselves and by society.
An example would be our housing tenure, which brings with it a set
of discourses that ascribe its relation to the wider society. This is in
addition to wider categories of class, gender, ethnicity, sexuality,
disability and so on. Ontological identity is how these are forged into
a coherent sense of self-identity.

Categorical identity is a key concept because it mediates between
society and ontological identity. Belonging to a category may be
associated with socially constructed norms of meaning and social
interaction. Fathers are responsible and mature, for example, or sons

are dutiful and loving. Categorical identity is one way in which the individual 'project of the self' relates to structural factors reflected in the expectations of both ourselves and others of appropriate behaviour. However, these categories and their meanings are reproduced or changed through the interactions of individuals – they are the product of the process of dialectical identification in which individuals reflexively live out the categories at one point in time. But this interaction is not simply a matter of individual choice, as categorical identities are forged through relations of power and authority that frame interactions. As Jenkins (1996, p 24) points out, "social identities exist and are acquired, claimed and allocated within power relations. Identity is something *over* which struggles take place and *with* which stratagems are advanced: it is means and ends in politics".

Collective identity also has elements of similarity and difference. Although the category may be defined through similarity, the distinction from other categories is maintained through the recognition of difference. For example, the categories formed around different ethnicities may be important in the formation of identity and its impact on housing and other areas of life. Membership of an ethnic minority category can open up members to discourses of racism that may influence their economic opportunities and reproduce deeply entrenched inequalities of income and wealth, as well as influencing personal identities, meanings and perceptions. Also, belonging to a particular ethnic category can influence a person's identity through the socialisation of cultural or religious norms or people and place allegiances, although these may vary considerably with age, length of time in Britain, and individual choice and circumstances. Some of these factors will affect many ethnic groups in the same way and to the same degree, but others may differ substantially in their impact on particular ethnic categories. Also, as Harrison (2001) argues, ethnicity is one of many categories to which an individual may belong. Therefore, Harrison uses the idea of difference within difference to illustrate the commonalities and differences that are associated with ethnicity. With regard to housing, he argues.

> Certainly it is difficult to 'read off' households' choices and housing careers from ethnicity, material positions or racisms in a simple way. Black and minority ethnic households face common problems in terms of discrimination, and also tend to be materially disadvantaged, but this commonality is overlaid or cross-cut by gender, ethnicity, disability and age, and by highly specific

differences between households and their goals. (Harrison, 2001, p 150)

Chaney (1996, p 4) defines lifestyles as "patterns of action that differentiate people... Lifestyles therefore help to make sense of (that is explain but not necessarily justify) what people do, and why they do it, and what doing it means to them or others". In general a lifestyle is "any distinctive, and therefore recognisable, mode of living" (Chaney, 1996, p 11). Lifestyles are related to the cultural values, attitudes and customs of a society, but are not necessarily determined by them and may not entirely reflect them. The pattern of action in a lifestyle is "a style, a manner, a way of using certain goods, places and times" (p 5). It is also a "distribution of disposable incomes" (p 12) and much interest in the concept has focused on its link to the consumption of goods and services. But it is much more than consumption, focusing on the way that people use places (such as the home or neighbourhood) and their time. Lifestyle is about the use of leisure time, but it may encompass individuals' choices about how to allocate their time between different groups of activities, such as work and leisure, as well as choices within a particular category. Lifestyles also encompass choices about household and family structure and the nature of the relationships involved. Lifestyles have symbolic aspects that may be related to questions of taste (Bourdieu, 1984). These may have a status dimension. In other words, lifestyles may serve as indicators of differential access to financial, educational or material resources and may be invested with normative significance. However, lifestyles are also existential projects or "processes of self-actualisation in which actors are reflexively concerned with how they should live in a context of global interdependence" (Chaney, 1996, p 86). People can reflexively choose and amend lifestyles. They can be "donned and discarded at will" (Chaney, 1996, p 12). Nevertheless lifestyles are 'embedded in the social order' and have both agency and structural dimensions. Lifestyles have elements of individuality and collectivity, and of sameness and difference.

The links between lifestyle and identity are strong. For example, Chaney (1996, p 12) argues that "people use lifestyles in everyday life to identify and explain wider complexes of identity and affiliation". Lifestyles are expressions of identity in daily life. At the same time they help to define our identity by patterning our interaction with others.

The search for identity through the construction of a lifestyle has important implications for housing. Saunders (1990) has argued that home ownership is an important source of this identity, but the impact on people's perception of housing is wider than a focus on tenure alone. Emphasis on the importance of what housing means in the lives of households is growing, as evidenced, for example, by recent work on the meaning of home (see for example Gurney, 1999). The key to this work is that housing is viewed as a means to an end rather than an end in itself. As King (1996, p 35) argues, housing "is a means of fulfilment that allows other human activities to take place".

In order to understand the fulfilment that housing provides, it is necessary to employ a framework that places the subjective nature of the meanings held by households at the centre of the analysis. King (1996) criticises the predominantly objectivist paradigm of both housing research and policy, and argues that it is responsible for the dehumanisation of housing policy and provision that has caused many of the problems evident in the current housing field. He sees housing as "a place of security and enabling for a household" (1996, p 22). Housing, he argues,

> ... is concerned with the relative notion of fulfilment, and thus not with generalised standards. What is sufficient in terms of the quality and quantity of a dwelling is for the individual household to decide. This notion, because it is a relative one personalises housing. It is a view that relegates the significance of aggregated physical structures and standards and places over it an analysis which is necessarily subjective. This subjectivity is because the analysis concentrates on the households who inhabit the structures and not on supposedly objective and rational economic players. It is thus a personalised view of housing – on what it does in people's lives. (King, 1996, pp 23-4)

The capacity to make choices and to search for a sense of identity and self-fulfilment through lifestyle choices brings with it increased risk. Some people find it difficult to compete in the deregulated flexible labour market, whether because of a lack of skills or training, or because of lack of access to employment opportunities. Short-term contracts and self-employment can lead to increased risk of unemployment in an economic downturn or in a rapidly changing technological environment where skills can become redundant or need constant updating. People disadvantaged in the labour market may find themselves both poor in a monetary sense and also excluded from the lifestyle choices open to others. Social exclusion is more than material poverty and, because of the individualisation and changing distribution of risk, can occur in different ways from in the past. An example is the distribution of mortgage arrears and repossessions in the late 1980s and early 1990s in the UK, which occurred in households across the income spectrum (see Chapter Four).

The changes associated with globalisation and individualisation have posed problems for individuals in terms of identity and risk. Also, the changes have set the agenda for governments, which have been forced to restructure housing policy in an attempt to economise on public expenditure in the face of constraints on taxation and an inability to use some policy instruments that impact on the deregulated financial and economic spheres. At the same time, they have faced new demands arising from their support for a flexible labour market, the advocacy and increasing expectation of consumer choice, and the fragmentation of traditional political affiliations.

Attempts to understand housing through a focus on government policy have decreasing relevance in an increasingly privatised and deregulated field, but other traditional approaches also have serious limitations in the new context. The similarities of the existing approaches outlined earlier seem to be disadvantages in furthering understanding of the complexities of housing in the postmodern world.

For example, the emphasis on simple and universal motivations of households and the assumption that they are rational actors are undermined by the importance of the search for identity and self-fulfilment through housing. The meaning of housing to individual households cannot be taken for granted or encapsulated in simple generalisations. A research approach is needed that places the meanings held by households at the centre of the analysis and involves a research method that can identify them. The primary limitation of current approaches is their positivist orientation. In a world of different and competing meanings the idea that there is only one truth or only one rational way of looking at things is problematic. What is needed is what Bauman (1992) calls the 'dissipation of objectivity': "The postmodern perspective reveals the world as composed of an infinite number of meaning generating agencies, all relatively self-sustained and autonomous, all subject to their own respective logics and armed with their own facilities of truth validation" (Bauman, 1992, p 35).

Towards a new approach

The aim of this chapter is to sketch the outlines of a different approach to the analysis of housing systems based on social constructionism, which overcomes some of the drawbacks of existing approaches and helps to fill some of the gaps in our understanding of housing in the current context. This approach forms the cornerstone of the book and is used as an organising principle for the structure and content of the book as a whole and for each individual chapter. Therefore, many of the issues outlined here will be covered in more depth in succeeding chapters.

The term 'social constructionism' has been used in very different ways and to mean different things. Nevertheless, a number of central arguments are shared by advocates of this approach. The fundamental tenet is that social life is constructed by people through interaction. It is through interaction that individuals define themselves and the world they inhabit, and so it is through interaction that the nature of individuals becomes apparent to themselves and to others. Much emphasis in social constructionism is on face-to-face interactions where individuals' subjectivity becomes available to themselves and to others through what they say and their body language. A key element in this interaction is the use of language, which is defined as a system of vocal signs. Berger and Luckmann (1967) argue that language is important because it enables interaction to be detached from the subjective 'here and now' of face-to-face interaction to become objectively available. Language allows interaction about individuals or objects that are not present and enables a vast accumulation of experiences and meanings to be available in the 'here and now'.

> Language is capable not only of constructing symbols that are highly abstracted from everyday experience, but also of bringing back these symbols and presenting them as objectively real elements in everyday life. In this manner, symbolism and symbolic language become essential constituents of the reality of everyday life and the commonsense apprehension of this reality. I live in a world of signs and symbols every day. (Berger and Luckmann, 1967, pp 40-1)

Language is capable of building up zones of meaning that serve as a stock of knowledge which individuals use in everyday life and which can be transmitted from generation to generation. These systems of meaning or discourse represent or describe the nature of the world or reality and come to be taken for granted. They tend to be seen as having an independent, objective reality that is above the subjectivity of individuals. This is partly because they are transmitted from generation to generation through socialisation, and so people perceive that they are the reality of the world into which they are born. They become reified, that is, seen as being other than human products, although social constructionists argue that they are merely the product of, and are sustained only by, human interaction. These discourses play an active part in people's construction of their worlds. Meaning is produced, reproduced, altered and transformed through language and discourse. Social objects are constantly constructed, negotiated and altered by individuals in their attempts to make sense of happenings in the world. In this way language and knowledge are not copies of reality but constitute reality, each language constructing specific aspects of reality in its own way. The focus is on the linguistic and social construction of reality, on interpretation and negotiation of the meaning of the lived world.

Discourses are built up into 'sub-universes of meaning' that define the taken-for-granted reality and include institutionalised codes of conduct that define and construct appropriate behaviour. With the establishment of sub-universes of meaning a variety of perspectives on the total society emerges, each viewing it from the angle of one sub-universe. Each perspective will be related to the concrete social interests of the group that holds it, although it will not necessarily be a mechanical reflection of those interests as it is possible for knowledge to attain a great deal of detachment from the biographical and social interests of the knower. The nature of social order in the society will depend on the ability of people to be able to sustain a particular version of reality as being the objective truth. This depends on the sub-universe of meaning being legitimized through being available to people and being plausible. Therefore, it will contain not merely a description of the world but also explanations and justifications of why things are as they are and why people should act in a certain way.

The social constructionist perspective has become a very fruitful and powerful one in sociology, and an increasing volume of research on housing adopts it (for reviews, see Jacobs and Manzi, 2000, and Jacobs, Kemeny and Manzi, 2004). However, it has not been integrated into mainstream housing analysis and needs some development, building on the criticisms of the approach, if it is to offer major insights into a wide range of issues in the current housing field.

There are numerous criticisms of social constructionism, but two in particular concern us here. The first is criticism of the emphasis on the social construction of reality. It is argued by positivists and 'realists' that there is a material reality that exists outside of language and discourse. In response, Gergen (1999) argues that it is not necessary to differentiate a material world from social interaction as "Relations among people are inseparable from the relations of people to what we call their natural environment" (Gergen, 1999, p 48). To create a dualism is unnecessary because 'the moment we begin to articulate what there is – what is truly or objectively the case – we enter a world of discourse – and thus a tradition, a way of life and a set of value preferences'. Therefore, he argues that the material world cannot be considered separately from language and discourse, which is the means we use to describe and understand it.

An example that has important implications for the study of housing is that of the human body. King (2002) follows Archer (2000) in criticising the supposed neglect of the embodied nature of selfhood.

> Individual subjects are embodied and relate materially to their environment as well as linguistically. Bodies have properties and powers of their own that are active in an environment that is wider than the concept of 'societies conversation' that constructionists claim is the creator of a sense of self. (King, 2002, p 77)

Similarly, Shilling (1993, p 13) argues;

> In contrast to social constructionism, it is important to recognize that the body is not simply constrained by or invested with social relations, but also actually forms a basis for and contributes towards those relations…Social relations may take up and transform our embodied capacities in all manner of ways, but they still have a basis in human bodies.

This argument is particularly important for attempts to understand housing in old age. The wish to escape the individualism and the neglect of social factors in the medical model of ageing (see Chapter Eight) has led many social scientists to stress the socially constructed nature of old age. As a result the importance of the ageing body has been downplayed. As Featherstone and Hepworth (1990, p 375) remind us:

> Human beings share with other species an embodied existence inevitably involving birth, growth, maturation and death. Our naturally endowed capacity to learn, to speak, to produce signs and symbols and to communicate knowledge through them should not make us neglect the unavoidable biological aspects of existence.

Identity is the product of the interaction of embodied individuals. Hockey and James (2003) show the importance of chronological age through categorisation into 'child' or 'adult'. Writers on identity in old age have focused on the 'mask of ageing', in which the attitude of others based on the appearance of the body does not correspond with the identity of older persons, who still sees themselves as the same persons they were at earlier stages of their lives. Craib (1998, p 7) acknowledges that as a middle-aged man he can present himself on the World Wide Web as almost anybody he chooses, but the physical body will intervene in any unmediated, face-to-face encounters. "Once I am seen, my ability to revise my identity is limited: I cannot become a blond teenage girl".

The relationship between the body and its social construction through language is a very difficult one to specify in general terms. However, in practice our focus in this book is on the impact of the body on the meaning of housing rather than trying to explain the material position of the body itself. A social constructionist approach is an appropriate way of doing this. Therefore, the position adopted in this book is what Sayer (2000) has termed 'weak social constructionism'. This recognises a material world outside of discourse, but argues that its nature and its impact on the social world can be understood only through its social construction. Thus, the ageing body is important to a study of housing in old age, but the nature and extent of its impact is socially constructed through interaction and language and discourse.

The second major criticism of social constructionism is the argument that it tends to focus too much on micro-level interactions and does not relate these to the macro-structures of society. Linked to this is the view that social constructionism does not pay attention to issues of power.

Social constructionism is a wide area with many different approaches and this criticism does have some weight with regard to some of them. For example, ethnomethodology following the work of Garfinkel (1967) does tend to focus entirely on micro situations. It is also true that the concept of power is not at the forefront of Berger and Luckmann's analysis, so it can be difficult to work out from their analysis why any one social construction of reality is accepted in society rather than others. Despite this criticism, much work in the social constructionist tradition has been concerned with the way that social institutions which pattern behaviour are constructed. It has often had an implicit view of power, even if it has been a pluralist view of many competing centres of power rather than of any one dominant force. Nevertheless, this area needs to be further developed.

Cicourel (1981) argues that social constructionism has tended to give primacy to individual agency in the creation of social worlds through micro interactions rather than seeking to integrate and give an equal causal role to agency and structure or the micro and the macro. This integrationist approach is the central concern of Giddens's structuration theory (Giddens, 1984), and the adoption of elements of his approach can add strength to a social constructionist analysis.

There is not the space here for a full exposition of Giddens's structuration theory (for a review, see Craib, 1992), but the essence of his approach is to reconstitute what he sees as the dualism of agency and structure in sociological thought as a duality. Structures do not have an independent existence but are produced and reproduced by human agency at both the individual and institutional levels, where they serve both to constrain and to enable action (Giddens, 1984).

Individual agents act on the basis of their practical consciousness, that is, the stored knowledge of what is appropriate in particular circumstances. In this way actors carry knowledge of social structures outside the moment of action. Action is consciously intentional but has the unintentional effect of reproducing structures. The key for Giddens is the analysis of social practices which, so he argues, have both a structural and an agency element:

> Social structure has always to be conceived of as a property
> of social systems 'carried' in reproduced practices embedded
> in time and space. (Giddens, 1984, p 170)

> The basic domain of study of the social sciences, according
> to the theory of structuration, is neither the experience of
> an individual actor, nor the existence of any form of societal
> totality, but the social practices ordered across timespace.
> (Giddens, 1984, p 2)

The centrality of time and space in Giddens' approach, which is built upon the time geography of Hagerstrand (1976) and others, has strong attractions for those interested in housing. As we shall show later, it draws attention to the social practices inherent in the movement of households through the housing field during their life course, and also to the locales of social practices, some of the most important of which are the home and the local neighbourhood.

There is much in Giddens' framework that can be reconciled with a social constructionist approach, and indeed some authors have bracketed him with social constructionists on the basis of his supposedly over-emphasising human agency (see for example Clegg, 1989). In particular, the emphasis on social practices with their agency and structural dimensions is a valuable one, which strengthens social constructionism and counters the criticism that it lacks a structural dimension. However, there are strong differences between Giddens' work and a social constructionist approach. Specifically, Haugaard (1992) points out that Giddens' concern is with individual actors who reproduce social structures through their actions. A social constructionist view would be that social structures are reproduced or changed through the *interaction* of individual actors; and it is here that power relations become important. Haugaard (1992) analyses different forms of interactions and argues that structures are reproduced only where a shared perception of a rule is affirmed. In other words, if one actor structures, in the sense of starting the interaction in a way that follows structural practices, the second party to the interaction can either respond in the same style, which means that the structure is reproduced, or can intentionally refuse to follow the structural practices (what Haugaard calls 'destructuration') or can not know how to respond in an appropriate way ('non-restructuration'). Interactions of this kind can take place in situations of consensus or of conflict over the appropriate rules to follow.

This analysis sits well with relational approaches to power, which see power as existing and being manifest only in the relationships between different actors. The individual is neither powerful nor powerless, as power outside of a specific context is meaningless (Clegg, 1989). Clegg (1989, p 20) views power as "best approached through a view of more or less complex, organised agents engaged in more or less complex, organised games". Clegg describes a world in which power is manifested through shifting and unstable alliances in a state of flux. However, relationships can be fixed or reified in the sense that they are patterned by mutually accepted 'rules of the game'. These may be fixed only temporarily and may be changed through exogenous factors or through the game itself. Clegg's concept of the rules of the game can be easily reconciled with Giddens' notion of social practices. The structural element of both is manifest in the way that they reflect social practices in the wider society. An example would be the way that the allocation priorities of a housing organisation reflect societal norms of a family. The agency element is the way that the specific interaction between a housing officer making a letting and the applicant can either reinforce or challenge these norms in the particular case (in Haugaard's terminology, either 'restructure' or 'destructure'). Over a period of time repeated interactions that destructured in a particular way may have some influence in changing the societal norms, although this will be dependent on the power relationships associated with the norms.

Clegg stresses that reification of power rarely occurs without resistance, which may take two forms. The first and most common is resistance within the existing rules of the game. An example is the way applicants for public rented housing may try to get the best deals they can within the current allocation policy. The major influences on the outcome of the game will be the organisation and tactics of the parties. By 'organisation' is meant the effective utilisation of resources at a party's disposal. In the case of housing applicants, they may have few resources at their disposal even if they have the ability to argue their case and an understanding of the allocation policy. In both these respects the housing officer is likely to have greater resources than the applicants and can deploy the sanction of withdrawing from the interaction. Applicants may have to resort to seeking help through a tenants' association or a local councillor or the press.

The second form of resistance is through contesting the rules of the game and attempting to change them. This may be done by contesting the meaning in which one is being implicated by others. Applicants may, for example, use the tenants' association to attempt to change the nature of the allocation policy so that it does not discriminate against certain forms of household, thus strengthening their cases. This may involve challenging wider concepts of the 'normal' family.

With the incorporation of ideas of structuration and relational power, the social constructionist perspective can be used to analyse housing in ways that can overcome some of the drawbacks of existing dominant approaches. However, in order to do this some mediating concepts are necessary to bridge the gap between the general theory and its specific application. The key concept in drawing together the threads of this approach is that of a housing pathway and it is to this that we now turn.

Housing pathway

Earlier, the importance was stressed in the postmodern context of the ability to make one's life through choice in the light of the loosening of traditional structures and the resultant differentiation in lifestyle. Therefore, an approach is needed which focuses on the household but which avoids the inadequacies of traditional approaches in economics and geography which assume universal and simple attitudes and motivations.

However, in clearing the ground for such an analysis it is necessary to confront the problem identified by Kemeny (1992) of the difficulty of identifying a household. He points to ambiguities in definitions used in, for example, the census, and argues that the forming, breaking and re-forming of households means that the concept is not a solid base on which to build analysis. Nevertheless, as Kemeny accepts, housing is consumed by individuals as households, which may consist of more than one person. Therefore, there is no practicable alternative but to use the concept of household as the basic unit of analysis in housing while accepting that there are substantial difficulties in its use.

The adoption of the household as a focus of analysis does not mean that individuals are ignored. Individuals have housing pathways, but large portions of most pathways are spent as members of multi-person households. These may be different multi-person households, for example, ranging from the family home in childhood to a shared house as a student, one or more marital homes and perhaps an institution in old age. There must be a twin focus on the individual pathway and on the pathway of the households to which persons belong during their life courses. Bengtsson (2002) rightly argues that life planning, identity and self-fulfilment are as much individual as household projects and so the household should be 'opened up' to the analysis of relations within it. There is already an interesting, although limited, literature on interactions within households which sheds some light on the negotiations, compromises and conflicts that are an inevitable part of living together (see Chapter Two). Important structural issues of gender relations, parent–child relationships, age-related roles and discourses of appropriate family life can all be implicated in these relationships. Power is a key element in the reconciliation of any different or conflicting expectations.

However, the important and interesting area of intra-household dynamics can be opened up without abandoning the focus on the household. The household focus is vital because it is the unit in which people consume housing and make decisions about it. It may well be that two adult members of a household hold different meanings of a home and different expectations and aspirations. But as a household they have to reconcile these in order to live in the same house or to make a decision about their housing circumstances. It is important to understand the composite household view of this situation, but it is not sufficient. It is also vital to understand the way this view is constructed through the interaction of the people concerned.

Therefore, throughout the book the focus is on both the individual and the household pathways.

The fundamental tool suggested here for the analysis of housing is the concept of a housing pathway. This is defined as patterns of interaction (practices) concerning house and home, over time and space. The concept owes much to Giddens' idea of social practices and his borrowing of the time-space geography of Hagerstrand (1976). It also builds on concepts of a housing career. Before expanding on the nature of a pathway it is important to be clear about the nature of the concept. It is used here as a framework of analysis – a way of framing thought. It is essentially the application of a metaphor and as such serves to illuminate some aspects of the housing field (and of course, like any framework, to hide other aspects). It is not a theory, although theories may be developed from its use from either empirical enquiry or analytical reasoning. Nor is it a research methodology, although it may provide a framework for one. The concept of a pathway is offered as a way of ordering the housing field in a way that foregrounds the meanings held by households and the interactions that shape housing practices as well as emphasising the dynamic nature of housing experience and its interrelatedness with other aspects of household life.

The housing pathway of a household is the continually changing set of relationships and interactions that it experiences over time in its consumption of housing. These may take place in a number of locales such as the house, the neighbourhood or the office of a landlord or estate agent. Previous work using the concept of a housing career has concentrated on the price, physical space and quality of the house that is consumed as well as the quality of the neighbourhood in which it is located (see for example Clark and Dieleman, 1996). Quality is usually objectively defined and graded, with price often being used as a quality indicator in a market situation. The focus in this kind of analysis has usually been on changes in consumption in terms of moving house (despite the acceptance that mobility is quite low). Mobility is characterised as involving the decision to exchange one house with a particular set of physical, tenure and locational characteristics at a particular price, for another house with another set of characteristics. Analysis has particularly focused on changes in tenure or in location. From this has developed the idea of a housing career in which households will achieve a set of preferences by moving house. This has been characterised as usually (but by no means always) an upward movement in housing and neighbourhood quality, which can be triggered by certain life-course events such as marriage or divorce or the birth of children or certain labour market-related changes such as a change of job or unemployment or retirement.

The concept of a housing career is a valuable one, and the pathways approach attempts to build on it. A housing pathway includes these elements, but also seeks to capture the social meanings and relationships associated with this consumption in the different locales. Therefore, at one point in time a household will be consuming a particular form of housing that will have different types of characteristics. There will be the physical characteristics of the house including the space, layout, and condition of the property. At the same time the house will have a particular set of meanings to the household which may relate to its use as a home and the patterns of interaction within it. The house may be an element in the identity of the household, and the individuals within it, and may be a factor in lifestyle choice.

Meanings are formed and expressed through interactions. In housing, such interactions may be with other households living in the neighbourhood or with professionals such as housing officers or building society staff. These interactions could involve different sets of meanings and involve the kind of power games highlighted earlier. For example, Clapham, Franklin and Saugeres (2000) examined the interactions between housing officers and tenants. These often involved disagreements over meanings associated with the category of tenant or the rules of the game that framed interactions. Tenants would put forward their situation as they saw it and the housing officer would interpret it in the light of predetermined categories based on organisational policies and procedures. Implicit in these policies and procedures, and the way they were implemented, were conceptions of appropriate behaviour by 'good' tenants. Behaviour that accorded with this norm was rewarded and inappropriate behaviour punished, for example, by refusing to use discretion to favour the tenant. In these interactions the housing officer was in a powerful position, with the tenant being a supplicant and not always possessing the knowledge or the skills to be able to challenge the judgement of the housing officer. Such interactions structured the nature of the landlord–tenant relationship.

Implicit in the social construction of the 'good' tenant, that is, the categorical identity of tenant, were wider structures. These included the concept of social exclusion, which defined the nature of poverty and framed the way poor tenants were seen. Conceptions of the appropriate role of council housing as a form of tenure and its role were also important. Implicit in the actions of some housing officers were also ideas of appropriate lifestyles and behaviour as a neighbour, which had a social class dimension. Housing officers usually came from a different social class than the tenants. Therefore, an understanding of a housing pathway is dependent on analysis of the more structural social constructions that framed interactions and the meanings held by households and others. In turn these wider structures were partly reproduced through housing interactions.

Government housing policy is often important in mediating between wider social structures and household pathways. The analysis of policy should involve not just the description of policy mechanisms and the way they are implemented, but also the language and meanings of policy documents. Discourse analysis of this kind has recently become recognised as an important element in understanding housing (see Hastings, 2000). The language of policy influences the meanings held by actors and therefore frames interactions.

One of the major strengths of the pathways approach is the recognition that changes in housing can involve a different set of social practices as well as the more widely recognised physical changes. In addition, the consumption of housing can be modified substantially even without mobility because of a change in social practices. For example, a change in the management policy of a landlord or the hiring of a new housing officer may change the nature of the social interactions around consumption of the house. A change in rhetoric used by government or the media may change the meaning that a household gives to its tenure position. Rising interest rates or a change in financial circumstances because of unemployment may also change the meaning that a household gives to a house, and influence identity and lifestyle.

One of the other major differences of the pathways approach from previous work on housing careers is the absence of any assumption that households have a universal set of preferences and act rationally in their attempts to meet them. Forrest and Kemeny (1984) in their discussion of housing careers discussed the idea of a strategy. They argued that some households have a clear idea of what they want to achieve and pursue a proactive strategy to achieve it. Others make decisions on a more ad hoc basis largely in reaction to external events. They have a coping strategy rather than a plan. Clearly households may have coping strategies at some times in their lives, but act on a more long-term basis at others. Therefore, the division is not a particularly useful one. Giddens (1991) uses the more neutral term 'life planning', which will be adopted here. In the housing pathways approach the focus is on ascertaining the perception the household has of its housing situation and the meanings that it attaches to it, without attempting to impose a predetermined set of assumptions as to what these will be and how the household will attempt to achieve them. This is particularly important because of the extent of lifestyle difference that postmodernity has brought with it. Households may vary significantly in the meaning they attach to the physical structures or location of houses.

Housing is not consumed in isolation from other aspects of life. Moving house may be triggered by employment or family issues. The meaning attached to a house may be part of a personal identity and lifestyle that includes type of employment, choice of clothing, type of car owned and so on. All of these elements need to be considered together as it may be impossible to disentangle them satisfactorily. Therefore, a housing pathway will run alongside and be closely associated with other types of pathway such as employment. Here the concept of life planning can be used as an integrating device for these different elements.

Households undertake life planning in a search for identity and self-fulfilment. The importance of identity has already been stressed and it can play a key role in the concept of a housing pathway. It has been argued that identity signals who people think they are and how they think they belong. It can be complex, fragmented and fractured. It is never singular but is multiple (Hall, 1996). It was earlier stressed that identity is not just of our own making but is influenced by the discourses which categorise and place us in society. Categories are ubiquitous in public policy and in common discourse in housing as in other fields. The example of tenure has already been given. Another example is the shock that home owners who have been evicted from their homes because of mortgage arrears experience in changing category from home owner to homeless person (Burrows and Nettleton, 2000). Categories are not always of our own choosing and do not all carry the same social standing. Clearly for home owners to become categorised as homeless persons carries a substantial reduction in social status. It will influence the way they are treated in society through the different discourses and practices that are associated with each category. These contain normative guidelines that reflect expectations of behaviour and attitudes both of those in the category and of others towards them. For example, Gurney (1999) has drawn attention to the normalising discourse around home ownership that ascribes it superior status to that of a tenant and contains the assumption that it is the natural state of affairs to be aimed at by all responsible citizens.

Wider categories may have a substantial impact on the housing situation of a household. The example of ethnicity was used earlier. Another example, considered in detail later, is the social construction of the discourse of old age that is related to the housing options available to older people. It is associated also with the expectations of older people themselves as well as of others towards them such as health-care workers and medical staff. The categorical discourse may carry expectations of appropriate housing behaviour in old age. An example is the expectations associated with the role of sheltered housing for older people. The form of this provision and the discourse associated with it are strongly linked to general discourses of old age.

The existence of categories and in particular the discourses associated with them are usually the subject of differing and competing views. For example, the discourses associated with physical and mental disability have been actively contested by professions, government agencies and interest groups in what has been called the politics of identity. It is here that the power games outlined earlier are played in which the actors attempt to mobilise their resources to ensure that their discourse is the one adopted in public policy and in general discourse.

Analysis of the politics of identity and the resultant categories with their associated discourses are an important element of any analysis of housing pathways. Categorical identity plays a vital role in mediating between ontological identity and the normalising discourse of social structure. Housing categories are related to, and have to be seen in relation to, wider social categories.

In their journey along their housing pathway households will face certain opportunities. The nature of these opportunities will depend on many factors such as government housing policy, the availability of housing in particular locations and the resources of the household. Housing usually has to be paid for and a major focus of the pathways approach has to be on the way that households pay for housing and the factors that influence their capacity to do so. These factors will include their income, labour market position, and the housing finance and subsidy institutional structure, and they may impact differentially on individual households and so lead to a pattern of inequality in the distribution of housing opportunities. As Giddens (1991, p 6) argues:

> Indeed, class divisions and other fundamental lines of inequality such as those connected with gender and ethnicity, can be partly defined in terms of differential access to forms of self-actualisation and empowerment.... It should

> not be forgotten that modernity produces difference, exclusion and marginalisation.

Household decisions on how much to spend on housing relative to other expenditures may also be an important factor on which little is known (see Chapter Four). We need more research that links the wider economic and financial institutional structures with household decision making. The pathways approach serves to highlight this linkage.

The value of the time element of a pathway has been shown in research on homeless young people. This has found the housing circumstances of some young people to be fast-changing as they move in and out of homeless situations. For example, it was common in a sample of young people in Glasgow to find that they would alternate between staying in the family home, staying with friends, living in a hostel and sleeping rough (Fitzpatrick and Clapham, 1999). Any snapshot of their situation at any one point in time would give a misleading impression of their circumstances.

Another example of the importance of a time dimension to an analysis of pathways is the housing situation of older people, which is strongly influenced by their circumstances in earlier parts of their life course. Clapham, Means and Munro (1993) draw the distinction between three different types of time in which housing pathways are structured: individual time (how old the individual is); family time (the stage of the family lifecycle); and historical time (the prevailing social, political and economic conditions). Different cohorts of people reaching retirement age, for example, will have experienced different circumstances, which will influence their housing situation. Households forming in the 1930s would have had opportunities to enter owner occupation not available in the 1920s.

Junctions in pathways are important points in a similar way to mobility in the concept of housing careers. The factors that are associated with a change in the pathway are key analytical foci. They could include, for example, the factors that enable a household to become owner occupiers or that enable a homeless person to gain access to and sustain a tenancy. Housing policy may be framed in terms of the desirable outcomes at junctions and certainly they can form an important element in the judgement of success of any policy. The pathways framework places emphasis on the dynamic element of the housing experience. The most appropriate way to judge public policies is on the basis of their impact on housing pathways over time.

The focus so far has been on the consumption of housing, but of course, production of the physical stock of dwellings is an important influence on this (see Chapter Five). There has been much research on the nature of the production process (see for example Ball, 1983) that has shed light on the goals and processes of the house–building industry. There has been less work on the nature of the finished product in terms of the design and its influence on the way that housing is consumed. The marketing strategies of house builders and estate agents are interesting in the way they link consumption of housing with lifestyle. Most volume builders have a small number of standard designs to which they give names such as 'Regency'. The basic shell of houses is often the same, differing only in decorative finish. Clearly there is a recognition here that buying a house is a part of lifestyle choice; and the meanings that households derive from their consumption of a house are important to their decision to buy.

The emphasis so far in this chapter has been on the pathways of individual households and the assumption that the primary focus would be on understanding these household pathways. It was argued earlier that a focus on an individual must not be lost because of the increasing flexibility and instability of traditional household forms. But another key issue is the move from the level of the household pathway to a broader level to enable generalisations to be made. One of the key themes of the book is the need for disaggregation and differentiation in assessing household meanings, attitudes and behaviours that have all too often been over-generalised in the traditional approaches. However, some degree of generalisation is necessary in order to understand the relative prevalence of different pathways or their constituent meanings, or to design national housing policy, or to characterise the housing system in comparison with other countries. In any analysis the basic unit is the pathway of the individual household, but it may be possible to discern general patterns and so to construct generalised categories of pathways. Some pathways may be small tracks with little traffic while others may be motorways in the sense that the route is shared with many other households. Clearly analysis of the motorways is a fruitful way of understanding the key features of housing in a country, although it is important not to lose sight of the range or spread of experience. Generalised pathways can be constructed from the results of empirical research or as ideal types based on theorising, which could then be used as hypotheses for empirical research.

An important feature of the analysis of pathways in the remainder of the book is the attempt to construct typologies of different household pathways. This is done to move beyond generalised analysis based on the view that all households have similar meanings and act in similar ways, while formulating categories that are general enough to enable understanding of the nature of the housing field as a whole.

Households will travel along a particular housing pathway over time. Sometimes the pathway will be a motorway and they will be travelling with many others. However, there will be junctions at which choices have to be made and part of a journey could be along a small track not often frequented, or even involve marking out a new trail. Nor does the journey necessarily lead to the same or even any predetermined destination. Travellers can travel in hope or enjoy the journey for its own sake. Neither is any destination necessarily further forward than the starting point. Journeys can be regressions or vary in direction. They may be straight or meander indeterminately.

Conclusion

The chapter has argued that current perspectives on housing are limited in that they all share a positivist orientation, assume simple and universal household attitudes and motivations, and do not effectively deal with the relationship between structure and action. It is argued that these limitations are important in a postmodern society where the emphasis on a search for identity and fulfilment through lifestyle choice makes the meanings held by households crucial to an understanding of housing. Housing is increasingly viewed by households as a means to the end of personal fulfilment rather than as an end in itself.

In these circumstances an approach to the analysis of housing is needed that is based on social constructionism and, therefore, can give due importance to the subjective meanings held by households. However, social constructionism needs to be developed to incorporate insights from Giddens' theory of structuration, which overcomes the common criticism of constructionism that it overlooks the structural dimensions of interaction. Through the concept of social practices, the agency and structural elements of interaction can be reconciled. Also added is a conceptualisation of power that can enable the outcomes of interaction to be explained and analysed.

With the use of this framework, the concept of a housing pathway is developed, which is defined as the social practices of a household relating to housing over time and space. The elements that need to be included in any analysis of pathways have been highlighted. Although the basic analytical tool is the individual household pathway, ways that pathways can be generalised in order to enable a wider-ranging analysis were discussed. These involved the identification of common pathways (motorways, to use the path analogy) or of ideal typical pathways.

The approach outlined here is not put forward as the only way of viewing housing. Like any approach, it foregrounds some issues and offers little insight into others. Nevertheless, it is argued that it is a useful addition to the conceptual armoury of the housing researcher. In a postmodern world, increasingly dominated by concerns about identity and lifestyle choice, the housing pathway concept offers a way of integrating these concerns into housing analysis and of understanding the meaning of housing in the postmodern search for self-fulfilment.

The concept of housing pathways offers a framework for the rest of the book. Each of the chapters is based either on factors that influence pathways or on particular stages in a pathway. The analysis in the chapters puts some flesh on the bare bones of the approach outlined here. In particular, each chapter focuses on the meanings and actions of the household while contextualising this by examining the structural forces that frame them. These are the discourses that shape the way that households view their housing and its relationship to other parts of their lives, as well as public policy and the form and practices of housing institutions and therefore the opportunities that households face. Meanings are socially constructed through interaction and so a particular focus will be on the interactions between households and housing organisations and the strategies that households adopt in order to achieve their objectives through these interactions. Where the information is available, attempts will be made to construct typologies of different kinds of household meanings and behaviour and the pathways that result.

TWO

Households and families

One of the key features of the pathways approach is that it puts the household at the centre of the analysis of housing. Insight into the attitudes and meanings held by households about their housing circumstances and their influence on their behaviour is crucial to an understanding of the housing field and is an important element of the search for identity. However, some problems with adoption of the household as the basic building block have already been alluded to in Chapter One. There are difficulties in defining a household precisely, especially as households continuously form, split and re-form. Nevertheless, people consume housing as households and so it is important to examine how the household functions. One criticism of much housing research (and policy) is that it has stopped at the front door, treating the household like a black box that responds in predictable ways to external stimuli. The difficulty is that, in practice, the responses are not always predictable and vary considerably between households. Therefore, it is necessary to go beyond the front door and attempt to understand how different households understand the world and why they act as they do.

The constant making and remaking of households is a problem, but it is also a process that is crucial to the housing field. For example, the rate at which households form and dissolve is an important determinant of the demand or need for housing. Changes in the size and structure of households can also influence the number, size and type of housing required. Understanding these processes is therefore essential to successful planning by governments and housing developers.

This chapter starts with a discussion of the difficulties involved in settling on a useful definition of a household. The concept of a household is compared with that of a family, and the relationship between the two is explored. The pattern of households is changing in the context of changing family structures. Contact between family members is diminishing and changing in form, but the evidence is that the family is an important element of many people's lives. The changes are influenced by competing discourses of 'family' that are present in political discourse and frame public policy as well as the decisions of people in their everyday lives. Two popular discourses –

one associated with the 'new right' that focuses on the so-called breakdown of the traditional family, the other associated with left-of-centre political parties that highlights family diversity – are examined. This discussion emphasises the normative element of household construction.

Some of the main trends in household size and structure and projections for the future are then examined briefly. Chapter One drew attention to arguments that the nature of the family was changing considerably in postmodern society; this section points to the increasing diversity that has two major implications for the study of housing outlined in Chapter One. The first is the difficulty in using any concept of a 'family life cycle' when experiences vary so widely. The second is the inappropriateness of assuming universal motivations of households when household structure and functioning vary so much.

The final section looks inside the household and examines what is known about the relationships between household members, in order to shed some light on how households make decisions, particularly in the field of housing. It is clear from the review that there are large gaps in our knowledge in this area, which must be a priority for future research.

Throughout the chapter examples from housing are used to illustrate the applicability of the analysis and the importance of the issues raised to the housing field. Many issues relating to the household will be considered later in the book, when their impact on housing pathways is explored. This chapter provides the background for these later discussions.

What is a household?

The common-sense definition of a household is one person or a group of people who live together in a house. The first problem is in defining 'living together'. The census traditionally focuses on collective housekeeping and eating arrangements as the essence of a household. But are older people in a household when they live in a residential home where meals are shared? What is the position of a group of students sharing a flat or a lodger in a self-contained room in a house with a family? How often do meals have to be shared? Are children away at boarding school still members of a household even though they are only there during the school holidays? Is a married couple living with one of their parents until they can afford to buy a house of their own part of the parents' household, or are they in an in-between phase in what has been called a hidden or concealed household?

The second problem is the precise definition of a house. Does it include communal living arrangements as in a nursing home? Are residents in an institution of this kind in one household, in a household of their own, or not in any household? These are difficult questions.

The intention here is not to put forward one universal definition of a household because the most applicable definition will vary according to the purpose for which it is to be used. For the purposes of this book the focus is on the consumption of a dwelling, and all living arrangements will be included on the grounds that all are interesting and important and closely linked to what may be called houses on any narrow definition of that term. In the same way, all people who consume housing of some kind will be included, even if it is not clear on what basis decisions on their housing are made.

It is important to distinguish between a household and a family. Ball (1974) defines the household as a spatial category where a person or a group is bound to a particular place. In contrast, a family is generally seen as a group of people bound together by blood or marriage ties. Of course, this definition is contested, as we will see later, and is increasingly challenged when the popularity of marriage is declining and the incidence of cohabitation of couples increasing. Nevertheless, the emphasis in definitions of the family is on blood or emotional ties. The definition of a household is based on the joint consumption of housing.

The difference in definitions of a household and a family is important because the two are not coterminous. As Muncie and Sapsford (1997) point out, families may form households but do not always do so. Parents may separate; children may be sent to boarding school. Conversely, a group of people may live under the same roof and not consider themselves to be jointly a family. A group of students sharing may each consider themselves to be part of their parents' family even though they are not living with them. Similarly, older people may consider themselves to be part of a family with their children despite living apart.

Although the definitions of a household and a family are conceptually distinct, the two are closely related in practice. The discourses associated with 'family' influence the living arrangements that people use, and vice versa.

'Family' discourses

The family as a social institution has varied over time and between countries and cultures. It is a social construction that is often contested with different normative conceptions of what it does and should involve. These both influence behaviour through the attitudes and perceptions of individuals and in turn are shaped by that behaviour. They are also influential in shaping housing policy, as we will see later. Policy instruments can contain implicit or explicit conceptions of what a family should be and how its members should behave and can be designed to reward behaviour deemed to be appropriate and to punish behaviour labelled inappropriate.

In the past 20 years in Britain there has been a hotly contested debate over the 'family', which has been reflected in political discourse and in policy documents and instruments. Two competing conceptions and their corresponding discourses will be explored here. One is the concept of the 'traditional' nuclear family as the norm. This has been particularly associated with the rhetoric of the 'new right' in both the US and Britain and with the policies of the Conservative governments in Britain in the last two decades of the twentieth century. The second is a conception associated with left-of-centre political parties in Britain, which recognises the importance of the 'traditional family' but which gives equal prominence to other family forms.

Support for the traditional family has come from a number of directions. Functionalist sociologists such as Parsons (1959) have argued that the family of a married couple with children evolved with the onset of industrialisation and was a major factor in economic success. He argued that its small scale enabled households to be geographically and socially mobile and provided support for the man to concentrate on the economic breadwinner role. Parsons identified a 'natural' division of labour in which the husband goes out into the rational, impersonal domain of work to earn money for the household while the wife stays at home and plays an emotionally supportive role. Parsons believed that this division of labour reflected biological difference between the sexes. For Parsons, the 'traditional family' has two main functions. First, it is the focus for the primary socialisation of children, inculcating in them the norms and values of society. Second, it provides a haven from the outside world, giving its members the emotional warmth and security they need to survive in a world that can be chaotic, stressful and impersonal. Jorgensen (1995) calls this the 'warm bath theory'; the husband arrives home from a stressful day at work and sinks into the warmth and security of the warm bath that his family provides.

More recently these ideas have been developed by writers of the new right associated with the governments of Margaret Thatcher in Britain and Ronald Reagan in the US (Abbott and Wallace, 1992).

For example, Mount (1982) has argued that the 'traditional family' was something natural, universal and enduring, an essential bulwark against the encroachment of the state into the private domain. It follows from this that the family is the natural place for all matters of care for the aged, the sick and children. This is an important point because it has influenced public policy in areas such as the care of older people, which will be highlighted later in the book. Although the traditional family was said to contain just parents and dependent children living together, writers such as Mount stressed that it included responsibilities for the well-being of family members outside the household such as older or disabled relatives. It was the duty of the family to make provision and care for these members, leaving the state to intervene only where the family is unable to exercise this duty.

The concept of the traditional family has also been linked to a normative family life cycle that emphasises that couples should marry before living together. It also places stress on the duty of care and socialisation for children. The duty of parents is to house and care for their children until they are self-sufficient and can earn their own living and provide their own shelter. Again, the role of the state is to act only as a last resort, and public policy should not encourage young people to leave home before they are independent by providing help for them. The implications of this for the situation of young people will be discussed in Chapter Seven.

The arguments for the traditional family have sometimes been linked to a concern with what was seen as a growing moral degeneracy and to campaigns against abortion and against the legalisation of homosexual practices. They also became linked to concern about an underclass detached from the norms of society as a whole and mired in a culture of poverty and crime reproduced from one generation to another through inadequate parenting. The most influential writer was Charles Murray, an American sociologist who published a series of widely read articles in the *Sunday Times* in Britain. Murray's starting point was the assumed supremacy of the traditional family: "I work from the premise that the traditional monogamous marriage, with children, is in reality, on average, in the long run, the most satisfying way to live a human life" (Murray, 1994, quoted in Jorgensen, 1995, p 98). Murray (1989, p 37) sees the family as a civilizing influence particularly on young men: "Young males are essentially barbarians for whom marriage – meaning not just the wedding vows, but the act of taking responsibility for a wife and children – is an indispensable civilizing force".

Murray saw trends of increasing permissiveness, sexual promiscuity, divorce and marital breakdown, increased cohabitation, rising rate of illegitimate births, and the increasing numbers of single-parent families as evidence of moral degeneracy. Without the responsibility of a family to support, young males lead dissolute lives and are tempted by drugs and crime. They are not attractive long-term partners for women and their children grow up without a responsible male role model and so run wild and later in life repeat the behaviour of their fathers. The state is implicated in this situation because it provides welfare benefits that act as a disincentive to finding and keeping work. The result is increasing crime rates; juvenile delinquency and hooliganism, drug abuse, educational failure, and a dependency culture.

The remedy for these problems is seen to lie in encouraging and strengthening the traditional family through public policy mechanisms. This involves reinforcing the male breadwinner role and encouraging women to concentrate on the care of homes and families. Welfare benefits and the provision of other public services such as public sector housing can be structured in such a way as to encourage appropriate behaviour. This analysis is supported by Morgan (1998), who implicates government policy in the demographic changes that have taken place, arguing that there is too much support for families other than the traditional two-parent norm. During the 1990s there was a number of 'scandals', highlighted by politicians and the media, of young girls supposedly having babies in order to jump the queue for council housing. John Redwood, when Secretary of State for Wales, drew attention to the proportion of lone mothers on council estates in Wales and particularly St Mellons in Cardiff. The implicit message in these stories was that the state, through council housing allocation systems, was encouraging irresponsible and immoral behaviour.

Murray's analysis has been supported by some people on the left of the political spectrum. For example, Dennis and Erdos (1993), who label themselves 'ethical socialists', point to the stabilising influence of the two-parent family, particularly in traditional working-class areas. They argue that all research studies have shown that children brought up in two-parent families do better, on average, in a wide variety of ways than other kinds of family. Like Murray, Dennis and Erdos focus on the lone-parent family as the particular problem and lay the blame on absent fathers as the key factor in what they argue is a growing level of incivility and crime committed by the irresponsible fathers themselves and by their children who are denied an appropriate role model.

The presumed superiority of the traditional family is ever present in political discourse, with the two main political parties in Britain stressing their support for the family. However, there are differences in emphasis between them, with the Conservative Party more clearly associating itself with the traditional family and putting forward policies to discriminate against other forms through the taxation and benefit systems as well as through housing policies.

At first glance, the 'decline of the family' often alluded to by supporters of the traditional family, may be supported by evidence from the British Social Attitudes Survey that contact with family has declined between 1986 and 1995 (McGlone et al, 1999). For example, in 1986 60% of people with a non-resident mother saw her at least once a week, whereas in 1995 only 49% did so. This was despite the fact that fewer adult children lived with their parents (around two thirds of 18- to 24-year-olds in 1986 and less than half in 1995), reflecting the trend of declining household size. However, contact between relatives was still high in 1995, with 60% of parents with a non-resident adult child seeing them at least once a week. Also, around 60% of people lived within an hour's journey of at least one close relative. Where families live at a distance, Mason (1999, p 174) concludes that: "living away from kin does not mean that kin relationships are insignificant, and there is a very real sense in which many people are prepared to contemplate, and to put into practice, 'long-distance kinship'". McGlone et al (1999) argue that most people are 'family centred', believing it important to keep in touch with close relatives and the extended family, including members with whom they have little in common. The family is seen to be overwhelmingly more important than friends by a margin of about 11 to 1. Therefore, although contact with family was declining it was not being replaced by friends, as contact with them was also less. The primary reason for this may be the increased participation of women in employment, as contact was much higher for females than males. In other words, the strong mother–daughter tie that Young and Willmott (1957) identified as the key element of the Bethnal Green community is still alive, but has had to adapt to the changing role of women. However, 'family centredness' was much higher among those over 45 than with younger people. This may reflect the stage of the lifecycle with people becoming more family-centred as they have children of their own. However, it may herald a reduction in the importance of the family in future if the less 'family-centred' attitudes are maintained.

Despite the growing number of older people living alone, their personal networks are dominated by family links. When Phillipson et al's (1999) sample of older people were asked to say who was most important in their lives, three quarters of those mentioned were family members, usually children. These constituted what Phillipson et al called the 'emotional core' of older people's lives. This was despite the growing number of children living some distance from their parents. Families varied in their capacity to overcome the difficulties of distance because of differential access to transport and telephones.

Dench et al (1999) show the continuing importance of the grandparental relationship, both to older people and to their families. In the British Social Attitudes Survey sample, 91% of grandparents said that being a grandparent was a very rewarding aspect of their life. Over three quarters said that they felt very close to their grandchild, and 43% saw them several times a week. Clearly, family is a very important feature of most people's lives.

An alternative discourse of the family has emerged which places more emphasis on a diversity of forms. It is not really one discourse but a collection of different discourses that each question the overwhelming superiority often attributed to the traditional family and favour tolerance and diversity in the way people live together.

An important element of this alternative discourse is the feminist critique of the traditional family. It is argued that this notion of the family is based on an unequal relationship between men and women that reinforces and supports a patriarchal society. Men are given the dominant and socially valued role of breadwinner and women are expected to support this through the undervalued and unpaid work of housewife and carer. This is argued to be oppressive to women. Feminists have also challenged the 'warm bath' image of the traditional family, arguing that it hides a life of domestic drudgery for women as well as a degree of domestic violence and child abuse. A number of studies have shown that family violence is widespread and is present across the social classes (see Dobash and Dobash, 1979; Pahl, 1985). Most of this violence is by men towards women and is argued to reflect the imbalance of power in the traditional family.

Recent changes in the make-up of the family are seen as being the consequence of the greater equality and financial independence of women. More women are choosing to live on their own and support themselves financially. The increasing rates of divorce are seen as partly the result of the increased ability of women to leave unsatisfactory or abusive or violent relationships because of the greater access of women to the labour market. Therefore, these trends are seen as the result of greater choice and power of women and are therefore to be applauded.

The evidence that children do less well in single-parent families is dismissed for a number of reasons. First, it is argued that the studies quoted are of children who grew up at a time when divorce was more stigmatized than it is now, and so children of divorced parents now will not suffer the same social opprobrium. Second, it is argued that the studies do not compare the life chances of children of divorced parents with those from families where there is substantial conflict, which would be the alternative if parents decided to stay together. Third, lone parents tend to be financially worse off than traditional families, and so it may be poverty rather than the breakup of the family per se that causes any problems with the attainment of the children.

Other minority discourses have been part of the 'diversity' discourse. Some critics of the traditional family have pointed to other forms of communal living such as the Jewish Kibbutz as alternative, successful ways of organising domestic life and bringing up children. New Age travellers or members of a commune are examples of people who have chosen to adopt a different way of living. The diversity argument also applies to members of ethnic minorities who may have different cultural and religious traditions of 'family' and may choose, for example, to live in extended families and to take part in arranged marriages. Gay and lesbian groups have fought for equal legal rights and social standing with traditional families in order, for example, to be able to adopt children or have legally recognised marriages.

The diversity discourse is well summed up by a quototation from a Labour MP, Harriet Harman;

> Family policy needs to recognise that families come in all shapes and sizes ... to claim that one kind of family is right and others wrong can do considerable harm by stigmatizing those who live in non-traditional family settings. Public policy cannot alter private choices, but it can mitigate the painful effects of change. (Harman, 1991, quoted in Muncie and Wetherell, 1997, p 59)

The two major discourses outlined here differ in their relationship to the 'reality' of the changing composition of households discussed in the next section. Whereas the diversity discourse accepts the different household forms that have emerged and argues that public policy should treat them equally, the traditional family discourse explicitly rejects current trends and argues for a return to a so-called golden age of the family. Therefore, it is argued that public policy should discriminate in favour of the traditional ideal and not undermine it through support for alternative forms of living.

The field of housing is deeply implicated in these discourses of family because the home is seen as the setting for family life. Therefore, the discourses surrounding the concept of home, which will be considered in Chapter Five, are strongly related to discourses of family. As a consequence, family discourses permeate housing policy and can be used to justify public policies in the field of housing as in other fields. One example is the allocation policies and practices adopted by public sector landlords to regulate access to their dwellings (as well as the practices of some private sector landlords), which may discriminate against particular forms of household. Homelessness legislation gives different rights to some single homeless people from those it gives to married households or those containing children. We shall look in some depth later at examples of public policy rhetoric and policy instruments that reflect one or other of the discourses outlined here when we examine the position of young people leaving home (in Chapter Seven) and of older people needing shelter and care (in Chapter Eight).

The discourses of family are also important in the study of housing because they frame the perceptions, attitudes and choices of people in their everyday lives, both in the shape of family or household they are part of, and in the roles within this household. People reproduce family and household forms through their actions and interactions. Dallos and Sapsford (1997) argue that the the family is a strong institution because of the desirability of its norms and goals. They point in particular to the sense of identity that people seek through their family and household. They argue that people look to the family to provide emotional support and social stability in the search for a settled sense of one's identity, capability and acceptability. Where it works, they argue that the family can provide a sense of solidarity and belonging. It can give a set of roles that enable people to locate themselves in the wider social order and to achieve status. It serves to socialise people into wider identities of class, ethnic group and gender.

The search for a sense of identity through the family (whatever its form) in the setting of the home is increasingly important in a postmodern society in which the pace and extent of change have led to increased risk and growing feelings of insecurity and isolation. It follows that the search for identity should be a major focus of the study of housing and be a major goal of housing policy.

Changing households

The discourses of family influence the make-up and shape of households. As mentioned earlier, recent trends have led to a diversity of household forms.

As in many Western countries, the overall population of Great Britain is increasing only slowly despite an increase in immigration, particularly from other European Union countries. The impact of longer life expectancy is offset by a declining birth rate, and the combined impact of the two trends means that the age structure of the population is changing. There is projected to be a fall in the proportion of the population under 25 and a large increase in the middle-aged (45-65) and those over 65 in the next ten years.

Despite this slow growth in the overall population, the number of households has increased substantially. For example, in England in 1991 there were just over 19 million households. This is projected to rise to 22.5 million by 2011 (ODPM, 2003a). The average household size was 2.47 persons per household in 1991 and is projected to fall to 2.24 persons per household by 2011 (ODPM, 2003a). One-person and lone-parent households are increasing the most, as the number of couples with children is falling. The increase in the number of households, even when the overall population is relatively stable, is causing problems for providers of housing and for government (through the land-use planning system) trying to keep up with the large increase in the number of dwellings required. This is particularly difficult because of the regional imbalance in the growth, with the greatest demand in South East England.

The growing number of lone-parent families is made up of different categories. Lone fathers are in a minority, with separated and divorced lone mothers making up over half the total, reflecting the increased rate of marital breakdown and divorce. However, a third of lone parents are single lone mothers who have an unplanned pregnancy or choose to have a child outside a stable relationship with a partner. Britain has the highest rate of teenage pregnancy in western Europe, and the rate has increased slightly during the 1990s. However, this does not seem to be the result of a positive lifestyle choice. Berthoud et al (1999) argue on the basis of qualitative research with young mothers that, given a choice, most of the women would have married before having their children. Either the option was not open to them or the father was considered not worth marrying, often because of poor employment prospects or personal irresponsibility. Their pregnancies were, for the most part, something that just happened to them, over which they felt that they had little control (McRae, 1999, p 10). Of those who did form cohabiting relationships with the father of their child, half were living on their own within one year of the birth (Allen and Bourke Dowling, 1999).

McRae (1999) draws attention to the circular links between teenage pregnancy and a disadvantaged family background. Daughters of teenage mothers are more likely to be teenage mothers themselves. Although many teenage mothers are able to escape poverty in the longer term, there is evidence that a teenage birth results in a greater likelihood of leaving home early, living in public rented housing, being in a manual job or unemployed and being welfare-dependent.

Teenage, never-married mothers are only one form of single-parent household. But, as McRae (1999, p 15) points out, "The problem of lone motherhood is poverty". Lone mothers have few chances of obtaining other than low-paid work, and the majority do not receive support payments from the fathers of their children. As a consequence the majority of lone mothers rely on state benefits. McRae argues that there is a divide among single parents. Non-benefit recipients were usually owner-occupiers, non-manual workers, better-qualified, had fewer children, were divorced or widowed, or were lone fathers. Benefit recipients were overwhelmingly public rented-sector tenants, manual workers, poorly qualified, had more children and were single or separated.

Single-person households have increased at an even faster rate than lone parents, and a large proportion of the total projected household increase will be accounted for by persons who live alone (see Scase, 1999). Single-person households span the age range. Some are young people living alone, while increasing longevity and the difference in mortality rates between men and women means that an increasing proportion of older people live alone. At the same time there has been an increase in the proportion of people in other age brackets living alone, partly because of the increase in divorce, but also because of choice. It is projected that one-person households will make up over a third of all households by 2011 (DETR, 1999). Hall et al (1999) show that younger one-person households are particularly concentrated among the professional and managerial classes, and more of them now own their property than follow the traditional path of renting. Employment seems to be a major factor in the geographical pattern of younger single households, which tend to be concentrated in London (particularly inner London) and other major cities. Men are more likely to live alone than women, but the number of younger female single-person households is increasing. For younger single-person households, living alone seems to be a positive choice. People who choose it stress the flexibility and fluidity of household arrangements and freedom and independence. None interviewed by Hall et al (1999) mentioned loneliness, and many had many friends and sometimes long-term loving relationships. Despite spending time with a partner they still considered themselves to be living alone.

Although married couples will still be the largest household type, they are projected to make up a minority of households by 2011. Married couples with children – the archetypal nuclear family – made up only about a quarter of all households in 2001 (ODPM, 2003a). Marriage rates in Britain are declining as cohabitation increases in popularity. In 1995 the number of first marriages in Britain was half that in 1970. In the mid–1960s, fewer than 5% of women cohabited before marriage while in the early 1990s, 70% did so (Haskey, 1996). Government actuarial projections suggest that the number of cohabiting couples could double over the next two decades. As cohabitation has increased, the number of births outside marriage has risen – to one third of births in 1996. Couple relationships are likely to continue to be transient for a growing percentage of the adult population with a high rate of breakup among those who cohabit. Buck and Ermisch (1995) found that cohabiting couples were between three and four times more likely to separate than married couples. The average length of cohabitation in 1995 was 34 months (Murphy, 1997).

The divorce rate is rising, with over one in three marriages ending in divorce – much higher than the average for western Europe. There is a link between divorce and economic disadvantage, with unemployed, disabled and welfare-dependent people more likely to divorce, and divorce itself sometimes resulting in economic hardship, particularly for women. Housing quality can decline on divorce. Flowerdew et al (1999) show that divorced men and women move more frequently than both single and married people. Moreover, divorce carries a high risk of losing owner occupation, with men particularly likely to move into their parents' home or to private renting and women into public rented housing.

Divorce can be a transitory phenomenon, with the number of marriages involving a divorced person increasing. This is leading to new forms of households in what have been called 'reconstituted' or 'reformed' households or 'step-families'. Allan (1985) argues that reconstituted families are inevitably more complex than first families as members bring with them "a history, a set of relationships antagonisms and loyalties, that inevitably influence the pattern of their family life" (Allan, 1985, p 119). This makes reconstituted families complex and gives them permeable boundaries as links are maintained with first families. Allan also points to the lack of socially defined 'rules' for step-parents, which can create dilemmas for step-parents over how closely to become involved in parenting and may reduce their legitimacy in the eyes of stepchildren.

Gorrell Barnes et al (1998) argue that reconstituted families or households can take many forms, which makes any simple definition misleading. In their research on the impact of 'step-families' on family links, Bornat et al (1999) point to the flexibility of the response to such situations among family members. The idea of family as a set of flexible, interconnecting, changing, supportive relationships coexisted in the minds of many family members with the prime importance given to the 'non-negotiable' blood tie of the parent–child relationship. Allan and Crow (2001) also point to the diversity of reconstituted families in the way that they see themselves and function. Some try to be as much like a 'normal' family as possible, with varying degrees of success, but others accept and 'celebrate' the differences from the traditional norm. Yet others see their situation as a transitional one until children grow up and leave home.

The proportion of the population over pension age is projected to rise substantially to almost a quarter by 2011 (Scase, 1999). One implication of this is that more women and men in late middle age and early old age will have both upward and downward generational ties. At the same time there has been a reduction in the extent of co-residence in inter-generational households, so that in 1991 over half of women and one third of men over retirement age lived alone. It is argued by McRae that this situation is brought about by the growing ability of older people to achieve their preference for independent living.

> What we are seeing in Britain today are increased opportunities for older people to achieve their wish to live independently: they are healthier and live longer, so there are more close friends with whom to socialize; there is better state support and more facilities (both state and private) to support independent living; and there is a significantly larger housing stock, so older people have somewhere to live. Had these conditions existed fifty or sixty years ago, it seems likely that many more older people would have chosen to live apart from their adult children. (McRae, 1999, p 23)

This overall demographic picture hides substantial variations. The average household size is greatest among ethnic groups from the Indian subcontinent and smallest among whites, although it seems that household size is declining in all ethnic groups. The pattern of household types varies between different ethnic groups. The proportion of lone-parent households is greater among African Caribbean people, which reflects the dominance of this form in the West Indies. The lack of strong involvement in child rearing and home life is compensated by a strong mother–daughter relationship. Goulborne (1999) shows how African Caribbean people in Britain have begun to reconstitute these links, sometimes broken by migration, and even maintain them across national boundaries. The proportion of inter-generational families is higher among Asian people in Britain. In their study of three locations in Britain, Phillipson et al (1999) found that almost all of the multi-generational households they found were made up of Indian or Bangladeshi people, although Murphy (1996) notes that at any one time such households make up a relatively low proportion of all households. The incidence of 'pensioner-only' households is low. Also, couples from these ethnic backgrounds were less likely to cohabit before, or as an alternative to, marriage. However, these are overgeneralisations that mask a changing and variable picture reflecting different and changing cultural values between people and different generations.

As mentioned earlier, within the UK there is a regional dimension to the trends. This is particularly marked with regard to household growth, which is much higher in some regions, most notably the South-East and East Anglia, than others, such as the North-East. Minority ethnic households tend to be geographically concentrated within particular parts of urban England. The regional differences mainly reflect historical differences in household types as well as differential geographical mobility largely caused by different economic growth rates and the resultant employment opportunities. This will be discussed more fully in Chapter Three.

A key element of the changing demographic trends is the increasing incidence of household types other than that of a married couple with children. There has been much controversy over the desirability of this change, which has been brought about by a variety of factors including a change of attitude to marriage and divorce, and a reduction in the birth rate. These changes support the analysis of postmodern theorists who have drawn attention to the increasing ability of people to make choices about their preferred living arrangements as part of life planning. The growing number of single-person households is evidence of the individualisation also said to be a key part of postmodern society. Beck-Gernsheim (2002) argues that individualisation of family has occurred alongside the flexibility of the labour market (to be discussed in Chapter Three) in a self-reinforcing cycle. She criticises government for promoting flexibility in the labour market while at the same time promoting the traditional family, arguing that the two are incompatible. The ever-increasing and changing demands of the flexible labour market are creating tensions within families, which are increasing the incidence of divorce. In turn the greater likelihood of divorce causes individuals to adopt defensive strategies to minimise risk of divorce. Beck-Gernsheim argues that these strategies themselves loosen the ties of marriage and make the traditional family more fragile.

It must be remembered that the distribution of households between the different classifications is a snapshot or a cross-section at one point in time. This hides the flow of households between different categories over time. For example, a lone mother may have been, as a child, part of a married-couple household, could have been a single-person household and may in the future cohabit or marry and so be part of a couple. The picture that increasingly emerges is of a more fluid situation than in the past. Households are being made, unmade and remade continually. This makes the concept of a family life cycle in which families move through a succession of stages (marriage, birth of children, children leaving home, retirement, death) increasingly problematic as a description of the experience of many households. As Clark and Dieleman (1996) point out, there was never agreement among researchers as to the appropriate stages to be used in an analysis, and the increasing diversity of household trajectories makes any useful categorisation very difficult.

Most of the figures quoted above concerning future years are projections rather than predictions. In other words, they are the forward projection of trends in the past few years. It is not always clear why these trends have appeared and so there can be no certainty that they will continue. Many factors may influence them, such as growing affluence and a changing labour market. The availability of housing may also be a factor. For example, the ability to access housing may be important in the timing of young people leaving home or of couples deciding to marry or cohabit. Therefore, there is a problem with using demographic projections to plan housing production when that production itself will influence the demographic trends to some degree.

Inside the household

It was argued earlier that much housing research has stopped at the front door of the home and has not been concerned with the household and its functioning. The household has been treated as a 'black box' with interest being shown only in the outputs – that is, the decisions made – rather than generating any insight into why the decisions were made and the factors that shaped them. This approach has been partly the result of the adoption of frameworks that assumed simple and universal motivations whereby households could be assumed to react to external factors in a predictable way. It was argued in Chapter One that this approach is inadequate and that it is necessary to understand more about the meanings, perceptions and attitudes of households if our knowledge of housing is to be adequate to meet the challenges of a postmodern world.

The household is the basic unit of a housing pathway. It is the grouping in which housing is consumed and decisions about housing are made. As the previous section has emphasised, the household is a social construction that has varied over time and is the subject of competing discourses of meaning regarding its appropriate constituents. In an increasing number of instances the household is made up of just one person, and so the focus is on the meanings and attitudes held by such persons. However, the majority of households are made up of more than one person and in most cases more than one adult, who would be expected to be part of the decision-making process. Households have to coordinate and accommodate the attitudes and behaviours of their members. A set of working practices and rules of behaviour will emerge from the interaction between the household members. "Each family or grouping can be seen as to some extent creating a unique interpersonal system of meanings and actions, a version of family life which develops from the amalgamation of its members' negotiations and choices based upon their personal and shared beliefs and histories" (Dallos, 1997, p 176).

Examples of the kind of areas that rules may cover include membership and rights of membership of the household (who is entitled to invite whom to sleep in the house, for example, and who can consume food). Working practices may be developed about the allocation of tasks such as cleaning or paying bills or about who is responsible for earning money. Mechanisms need to be derived for deciding who has use of the facilities of the house and when (Anderson et al, 1994). Other important questions concern the allocation of household resources between different uses. For example, how much money is to be devoted to repaying a mortgage for house purchase as against paying for holidays or other household expenses?

In each household of more than one person there will be a mixture of shared and individual meanings and beliefs. The balance between the two may vary from one household to the next. Where there is a disagreement over how to view a particular issue, there will have to be a means of dealing with this, particularly if action is required. Over time there is likely to emerge out of the interactions of members a set of rules or norms within the household over how to manage particular situations. For example, it may become accepted that a male adult of the household chooses the internal decor in consultation with other members, but a female member has the major say over when redecoration occurs. Decisions over important issues, such as when and where to move, may involve a long and complex pattern of interaction between members of the household, perhaps including negotiations and trade-offs. Decisions may also involve interactions with members of the family not in the household, such as parents who may need care or children who need support. For example, in her research on family care, Finch (1989) identifies substantial variations in the caring links between family members. She argues that support and care (whether financial, practical, emotional, or involving personal care or child care) among family members was not inevitable, despite the sense of obligation most people felt. Rather, it was negotiable without a clear set of rules within which to work. Finch (1989) identifies a number of principles that guide the negotiation, such as reciprocity and the desire for each adult to keep an appropriate level of independence. Expectations of gender differences are also important.

The process of interaction will be influenced by power relations within the household and between wider family members, which in turn will be influenced by the tactics and strategies of the participants and the making and remaking of alliances. Wider norms and values will influence both the power relations and what outcomes are considered appropriate. For example, the ideology of the traditional family may influence households to give precedence to the views of the man in decisions about moving house because of the importance of the breadwinner role, whereas women may be given more say over decisions regarding the bringing up of children or the interior appearance of the home. Different ethnic and cultural backgrounds may lead to different views of appropriate family functioning.

There are different views on the distribution of tasks and influence within the household. Young and Wilmott (1975) argued, on the basis of a study in London, that the involvement of men and women in family life has become, in the twentieth century, more symmetrical, with a more egalitarian relationship between them. Other authors such as Oakley (1974) dispute this and argue that men play little part in domestic life, with women still undertaking the vast majority of housekeeping and child-rearing tasks. Edgell (1980) examined decision-making in a number of middle-class families and his findings cast doubt on the symmetricality thesis. Particularly interesting for housing pathways is the influence that men are reported to have over issues to do with moving house and finance. However, house improvements are said to be decided by both husband and wife, and decisions on interior decorations are said to be taken by the wife.

Allan and Crow (2001) criticise the simplistic nature of this kind of decision-making approach. The processes behind any decision may be more complex than can be described in terms of a simple ascription of responsibility. Some important issues are non-decisions in that they are never openly discussed but implicitly taken for granted. In some cases there may be substantial negotiation over an issue that could signal an equal partnership but may reflect one partner fostering compliance. In addition, people may make a decision but consciously put the interest of others over their own. Thus, a wife may make decisions that prioritise the needs of her husband and children. Harrison (2001) argues that reality may not be as it seems in some ethnic minority households, where the appearance of female passivity may be deceptive. Allan and Crow (2001) argue that there is more equality of work and influence in cohabitation households than in married ones. They ascribe the difference partly to the less established role expectations and the emphasis that many couples place on the 'construction' of their own personal relationship to match their own particular desires and ambitions. Allan and Crow (2001) also argue that people in households based on gay relationships both desire and achieve more equal relationships than married couples.

Working practices are not unchanging but are continually made and remade as circumstances change. For example, the membership of the household may change because of divorce or separation or the leaving of older children. The birth of children may involve a substantial reworking of existing practices. However, Allan and Crow (2001) argue that many changes in the detailed management of the home and the responsibilities for tasks are superficial and do not alter the underlying division of responsibilities which is set early in the household's existence and which is highly gendered.

Households may develop a long-term view of where they would like to be in the future, and to formulate a strategy in order to achieve this that will frame individual decisions. The use of the concept of strategy, and the questions whether and to what extent households have strategies, have been controversial in studies of the family. Crow (1989) has argued that the term 'strategy' has been used in many different ways and has no clear and accepted meaning. Nevertheless, he does not wish to dispense with the term. He wishes to use the term to "imply the presence of conscious and rational decisions involving a long term perspective" (Crow, 1989, p 19). The existence of a strategy is a guide to the extent to which households engage in what Giddens (1991) called 'life planning'. That is "the extent to which they, rightly or wrongly, perceive themselves as actively and with foresight seeking to organize, plan, control or influence the paths taken by their present and especially future lives" (Anderson et al, 1994, p 21). Anderson et al (1994) found in their sample of households that a high proportion showed evidence of conscious strategic thinking in at least some parts of their lives. Interestingly, this varied with the gender of single households, single women being more likely to have a strategy than single men.

Between a third and a quarter of Anderson et al's sample had a clear long-term housing strategy. When all in the sample were asked about their general plans, nearly 40% mentioned housing issues, including home improvement and moving house. This was concentrated on the younger age groups; the older groups were more concerned with holidays and leisure.

> Indeed we can see a clear pattern where younger men and women focus their hopes and expectations on acquiring and improving their accommodation and to a more limited extent on family, work and leisure. Then, as they enter middle age they become much more restricted in their proactive planning and focus it largely on continued home improvement and plans for holidays and travel, probably because they have either achieved their housing, work and family ambitions or have come to believe that this is no longer possible. (Anderson et al, 1994, pp 52-3)

McCrone (1994) found that the incidence of housing plans was strikingly high in his sample of households, both among those who claimed to plan strategically and those who did not. Clearly, housing issues are major elements of the life planning and lifestyle choices made by households.

It cannot be assumed that all households have housing strategies or plans. For example, Allen and Bourke Dowling (1999) studied the behaviour of teenage mothers. They found that, in general, their pregnancies were unplanned and sometimes caused substantial turmoil and conflict involving relationships with parents and the fathers of the children as well as others. Decisions about residence were tied up with other decisions about whether to continue with the pregnancy, the role of the father and parents in the care of the child, and their employment and economic status – for example, whether to leave school or employment. The housing circumstances of the teenage mothers studied by Allen and Bourke Dowling changed substantially after learning of their pregnancy. The proportion living with parents dropped from nearly one half to one quarter. The proportion cohabiting remained constant at just under one third, although this masked considerable household change because nearly half of the original cohabiting relationships had broken down. The proportion living with a husband increased from 11% to 18%. However, the most striking change was the sharp increase in the proportion of those living alone, from 7% to 29%. Allen and Bourke Dowling comment that very few of their sample had intended to end up as lone mothers, but around half of them had done so.

Allen and Bourke Dowling (1999) studied the decision-making behaviour of the teenage mothers and the discussions they had with parents, the fathers of their children and others. They concluded:

> It was clear that decisions on housing and living arrangements were often not the subject of rational discussion, particularly those which involved a move. Moves were often precipitated by relationship breakdown, which was perhaps not the most comfortable situation in which to have reasoned discussions about where and with whom to live, particularly late in pregnancy or with a tiny baby. There were many indications in the housing histories of the women that they often felt that the moves were out of their control, not only in deciding where to go but also when they would move. It was clear that many of them had expected to stay in accommodation longer than they had, but that other events, including relationship breakdown, had dictated otherwise. Again, there was a strong impression that many of these young women were often following rather than controlling what was happening to them, and

> that they felt powerless to influence the course their lives
> were taking. (Allen and Bourke Dowling, 1999, p 344)

This section has put forward a framework for the analysis of the workings of households and has examined some of the existing knowledge of how households operate, particularly in terms of issues related to housing. From this review it can be seen that existing knowledge is slight and that we do not really yet understand the process by which decisions on housing issues are made and the factors that influence households in those decisions. Most current knowledge concerns traditional households, which as we have seen are becoming less common, and there is little information on how other forms of household operate. Also, housing issues have been explored as part of a much wider agenda and so housing issues have not been given much prominence in research studies. There is a need to increase our understanding of what happens within the household if we are to further our understanding of the housing field.

Conclusion

This chapter has begun the exploration of housing pathways by focusing on the household, which is the unit in which housing is consumed. Some of the difficulties of its definition were outlined, and it was argued that there was no universal and watertight definition and that the concept had to be defined according to the purpose for which it is to be used.

Chapter One pointed to the conclusion of many writers on postmodernity to the effect that the traditional collective institutions such as the family were changing and this was borne out by an examination of trends in the distribution of types of household. The major growth is in lone-parent and single-person households. The declining incidence of marriage and the growing rate of divorce mean that households are constantly forming, splitting and re-forming, making a dynamic perspective imperative. The importance of taking a twin approach on both individual and household pathways outlined in Chapter One was reinforced by the volatile nature of household change described here. Individuals pursue housing pathways that at some times may involve membership of one or more different households. There needs to be a focus on the individuals but also on the functioning of the households of which they are a part.

The shape and functioning of households is influenced by discourses associated with different views of what family life should be. These discourses are closely related to public policy and they influence the attitudes and behaviour of individuals. Therefore, they are crucial influences on housing pathways. However, individuals make their own choices and the impact of the discourses is mediated by issues of ethnicity and gender.

The chapter considered the internal dynamics of households, and the lack of information on the way that households make decisions on their housing pathways was emphasised. This is clearly an important gap in our knowledge of housing, which will be highlighted in the following chapters. In order to understand how households achieve their search for identity and fulfilment through housing, we need to know much more about the way that different perceptions and attitudes are reconciled within the household and how a household perspective emerges that results in the making of housing choices. Without this knowledge our understanding of the housing field is limited, as discussions in the following chapters on decisions about how much to spend on housing, and when and where to move for employment, will show.

Finally, it was noted in the chapter that households differ in their willingness and ability to plan strategically for their future. The research on single mothers shows that many do not feel in control of their lives and react to external circumstances on a day-to-day basis. It is easy to see how this can lead to inequality in housing opportunities and outcomes.

THREE

Work

The chapter assesses the links between employment and housing at the levels both of policy and of individual households, following the pathways framework. At the level of policy the chapter traces the influence of the discourse of a flexible labour market on housing policy. The main theme is the dominance of the discourse in setting the agenda of housing policy. At the level of individual households, the chapter reviews existing research and calls for more studies examining the relationship between employment and housing decisions.

Employment is one of the key factors underlying family and household structures. It has an important influence on changing patterns of housing demand and need. It is also an important factor in the income of a household and its ability to afford access to housing. Clearly, households need to be able to pay for housing and, for many, employment provides the income for this. Employment position is a key influence on differential access to parts of the housing field. This may be through the ability of a household to afford particular housing options, such as owner-occupation, or to access certain parts of a housing sector or particular areas. In addition, because employment opportunities are spatially differentiated, they may influence where a household may wish to or be able to live, and therefore influence what households expect from housing.

At the level of the individual household, employment and housing pathways are usually closely linked. Decisions on one will usually have implications for the other, and so the two will often be considered together. There may be trade-offs between the two, or one may be dominant. For example, a decision to remain in an existing house or area may constrain the employment opportunities available. Conversely, a decision to move areas to take up an employment opportunity may result in housing dislocation and possibly a reduction in housing quality. An understanding of how these trade-offs are made and how the housing and employment pathways intertwine is important to a general understanding of the place of housing in people's lives.

The chapter starts with a very brief review of economic changes that have been given the label 'globalisation'. As argued in Chapter

One, the discourse of globalisation has dominated public policy in Britain in many fields and has had a strong impact on shaping housing policy. The main focus in this chapter is on the impact of globalisation on employment trends in Britain, concentrating on the discourse of the 'flexible labour market', which has been seen as the appropriate response to a globalised economy. The chapter continues by exploring the implications of the discourse for housing, focusing on the discourse of a flexible housing field. Three main elements of flexibility are highlighted here. First, are houses being built in the right places to aid economic development? Second, can households move house easily to access employment opportunities? Geographical mobility has been a major policy focus, and the resultant emphasis on increasing mobility in different tenures is assessed. Third, does the organisation of housing enable unemployed households to access employment? An important aspect is the attempt to create employment for people living in deprived estates who may not be able or willing to move to take up employment opportunities.

The flexibility discourse also raises questions concerning the organisation of housing finance to enable households to afford appropriate housing and to cope with fluctuations in earnings. The ability of households to afford and sustain payments for housing, and the financial incentives they experience, will be considered in Chapter Four.

Finally, the implications of employment on housing pathways is explored by examining how employment and housing issues interrelate at the level of the individual household.

Globalisation

The global economy has seen substantial changes in the recent decades led by the rapid international mobility of financial capital. The impact of decisions taken by companies on the location of production can be vital to local employment markets. For example, in the 1990s a number of south-east Asian information technology (IT) manufacturers chose to locate some of their production plants in Britain to serve the European Union market. This foreign investment was part of the particular South Korean reaction to globalisation, and involved what Phelps and Tewdwr-Jones (2001) called the selective internationalisation of markets and sources. Britain was chosen as one of the sites of investment partly because labour costs were cheap and there was a plentiful supply of labour because of reductions in the traditional manufacturing sector and the coal and steel industries.

Another reason was the ability and willingness of the UK government through the regional arms of the Welsh and Scottish Offices and the regional development agencies in England to provide support and financial help. This involved fast-tracking planning procedures as well as direct financial backing. However, the downturn in the south-east Asian economies in the late 1990s and the early years of the twenty-first century led to a change of strategy by the South Korean companies and a substantial reduction in production capacity in Britain, with plant closures and employment loss. The regional agencies in Britain were powerless to influence decisions taken many miles away in response to factors well outside their control (Phelps and Tewdwr-Jones, 2001).

In Chapter One it was argued that the discourse of globalisation has emphasised the inevitability of the free flows of capital, seeing globalisation as a natural force that governments are ill-advised to attempt to resist. This is true of successive British governments, which have accepted globalisation. For example, in the British government White Paper *Opportunity for all in a world of change* (DTI, 2001), a number of phrases mark out the perceived limits of government action. "We cannot and should not try to resist the profound structural changes facing businesses and individuals" (p 1). "There are limits to what national governments can realistically achieve on their own"(p 7). "We cannot force companies to invest or to continue to invest in particular places" (p 7).

The response of successive UK governments, and many other governments in the advanced capitalist countries, to 'globalisation' has been to seek to provide favourable conditions for investment and employment growth through a mixture of macroeconomic management and supply-side policies designed to increase the flexibility and productivity of labour. In *Opportunity for all in a world of change*, mention is made of "equipping individuals with the skills, abilities and know-how they need to be successful in the modern economy" and "ensuring that the communities and regions within which people live have the capacity to grasp the opportunities offered by change" (DTI, 2001, p 4).

Over the past 20 years the British economy has been transformed through the decline of manufacturing and the growth of service occupations. Scase (1999) illustrates the change in a dramatic way by highlighting the fact that more people in Britain now work in Indian restaurants than in shipbuilding, steel manufacturing and coal mining combined. He also states that there are three times as many public relations consultants as coal miners, reflecting an overall increase in the proportion of managerial and professional occupations, and a related decline in skilled and semi-skilled manual jobs.

This restructuring has also coincided with a growing inequality in incomes. Jobs in the growing service sector tend to be at the two ends of the income spectrum. Some skilled jobs are at the top of the earnings scale, but others, such as office cleaning, tourism, catering, retail or caring, tend to be relatively low paid. This element will be explored further in Chapter Four.

The 'flexible labour market'

The government response to globalisation in Britain has been to promote and sustain changes that together have been labelled a 'flexible labour market'. The term encapsulates a discourse that is both a description of certain labour market trends and a guideline for labour market policy. Successive governments have emphasised flexibility as the aim of policy. A flexible labour market is said to improve the productiveness of the economy by increasing the productivity of labour and allowing industries and individual companies to respond flexibly to changing tastes and demand.

The core of flexibility is held to be the understanding that there are no longer 'jobs for life' and people should look towards changing their employment and even their career a number of times during their working lives. The cause of this is said to be the growing pace of technological change, which can render whole occupations, production processes and industries obsolete. An example is the growth of call centres, made possible by the use of information technology, which have led to closure of bank branches and a change in the type of office buildings required. However, call centres may have only a limited life as technological changes will make it possible for people to increasingly undertake their own transactions via the internet (Bristow et al, 2000).

The rapidly changing technology is said to highlight the need for an educated and trained work force. But training may be required at many points in the life cycle as technologies change. Skills can be made obsolete quickly and re-skilling required.

To what extent does the British labour market correspond to this picture? Evidence of flexibility is provided by the growth of what is usually termed 'non-standard' employment. This includes part-time work, flexible working hours or self-employment. Part-time work has risen from 14% of all employment in 1971 to 25% in 2002, and is predicted to increase further (Scase, 1999). Horrell et al (1994) argue that flexible work patterns affect a high proportion of all workers with a consequent impact on average hours of work, the predictability of working time patterns and the spread of working time throughout the day, week and year. These factors can have a substantial impact on the time spent in the home. The work–life balance may also have an impact on family life and, therefore, on activities in the home and on the time pattern of use of the home (see Chapter Five). La Valle et al (2002) found that, among dual-income families, those working 'atypical' hours were in a majority. This often resulted in what they termed 'shift parenting', with fathers and mothers taking it in terms to look after the children. Combined with a 'long working hours culture', this resulted in parents being concerned about the time they could spend with their children and the demise in many households of the 'family meal'.

The huge increase in the number of women in employment has been one of the major trends in the labour market. In 1951 a third of women were employed; this figure had risen to 70% by 2002 (ONS, 2003). Hochschild (1997, p 247) argues that employment provides women with "a source of security, pride, and a powerful sense of being valued" which they do not enjoy in the lower-status role of housewife. The changing attitude of women towards work is associated with the changing discourse of the family, including attitudes towards the desirability and timing of child-bearing as well as different roles within the home. Chapter Two discussed the different discourses that have formed the framework for debates over the appropriate roles of women in the family. Perhaps most disputed has been the desirability of women with young children working. In 1995, 51% of mothers with children under five were in part-time or full-time employment; this figure rose to 80% of those with children over 10 years of age (Allan and Crow, 2001). There has been controversy over research that seemed to show that very young children left with childminders performed less well at school than those who had a mother at home. These findings have been taken up by advocates of the traditional family, who have argued that the place of every new mother with young children is at home. Others have disputed the findings and argued that the key is to improve the quality of childcare to enable mothers with young children to have the choice to work (for a review, see Allan and Crow, 2001). Hinds and Jarvis (2000) found that 42% of men and 58% of women in 1998 thought that a woman with a pre-school child should be free to choose whether or not to work.

The number of people who are self-employed has increased across the skills spectrum. This is partly a reflection of employers seeking to transfer the risk of low or seasonal demand to their workforce. If demand falls, self-employed workers can be easily laid off with no obligation to continue to pay employer contributions to national insurance or pension costs. However, the growth of self-employment is also a reflection of the changing industrial structure and, in particular, the growth of the service sector. The growing importance of small businesses in a situation where innovation is key to success, and the outsourcing of tasks by large companies is growing, means that long-term careers and employment in a small number of large corporations is likely to decline. Jobs are likely to be fixed-term and tied to performance expectations. Employees are likely to be forced to become more adaptive, shifting between companies with greater frequency as well as embarking on periods of self-employment.

At the same time, technological change has meant that it is possible to work in remote locations away from the traditional office. Data from the Labour Force Survey (ONS, 2003) shows that in 2001, 2.2 million people in the UK – 7.4% of the employed population – were 'teleworkers', a rise of 65% since 1997. Teleworkers are defined as people who work from home for at least one day a week. Around half of teleworkers had an office where they spent most of the week, doing only specific tasks at home, but others worked solely from home. Teleworkers tended to be self-employed or managerial staff. Scase (1999) argues that between 40% and 50% of the work tasks of many managerial and professional jobs are likely to be undertaken at home in the future.

The iconic 'flexible' workers are the so-called portfolio workers who are self-employed, selling their expertise to a wide range of clients, and working from home in a small town or in the country in their 'electronic cottage', keeping in touch with the world through the Internet. It is unclear how many there are, but they are clearly a growing part of the labour market. Portfolio workers live by selling their knowledge and skills. Therefore, it is vital for them that they invest in training to ensure these skills are up to date and relevant.

Scase (1999) argues that changes in the labour market will alter what he calls 'the psychological contract' to employment. He argues that individuals will have few expectations of long-term careers and will tend to regard employment contracts as essentially short-term, negotiated arrangements. Uncertainties and insecurities will increase due to a greater frequency of job changes. People will be required to be psychologically and emotionally more mobile, and to adapt more easily to change. This will foster a more self-reliant and independent culture among workers, and place emphasis on what Giddens (1991) called 'life planning'. There is little evidence that people are changing employment more often, but there is some evidence that people are feeling more insecure. Felstead et al (1998) found that workers in 1997 felt as insecure in their jobs as those in 1986, even though employment conditions were much more favourable, with a much lower level of unemployment. They argue, there has been an upward shift in perceptions of job insecurity, particularly among professional and higher-paid workers who were previously used to relatively safe jobs. Beck (2000) argues that labour market flexibility means a redistribution of risks away from the state and the economy towards the individual. This has profound effects on people's state of mind, their biography and their family life. As discussed in Chapter Two, Beck-Gernsheim (2002) notes that the individualisation of work is associated with an individualisation of family life, which is leading to a 'fracturing' of the traditional family and a restructuring of household forms.

Flexibility in employment can be viewed in two lights. On the one hand it may liberate individuals by offering the opportunity to pursue their own work goals and to find their own balance between work and other parts of their lives. On the other hand, many of the 'flexible' jobs are low-paid and open to exploitation, and these are more likely to be undertaken by women.

Alongside the changes in the labour market, prolonged economic growth since the mid-1990s has resulted in a decline in unemployment. This has been aided by government programmes designed to support training and to encourage people back into work. Although unemployment has fallen from its heights in the early 1980s to about 5% in 2002 (according to the International Labour Organisation definition), it is still at a historically high rate. Unemployment is higher among unskilled than skilled workers and particularly affects people under the age of 24, many of whom are on government-funded training schemes. About 20% of unemployed people have been without a job for more than one year (ONS, 2003). There is a disparity between 'work rich' households with one and a half or two jobs and 'work poor' households with no job at all. In 1992 60% of employed men had a partner who was also in employment, but 80% of unemployed men had partners who were also out of work.

Although regional unemployment rates have converged over the last two decades, there are still strong regional disparities in economic growth and in unemployment. Regional differences in economic growth increased between 1990 and 1998 (DTI, 2001). Fothergill (2001) argues that unemployment figures substantially underestimate the extent of regional inequality. This is because the decline in traditional employment tends to be associated with a substantial withdrawal of people from the labour market. They become what MacKay (2003) calls detached or discouraged workers. Some retire prematurely and others respond to the incentives in the social security system for people to be registered as long-term sick or disabled rather than unemployed. This results in many people ceasing to look for work even though in a fully employed economy they could reasonably be expected to be in work (Fothergill, 2001). Citing figures that include the 'hidden unemployed', Fothergill (2001) argues that the unemployment rate in Wales in 1997 at 21% was more than double that of East Anglia at 10%.

Within regions, there is a concentration of unemployment and poverty within particular localities, reflecting both local labour markets and housing markets. There is a strong tenure pattern to unemployment. The proportion of heads of households in employment in the council-rented sector was 23% in 2001, compared with 86% of owners with a mortgage (Wilcox, 2002).

A flexible housing system?

The discourse of labour market flexibility highlights the interactions between the labour market and housing. It is argued that, as a result of the political importance attached to the discourse, it has been used as a lens through which successive governments have viewed housing policy. A key question posed by the discourse is whether the organisation of British housing is currently suited to enabling households to cope with flexibility. Is the flexible labour market being supported by a flexible housing field? This question, which has dominated housing policy, can be broken down into a number of sub-questions. Are houses being built in the right places to help labour market functioning? (This raises issues concerning the link between economic development and housing at the regional level.) Is the housing production industry prepared to provide the appropriate housing? What role does the land use planning system play? Is there sufficient coordination between government housing and economic development strategies?

Doogan (1996) argues that the flexibility discourse that emerged in the 1980s has emphasised labour mobility, which has been defined as geographical mobility. Therefore, the second set of questions concerns the ability of households to move from one area to another to access employment opportunities. The third set of issues is concerned with providing housing for unemployed people and the low-paid. Are long-term unemployed people able to access appropriate housing? What role does housing play in enabling them to access employment opportunities? A fourth area of interest surrounds the affordability of housing. Does the structure of housing finance and government financial support enable people to access affordable housing and to sustain their homes during periods of reduced or fluctuating earnings, which may be more likely in a flexible labour market? Are there appropriate financial incentives to take up employment opportunities? This final set of questions will be considered in Chapter Four. The first three sets of issues will now be examined in turn.

Housing production and economic development

The regional disparities in economic growth and employment have already been described. In Britain, the principal area of economic growth is London and the south-east of England, spreading west along the motorway corridor and north-east into East Anglia.

There has been considerable political pressure, on successive governments, from trades unions and political leaders in the less affluent areas, to adopt a regional economic development policy to attract industry away from London and the south-east and towards other, less affluent areas where unemployment is higher. However, successive governments since the mid-1970s have rejected this approach, focusing instead on encouraging foreign investors and supporting indigenous growth through supply-side improvements involving support for new firm foundation and encouragement of enterprise, innovation and competitiveness. Recently, emphasis has been placed on encouraging labour skills and knowledge (DTI, 2001). This focus on employability is based on a perception that exclusion from employment is mainly an issue of individual failings in education and training rather than a lack of job opportunities (Gripaios, 2002).

The government position has been to cast doubt on the effectiveness of previous regional policy (DTI, 2001). MacKay (2003) argues that the mobile firms influenced by regional location policy in the 1950s and 1960s were progressive, dynamic and successful, and made a long-term impact on the areas in which they located. According to MacKay (2003), the reduction in regional assistance since the mid-1970s has led to an increasing prosperity gap between the affluent regions and the rest. Other evaluations have supported this view. For example, Anyadike-Danes et al (2001) admit that the jobs created through previous regional relocation policy have been expensive because of what they call the 'deadweight' of automatic grants paid to firms that would have located there anyway. Also, some jobs created were not sustained during the deep recession of the early 1980s. Nevertheless, they argue that a mixture of automatic grant entitlement and tax incentives for business relocation would help to narrow the existing regional employment imbalances.

Recent government policy has been to support supply-side measures in all regions and to reject calls for additional selective regional assistance (DTI, 2001), arguing that differences within regions are as great as differences between them. It is implicitly assumed that jobs cannot be steered towards people in anywhere near the required degree, and so people have to be able to move to regions where jobs are available.

The regional economic imbalance has created an unbalanced housing system. In the growth regions of the south, housing shortages have led to high house prices and affordability problems for low-income workers. In the low-growth areas of the north and west there are problems of low demand and, at the extreme, abandonment of some unpopular neighbourhoods (Bramley and Pawson, 2002). There are two key issues for housing policy here. The first is whether resources are allocated to public sector housing in a way that accords with economic forces and promotes economic development. The second is whether the production process for private sector housing, including the statutory land use planning system, which is meant to ensure that appropriate land is available, are supporting economic development through the provision of housing to ease shortages.

The first issue strikes at the heart of conflicting conceptions of the role of public sector housing. One conception is that the sector exists primarily to cater for those in most acute housing need. If this is accepted, the allocation of resources should follow indicators of housing need, as has happened for many years in Britain. The result is that most resources have been targeted at the regions of slow economic growth, where housing conditions are worst. A number of well-publicised examples of new public sector schemes in these areas have had to be demolished after a few years because of low demand (Bramley and Pawson, 2002). But, more importantly, even if the houses had been let, the policy can be criticised for supporting population stability rather than allowing people to move.

In more recent years, the formula for allocating funding has been changed, with less emphasis on housing need and more on housing shortage (Bramley and Pawson, 2002). The result has been a reduction of resources directed at less affluent regions and an increase in resources for the regions where economic growth is higher, particularly London and the south-east of England. The primary argument for this change is that it supports economic development and allows people to take up employment opportunities in areas of the country where there are shortages of relatively less expensive housing. The approach has been linked with particular labour market shortages, particularly the lack of public sector workers such as nurses, teachers and police officers in London. However, this emphasis can be criticised for ignoring people in housing need in the deprived areas of the country and helping only those with the ability to move. What happens to those who are too old, sick or disabled to move? The same arguments apply to the criteria for the allocation of resources within regions as well as between them.

The dilemma strikes at the heart of the public sector role. Is it there to cater primarily for those who are not in work and so cannot compete in the private market? Or is it a sector catering for a wide range of needs and demands, and an instrument for the achievement of a wide range of public policy objectives, including the promotion of economic growth? The major problem with catering primarily for those in most need is the creation of a sector of last resort that caters only for those unable to access other tenures. This has been the case for the last 30 years in Britain, resulting in a residualised and stigmatised sector whose popularity has fallen.

The major difficulty with a wider role is the subsidy structure through the housing benefit system, which can provide disincentives to work for council tenants (see Chapter Four). Public sector rents have increased substantially in real terms over the last few decades, and so where house prices are affordable, most households have the financial incentive to enter owner-occupation. It is only in places where house prices are relatively high and entry to owner-occupation unaffordable for low-income working households that the public rented sector will be considered by many working households. This situation is most likely to occur in areas of strong economic growth such as London and the south-east of England. It may also apply in some rural areas where the ownership of second homes or retirement homes by affluent, usually urban, dwellers can render house prices unaffordable for households working in the seasonal tourism industry or in low-wage agriculture. The problem is that working households may have difficulty getting access to public sector housing in these areas because allocation policies are based on housing need. Also, high public sector rents may cause problems for households whose incomes are above the thresholds for the receipt of support through Housing Benefit.

The second major issue highlighted above was the production process for private housing in areas of high economic growth. The focus here is on owner-occupation; the private rented sector will be considered later. Private developers are content to build new houses in areas of high economic growth where there is an assured market and high land costs can be recouped through high house prices. However, the major concern is the extent of this supply, which seems to be consistently below levels of demand. Barker (2003) shows that the UK has a lower level of responsiveness of house building to demand than most other countries. This is partly due to the reaction of developers to the uncertainty created by volatility in house prices, which means that they see their interests being served by restricting supply to reduce the risks of unsaleability. They are able to do it without suffering competitive loss due to the lack of competition in some parts of the industry. Apart from the risks associated with volatility, Barker (2003) argues that the house-building industry faces site-specific risks that developers seek to contain. This manifests itself in risk-averse behaviour such as outsourcing of many functions, a low level of innovation, and a reluctance to take on complex developments that may be associated with some 'brownfield' sites. Another issue that constrains a high level of housing completions is said to be skill shortages in the industry, particularly in areas of high demand (Barker, 2003).

Another major problem is the availability of land. The land use planning system is at the heart of this issue (Barker, 2003). It is the duty of local planning authorities to ensure that there is enough development land allocated in development plans to meet the predicted increases in demand. However, in areas of housing shortage there is often a lack of suitable land and political pressure from existing residents to constrain further development. There is also pressure from other land uses, such as recreation, or pressure to protect wildlife or the landscape. In addition, the government has set targets for the use of brownfield sites for development in order to restrain urban sprawl and to increase densities in cities to promote environmental sustainability.

The planning machinery designed to achieve land availability for house-building in Britain has been subject to considerable criticism (Barker, 2003). It is said to be too complex, with an over-reliance on discretion in individual planning agreements, which makes it difficult for developers to predict accurately the costs and timescale of development. Central government has set targets for local planning authorities to meet on the basis of projected housing need, but lower targets have been adopted in some areas by planning authorities responding to local political pressures.

The overheating of the housing market in the south-east of England is seen by the government as a major factor in the instability and volatility of the market as a whole. The Treasury has become very concerned about its perceived impact on economic convergence with the Eurozone; hence the government's drive to increase the rate of new house building. Many elements of the Labour government's strategy came together in the White Paper *Building sustainable communities*, published in 2003 (ODPM, 2003c). The primary aim is said to be to focus government effort and resources on the creation of new communities in the south-east of England in order to meet the large demand for houses driven by economic prosperity and employment growth. At the same time there is a weaker commitment to helping some areas of low demand in the north of England, although it is unclear how government intervention will increase demand in the face of declining employment opportunities.

Even if appropriate housing is available, the regional imbalance in employment opportunities and the perceived failure of regional economic policy to alleviate it shifts the focus to the mobility of households. Are households prepared to move to take up employment opportunities?

Mobility and housing

The migration rate of manual workers in the UK is very low compared with some other countries such as the US (Hughes and McCormick, 1990). Hughes and McCormick argue that council tenants are less likely to move for job-related reasons than either owner-occupiers or private tenants, even though they have no less intention or desire to move. Therefore, they conclude that the organisation of public rented housing and the access procedures and priorities need to be changed in order to encourage greater mobility.

McGregor et al (1992) question this interpretation of the data and argue that the income and social status of the household are the most important factor in influencing mobility. In a housing field where there is substantial income differentiation between tenures, it is argued that mobility rates between tenures will vary substantially. A high proportion of all moves are job-related within a company, and these are more likely to be offered to more senior and more highly-paid staff. Households in this situation are likely to be offered substantial help to enable them to move (Doogan, 1996). This can include payment of transaction costs such as estate agent and solicitor's fees in buying and selling houses. Other costs such as removal expenses or the costs of furnishing a new house may also be paid. These inducements may be offered to skilled employees in order to encourage them to change companies as well as to those moving within the same company. In contrast, low-paid employees are more likely to be recruited from the local labour force and there is unlikely to be any help with moving home to retain employment or find new work. However, Doogan (1996) also shows that employers' help with housing can often be used to obstruct mobility rather than to promote it. He refers to employers who termed their long-term housing support 'golden handcuffs' because it was designed to tie key staff into the organisation, thus reducing staff turnover and maintaining the commitment of key members of staff.

It is very difficult to unravel the various influences on mobility of income and tenure as the two are so closely related. Nevertheless, it is clear that barriers to mobility are inherent in all tenures in Britain. In the owner-occupied sector there are substantial transaction costs in moving. Professional fees usually have to be paid to estate agents, surveyors and solicitors. The house moving process in Britain has been said to be one of the most efficient in the world (Diamond and Lea, 1992). Nevertheless, there is an increasing government focus on the transaction of buying and selling houses. Reforms have been suggested to minimise the incidence of 'gazumping' (that is, transactions being broken off when a higher bid is received by the seller, resulting in uncertainty and possible abortive costs for the buyer) and to cut down on delays in the purchase process. There have been attempts to simplify the acquisition of information needed for purchase and to require the seller to provide the information.

Other barriers to mobility relate to specific conditions in the owner-occupied market. During the 1990s there were particular problems with households that found themselves in negative equity. This occurs when falls in house prices reduce the current value of a house below the outstanding debt owed by the mortgagors. This phenomenon will be considered further in Chapter Four, and its roots in the deregulated financial system and in the lending practices of banks and building societies, explored. However, it is clear that a household in negative equity will find it hard to decide to sell its house if it is left with a substantial debt that will have to be repaid. The obvious strategy for households in this situation is, if possible, to sit tight until house prices rise enough to cover their debt.

Another major barrier is regional differences in house prices and demand for housing. Regional house price differences are large. For example, the average price of a house in the north of England was

£71,117 in 2001 compared with £182,534 in Greater London (Wilcox, 2003). If a household wishes to move from the north of England to London in pursuit of employment, regional house price differences mean that it will have to substantially increase its housing costs or reduce the quality of its housing (or accept a mixture of both). It also faces the problem of selling its existing house in what may be an area of low demand and to purchase one where demand may be strong and the availability of houses restricted. Owner-occupiers in the high-price regions are reluctant to move to a low-priced region for fear of being priced out if they want to return (Barker, 2003). The differences in house prices may be offset to some degree by differences in regional wage rates. However, the existence of large regional house price differences is clearly a barrier to inter-regional migration.

The barriers to mobility for public rented tenants are a function of the way that the sector is organised and managed, which is primarily through local authorities that own and manage the majority of stock. There are some central government directions and constraints on the methods whereby they manage their housing stock. These have increased in recent years as central government has sought to increase its influence by responding to what it perceives as inefficiency and a poor service to tenants on the part of some local authorities. Intervention has taken the form of legislation, monitoring through regulatory bodies such as the Audit Commission, and demonstration projects designed to show how it should be done (an example is the Priority Estates Project; see Power, 1982). Within the broad constraints set by this intervention, local authorities are largely free to manage their stock as they wish. This freedom includes the ability to set their own allocation policies. As a result, local authorities tend to give priority to local people, who of course are their local electorate. Within points-based allocation schemes some priority is usually given to connection with the local area. In addition, most schemes involve waiting in a queue for the offer of a tenancy. People moving into the area for employment reasons are not likely to be able to wait long for accommodation. Some local authorities give an element of priority to workers moving into the area by, for example, reserving a proportion of lettings for this group; but how widespread this practice is, and the number of dwellings involved, are unclear

A similar picture exists for housing associations. In England, a few associations are national in scope and so can enable tenants to transfer from one part of the country to another. However, this is not true for Scotland or Wales, or for the vast majority of associations in England, which are generally based in particular localities or regions. Therefore, local administration militates against mobility, although there is some evidence that housing associations may be more flexible in their allocation policies and procedures than local authorities, and the lack in many cases of strong local democratic accountability allows them to resist local pressure for priority for local people.

One response by central government to these problems has been to establish the HOMES mobility scheme, which is specifically intended to aid mobility for employment. Under the scheme, local authorities make available a proportion of their lettings to households moving into the area for work. The problems are that local authorities tend to put forward the properties they find difficult to let, which of course tend to be the most unpopular ones. In addition, there is a shortage of properties available for letting in areas of high demand, which is usually where households wish to move. Therefore, the scheme needs to overcome these problems if it is to provide a significant answer to mobility problems.

Private renting

This sector is often regarded as the one which offers fewest barriers to mobility and the easiest and quickest access for households. Access to the tenure is usually determined by the availability of appropriate stock, the perceived suitability of the tenant in the eyes of landlords or letting agents, and the ability to pay the access costs. These are usually made up of one month's rent in advance plus a bond (usually of one month's rent) as security for damage to the property or failure to make rental payments, and possibly commission to a letting agent.

The availability of dwellings in the private rented sector has been the subject of considerable analysis, mostly focusing on the decline in the sector from around 90% of housing in 1914 to 9% in 1988. The reasons put forward for the decline are many and complex (for a review, see Crook, 1992; Kemp, 1993). The most often-cited reason is the existence of statutory rent controls during most of this period. Rent controls were first implemented in 1915, during the First World War, largely as a result of civil unrest on Clydeside and elsewhere, over rising rents in a period when the government was concerned about the impact of low morale on the war effort and was looking over its shoulder at events in Russia. Rent controls were viewed by the government as a temporary expedient that would be removed once the war was over and the private market was able to reassert itself. However, once implemented, it became difficult politically to remove the controls, and they remained in one form or another into the 1950s.

In 1957 there was an attempt to deregulate the tenure, but the form of deregulation (on vacant possession) led to the harassment of tenants, and political uncertainty relating to the intentions of future governments encouraged landlords to cash in while they could by selling their properties. Therefore, deregulation hastened rather than halted the decline of the sector, and there was little sign of new investment. Rent regulation was reimposed during the 1960s, but gradually scaled down during the 1980s until it ceased to be a factor for all new dwellings or for most existing ones.

During the existence of rent controls there was little new investment in the private rented sector. This reflected low returns to investors, which both put off new investors and also restricted the return for existing landlords. This resulted in a lack of money for maintenance and repairs for existing properties and a consequent decline in the quality of the stock in the sector. The rate of return from private renting as compared with other investments was further depressed by the taxation position of private landlords, who were not able to take advantage of the depreciation tax allowances available for investment in capital projects such as industrial and commercial property. Also, owner-occupiers with a mortgage were able to claim income-tax relief on their mortgage interest payments. There is some dispute over the benefit that owner-occupiers received from this tax relief as some or all of the relief may have found its way through to land prices. However, to the extent that owner-occupiers benefited, the costs of owning were reduced relative to renting, thus changing the relative financial desirability of the two tenures to households. There has been no change to depreciation allowances, but mortgage interest tax relief has now been abolished and private tenants, like their public sector counterparts, may be eligible for income-related Housing Benefit on their rental costs. Although there are limits to the amount of payment, rents are assessed as market rents.

The decline of the sector up to the 1980s left the sector with four main roles. The unfurnished sector largely catered for older people who had lived in the sector for a considerable time, generally in old property often with poor facilities and in poor repair. The furnished sector was often inhabited by students or other young people as a first step in their housing pathway, because of the entry costs of other sectors. The tenure also functioned as a temporary housing solution for people who may have moved for employment or family reasons, such as a marriage breakup. Finally there was a small luxury sector with high housing standards and high rents. The sector was geographically concentrated in major cities and particularly university towns, and tended to be in older and less popular parts of the city such as inner-city residential areas. The majority of private lettings were by individuals as landlords (over two thirds in 1978; Todd et al, 1982). Therefore, the focus of government intervention has been to attempt to persuade institutions to invest in the sector.

Since 1979 there have been a number of attempts to stimulate more investment in the sector, particularly through the Business Expansion Scheme. Although the take-up of this was relatively good, investors were primarily interested in a short-term return, and it did not result in a long-term increase in the amount of stock available (Crook and Kemp, 1996). Further attempts to stimulate investment and encourage institutional involvement were made through the introduction of Housing Investment Trusts, which also had little impact (Crook and Kemp, 2002).

Despite the very limited success of government policies designed to stimulate investment in the sector, the long-term reduction in the size of the sector was halted in the 1990s and early 2000s. It has stabilised at about 10% of the stock. The fortunes of the sector now seem to be closely tied to the fluctuations in owner-occupation. During the early 1990s, with problems of declining prices and increasing mortgage costs in the housing market slump, the informal end of the private rented sector increased as households, having problems in paying their mortgages, let out rooms to increase their income, and some households in negative equity let out property that they were unable to sell (Crook and Kemp, 1996). Since then house prices have increased steadily, and the private rented sector has been boosted by 'buy to rent'. This mainly involves investors buying property in popular areas where prices are increasing, in the hope of capital returns on future sale, but letting the property in the short term. This activity has reinforced the picture of the sector being mainly composed of small landlords, but it has boosted the top end of the market, in particular with the availability of more new and good-quality stock.

There is little recent research on the third possible barrier to entry, which is the attitude of landlords towards potential tenants. In the past, there has been concern over the discrimination against minority ethnic groups and households with children. There is some anecdotal evidence that some landlords are reluctant to take households that are dependent on housing benefit, whereas some parts of the sector cater specifically for this group.

Some emphasis has been placed on the private rented sector because a number of commentators have argued that the perceived problem of labour mobility in Britain could be solved through an increase in the private rented sector (Maclennan, 1994). As an easy-access tenure, it is argued that it is best placed to allow households to move for employment reasons without causing substantial housing dislocation. At the same time it is argued that a larger and more attractive sector will enable households to postpone their entry into owner-occupation until later in their employment pathways, which it is assumed will be more stable. A larger private rented sector is also put forward as a way of stabilising fluctuations in the owner-occupied sector by providing a safety valve. We will return to this in Chapter Four. The key questions for advocates of this approach are how, and to what extent, the sector can be encouraged to grow.

Bringing jobs to people

There has been little emphasis in the last few decades on attempting to move jobs to people because of the government's perception of the failure of earlier policies of encouraging industry to locate in disadvantaged regions. In addition, government has argued that the importance of regional employment imbalances has been overestimated and that differences within regions are just as important. Therefore, policy attention has been focused on the concentration of unemployment in particular disadvantaged neighbourhoods; and the Neighbourhood Renewal programme designed to deal with this problem has been seen as an element of economic development policy (DTI, 2001). The problem has been defined as a lack of motivation and job skills among people in these neighbourhoods. Although there is a general policy to deal with these issues through the New Deal programme, it is admitted that this approach on its own will not necessarily bring employment to the socially excluded communities where access to employment opportunities is poor, mobility is difficult, and job skills, confidence and motivation are lacking. The New Deal programme, introduced in Britain in 1998, has been aimed at improving the skills of the long-term employed to bring them back into the job market (as well as making benefits dependent on job searching behaviour, thus reinforcing the work ethic). In addition, as part of the social exclusion and neighbourhood renewal programmes, there has been an emphasis on increasing employment in disadvantaged areas (Clapham et al, 1995). The New Deal does not usually create jobs but increases the employability of individuals. The social exclusion approach often involves a mixture of employability elements as well as attempts to target jobs at the people and areas alleged to be in greatest need.

A number of approaches can be adopted separately or together. The first is to attempt to improve the job skills and motivation of households. This may take the form of personal and vocational skills development, and employment advice and counselling. Assistance in applying for employment and specific training or job placement can also be given, along with help and advice in establishing a small business. Work-spaces may be created as part of a housing regeneration programme. Childminding schemes may be established both to enable people to go to work and to provide employment.

Employment opportunities related to housing areas may be targeted on local residents. Opportunities may arise as part of rehabilitation of the housing stock to employ local people and train them in building skills. Ongoing management activities such as housing maintenance and repairs, security, and gardening and landscaping may offer the same opportunities. One approach to this has been to establish community businesses. These are non-profit organisations that usually aim to employ local people while providing a local service such as those outlined above, or local shops or cafes. Finally, alternatives to traditional employment may be developed to enable those without work to make ends meet more easily. Examples are credit unions, food co-ops or local economic trading systems (LETS), which operate a formalised exchange for people to offer their own skills in exchange for those of others without a cash payment.

Schemes to improve economic life on socially excluded estates have encountered difficulties of funding. They are also criticised for merely redistributing employment without creating new jobs. It is argued that housing-related schemes have often given rise to only short-term employment and have trained people in marginal occupations such as construction, which are subject to fluctuations in employment opportunity. Thus they have contributed to what has been called labour market churning, with marginal people moving in and out of jobs rather than experiencing a long-term change in their employment prospects. Gordon (2003) notes three disadvantages of locally targeted job creation. First, the costs per job created are higher than in more general schemes. Second, there is substantial 'leakage', as people who gain employment move out of the area and are replaced by others who are unemployed. Third, it distracts attention from the measures necessary to ensure that disadvantaged people are competitive for 'mainstream' jobs.

Anyadike-Danes et al (2001, p 21) argue that the local focus confuses labour market effects with housing effects: "People are not unemployed because they live on run-down council estates. Rather they often live on run-down council estates because they are unemployed". They argue that unemployment is not a neighbourhood phenomenon but a feature of local labour markets that are larger than neighbourhoods, and government action to deal with the problem should be aimed at this level.

Cheshire et al (2003) draw attention to the spatial interactions of the labour and housing markets that lead to the segregation of different income groups. They argue that this segregation has increased in recent decades because of the greater income inequalities in a flexible labour market. Where people in a deprived neighbourhood improve their position in the labour market, for example by getting a job, they tend to move to a more desirable neighbourhood as their income increases. This highlights a seeming paradox: the more successful the employability programme, the higher will be the unemployment rate in the neighbourhood because of the increased mobility.

Flexible housing?

The dominance of the flexible labour market discourse has both placed an emphasis on housing and shaped the way that housing policy has been seen. A particular focus has been on the way that the institutional structure of housing hinders households from moving to take up employment opportunities. This has led to a policy emphasis on reducing transaction costs in owner-occupation and on enabling the private rented sector to grow. However, it is unclear whether housing policy changes have increased labour mobility. The policy mechanisms have been marginal in comparison with the scale of obstacles to movement created by market conditions in the owner-occupied sector and the barriers of institutional structure and localised lettings policies in the public rented sector. The private rented sector has not grown sufficiently to provide the large, easy-access sector that some have advocated. Despite the limited impact of these policy mechanisms, it is important to recognise the importance of the flexible labour market discourse in defining the policy terrain. For example, without this discourse it is unlikely that there would have been policy interest in sustaining the private rented sector, given the image of the sector and the political imperative of support for owner-occupation.

The importance of the flexible labour market discourse can clearly be seen in concern with the affordability of housing in growth regions. Here, the perceived needs of the labour market have led to funds for new public sector housing to be reallocated away from the traditional aim of meeting need towards the aim of supporting employment objectives.

Doogan (1996) argues that the roots of the flexibility discourse are embedded in neo-classical economics and the assumption of the superiority of free markets in labour and housing. Therefore, the policy prescriptions that have flowed from the discourse have stressed deregulation and the dismantling of supposed barriers to flexibility on the assumption that their demise would lead to greater mobility. However, the importance of these barriers can be disputed. An alternative discourse could see mobility (the key component of flexibility) as being what Doogan terms a process of 'structured opportunity' that is determined by people's labour market positions as well as their personal characteristics. The structure of the labour market, and individuals' positions within it, strongly influence the choices open to them both in employment and in housing. Within this context, immobility is not solely determined by the inflexibility of the organisation of housing, or by the personal preferences of households, but by the interaction between these often complex factors. An understanding of mobility needs to examine the complex interaction of these factors at the level of individual households and their housing and employment pathways.

Households, jobs and housing

At the level of the individual household, decisions about housing and employment will often be inextricably linked. One of the major functions of a home is to provide access to employment opportunities, and of course employment usually provides the money to pay for housing. Households may be faced with trade-offs between housing and employment goals. For example, the main earner in the household may wish to take advantage of employment opportunities in another location. This situation could lead to a complex household decision-making process in which factors such as the benefits of the existing home and locational stability may be compared with the benefits of a new home and job. There may also be an option of long-distance commuting, which may have different costs and benefits for different members of the household. Different household members may have different views, and these have to be reconciled through a decision-making process in which members have differential bargaining power. It was mentioned in Chapter Two that research has shown that men generally make these important decisions in the household. McCrone

(1994) found in his sample of households in Kirkcaldy that the woman's employment and home situation was usually subordinate to the man's.

> Apart from the few cases where the woman has had to become the main breadwinner, in most households the woman's work patterns have to accommodate to the man's. This can take the form of uprooting the household to follow the male career, or adapting working hours and practices to fit in with male routines of work. (McCrone, 1994, p 83)

Nevertheless, McCrone found that males generally adapted their work patterns to fit into the wishes of the household.

For single-person households this decision-making process may be simpler in that only one person's views may have to be considered. However, single people may still have close personal relationships with friends, lovers or family members that impose locational constraints. In other words, people outside the household may be considered and may have substantial influence over work and housing decisions.

There is little empirical evidence on household strategies and decisions concerning work and home. This reflects the research emphasis on the duality of structure and agency identified in Chapter One. One study is worthy of attention because it reflects the type of approach needed if the gaps in knowledge are to be filled. The study was carried out some time ago by Forrest and Murie (1987), who focused on a selection of affluent owner-occupiers in one area of Bristol. Their research technique was the biographical interview designed to illuminate what they called the housing histories of their sample. The people interviewed by Forrest and Murie were, variously, self-employed, professionals in the public sector, executives working for expanding multinational companies, or small businessmen. A number were described as 'localist', having spent all or almost all their housing pathway in the Bristol area, mainly because they were tied to family businesses in the area. However, most were mobile, having lived in a number of places because of career moves, and expected to move again in the near future. These moves were either with the one employer or involved changing employers, but they were usually supported by employers through financial and practical means. The high level of mobility of this group influenced their attitude towards the purchase of housing. They were generally concerned to maximise the equity value of their houses by choosing dwellings considered to be highly saleable and by investing as much as they could afford. This was done, not to generate wealth, as they were already well-rewarded through their jobs, but to facilitate mobility. Many had thoughts of moving to high-value areas such as London, because that is where employment opportunities were concentrated, and wanted to be able to do so without sacrificing too much in terms of housing quality.

Forrest and Murie concluded that the housing pathways of the households in their sample were dominated by their employment circumstances. In particular, the male job was the driving force, even though a number of their wives were in employment. The husband's work came first and the housing situation was designed to support this. Breugel (1996) draws attention to the implications of the dominance in some households of the male career in determining migration decisions for what she calls the 'trailing wife'. She argues that trailing wives are as prevalent as ever, despite the increasing number of women in employment. In many cases the market for 'women's work' is local and so many wives feel they can pick up equivalent employment in a new location. For Forrest and Murie's movers, employment considerations determined their general location – that is, the city they lived in – and so they were dependent on the geography of their industry. Nevertheless, the specific location or neighbourhood was strongly influenced by family considerations such as the availability of good schools for the children.

The fieldwork for the research was undertaken over 20 years ago, and Forrest and Murie comment on the historical specificity of the experiences of the households. However, the research highlights a group of people for whom housing choices are strongly influenced by their employment circumstances and whose housing pathways were dominated by their employment pathways.

This study is an example of the kind of research that can illustrate the links between work and housing at the household level. However, the employment categories covered are very narrow and specific. Much more needs to be known about households in other employment circumstances and with different priorities between work and housing. The aim should be to construct typologies of different kinds of households in terms of their orientation towards work and its relationship to their housing pathways.

Conclusion

This chapter has argued that the discourse of 'globalisation' has had a significant impact on housing mediated through the discourse of a 'flexible labour market'. Flexibility has both provided the context for the behaviour of employers and workers and been an influential framework for housing policy. It has been argued that the adoption of the flexibility discourse and the priority accorded to it by government has led housing policy to be primarily seen as an instrument of employment policy. The chapter has shown the importance of the flexible labour market discourse on defining policy issues. There is an emphasis on using housing policy as a way of supporting economic growth, through, for example, providing new housing in growth areas and easing the process of moving home to improve labour mobility. The continuing focus on the health of the private rented sector can be traced in large measure to its perceived role as an easy-access tenure that can aid labour mobility. Therefore, housing policy can be seen, at least in part, as an element of labour market policy.

A flexible labour market has increased a sense of insecurity, which may have an impact on the way that people view their homes and what they want from them. It may also influence their willingness and ability to pay for them, as we shall see in Chapter Four. It has also changed the pattern of use of the home for some households. For some dual-income families with an 'untypical' pattern and long hours of work, the amount of time spent in the home is small and the pattern is based on 'shift occupation' rather than on communal activities such as the 'family meal'. Others who are 'portfolio workers' may spend a substantial amount of time at home, which may function as an office as well as a place of relaxation and leisure.

Households are faced with a complex array of factors concerning their housing and work situations. We know very little about how they deal with this on a day-to-day basis and how they reconcile different pressures and concerns. In what circumstances do employment considerations take precedence over home issues, and in what way? Do households vary in their orientation towards work and home, and what different forms does this take? How are different views within the household reconciled? There are few answers to these questions because of the lack of emphasis in housing research on the household and its functioning. The pathways approach provides a framework for further empirical examination of these questions by bringing together analysis of discourses and action. As Doogan (1996) argues, issues such as geographical mobility can best be understood as the outcome of a complex interaction of discourses and household perceptions, attitudes and behaviour.

FOUR

Paying for housing

This chapter assesses the way that households pay for their housing. In line with the pathways framework, the emphasis is both on the discourses and related institutions that structure opportunities and on the behaviour of households. The interaction between households and the institutional structure is examined in particular through the experience of households that encounter problems in meeting housing payments.

Institutional structures have been socially constructed in order to enable households to pay for housing. Payments can be a large proportion of a household's expenditure as housing can be a costly and relatively large item of consumption. These institutional structures are organised on the basis of housing tenures, which impose on households different rights and obligations and different types and sizes of financial payments. The institutional structures are based on the need for tenants to make rental payments or for owner occupiers to fund purchase usually through borrowing on a loan or mortgage. Government in Britain has been heavily involved in the construction of these institutional structures and has subsidised housing payments. The justification for this intervention has varied over time and been the subject of political debate and conflict, but a common element is the belief that housing is a basic requirement that all households should be able to enjoy. Given the high cost of housing, some households may not be able to acquire the use of what is perceived to be an appropriate standard of accommodation without government financial support. This support has been given primarily in the form of housing-specific grants or allowances rather than general income supplements in order to ensure that it is spent on housing rather than other commodities.

In addition, it has been recognised that housing, because of its location, is a means to enable access to a wide range of public and private resources. The ability to purchase high-quality housing by paying a high price can lead to advantages in accessing other opportunities such as well-paid employment and 'positional goods' such as good schooling or a pleasant environment. Conversely, those households that can afford to live only in low-price, unpopular neighbourhoods may find themselves at a disadvantage in attempting to gain employment or to access positional goods. Therefore, housing influences life chances through enabling the purchase of healthy environments that offer good access to employment and public and private facilities. In addition, housing can impact on the acquisition of wealth, as the ownership of housing has been an important element of household wealth in the UK (Forrest and Murie, 1995). In short, the differential ability to afford housing is an important factor in the creation and persistence of income and wealth inequality. Therefore, government intervention in the financing of housing has sometimes been defended as a means of achieving wider egalitarian aims, although it has been strongly criticised for not achieving them in practice (see for example Le Grand, 1982; Hills, 1991).

The first part of the chapter sets the scene by examining some of the factors that influence household attitudes and behaviour by shaping opportunities and constraints. The impact of the discourse of the flexible labour market, discussed in Chapter Three, is outlined, and the associated discourses of social security and poverty are introduced. All of these discourses influence the income of the household, which is an important factor in enabling households to meet housing costs. Therefore, recent trends in household income are described, focusing on the degree of inequality between households which will structure the degree of inequality in access to housing.

Spending decisions impact on the consumption of housing through the mediating mechanisms of the institutional structures of housing finance, which influence the choices and opportunities open to households on their housing pathways. Therefore, the chapter continues with an analysis of these structures in the different tenures. In the owner-occupied sector, the structures consist of financial institutions such as banks and building societies as well as government involvement through regulation. The chapter focuses on changes in these structures made in the 1980s, which have shaped the sector as it exists today and show, in sharp relief, the underlying perceptions behind them. In the public rented sector there is a complex system of government funding through housing associations and local authorities, with housing associations also borrowing from private lending institutions. There is not the space here to describe in detail the specific arrangements in each sector. Readers are referred to Gibb et al (1999) for this information. The aim here is to emphasise the socially constructed nature of these structures and to examine some of the discourses that have been used in this construction and trace their relationship to wider discourses of globalisation and labour market flexibility. In all sectors there is substantial government intervention through regulation or subsidy, and this is associated with policy discourses that reinforce and justify the extent and nature of this intervention.

The housing pathways of households are influenced by the interaction between household decisions and the institutional structures that shape the choices and opportunities open to them. Therefore, the focus of the chapter then moves to the attitudes and behaviour of households. The chapter reviews what is known about the way that households handle their personal finances and budget for their expenditure. A key issue is the proportion of their income households are willing to devote to housing. A review of the evidence shows that households in similar circumstances devote very different amounts to housing.

The emphasis then moves to household wealth and its relationship to housing. Some households view the purchase of a house as a financial investment that will result in the accumulation of substantial wealth. This may be used to fund household consumption or passed on to subsequent generations through inheritance. The chapter reviews what is known about the influence of investment issues on household decision-making and planning in terms of mobility and repair behaviour.

The chapter continues by focusing on two situations in owner occupation and public renting where households experience difficulties in paying for their housing. The first is the situation in the public sector where households are unable to meet their rent payments. The second is mortgage arrears where households are unable to meet their financial obligations to make regular mortgage payments to a financial institution. Again, the major focus is on the early 1990s because this was a time when arrears were at their height and were the focus of much research and policy interest. The reasons for mortgage arrears are explored, and the social practices of government and financial institutions, and the reaction of households to them, are examined. A particular focus is the strategies that households pursue in attempting to cope with these difficult circumstances. These examples show the way that housing pathways are shaped by the interaction of households with the institutional structure.

Discourses of housing finance

Chapter Three described the impact of the globalisation discourse on the labour market through the associated discourse of 'labour market flexibility'. Employment is the major source of income for many households and so changes in the labour market can impact on households' ability to pay for housing. Labour market flexibility has been associated with a widening of income differentials. Hills (1998) notes that earnings growth for the richest tenth of the population between 1979 and 1995 was over 60%, compared with a growth of 40% in average income and 10% for the poorest tenth. During the 1990s income differentials did not widen as much as they did during the 1980s. Nevertheless, inequality was still greater in the mid-1990s than at any time in the previous 40 years. The index of inequality (the Gini coefficient) was greater for the UK in the early 1990s than for any country apart from the US, and had grown faster than any other country since the 1980s. Between 1994/95 and 2001/02 there was similar income growth across the income distribution, and the ratio of incomes of the top fifth to the lowest fifth showed little or no change (Palmer et al, 2002). Therefore, although the UK is a very unequal country, the inequality is presently relatively stable. However, the extent of income inequality will underpin the unequal opportunities open to households in pursuing their housing pathways.

For some households, income from employment is supplemented by social security payments. For others, welfare benefits may constitute the sole income. Meeting the housing costs of welfare claimants has been a problematic element of social security. This is partly because there can be very different levels of payment for the same quality of accommodation between geographical areas or between different public sector landlords (because of historical factors associated with the funding structures). Also, households may devote different proportions of their income to housing. A failure to meet these costs through social security benefits may lead to the loss of a home. Therefore, housing costs have been treated as a separate element of social security payments and dealt with on an individual, means-tested basis. For tenants, housing costs may be met in full or part by Housing Benefit, which will be described later. Owner-occupiers may get help in meeting the interest costs on their mortgage. Therefore, as we shall see later, the discourses of social security will have an important impact on the amount that some households will receive to meet their housing costs and the form that the assistance takes. An important element of the discourses concerns the relationship between benefits and the labour market. The desire not to undermine the financial incentive to engage in paid employment is one of the key features of the social security discourse and the policy mechanisms designed to deliver benefits. The example of Housing Benefit will show how the flexibility discourse has been associated with strong criticisms of the current system because of its alleged impairment of flexibility by undermining incentives to work and its inability to cope with fluctuations in household income.

The structure and discourses of social security will depend to a large extent on the discourses of 'poverty', as the alleviation of poverty is one of the key aims of policy. Poverty discourses usually contain elements that define poverty and explain its causes as well as appropriate mechanisms for dealing with it. They may be divided into discourses that focus on the individual and those that stress the importance of structural factors. In addition, discourses vary in the importance they attach to monetary income and in the priority given to monetary payments to increase income as an appropriate policy response to poverty. For example, discourses of the underclass, multiple deprivation and social exclusion, include a wide variety of factors in their definitions of poverty such as poor access to public and private facilities, poor health and environmental conditions and so on (see Chapter Six).

Given these different discourses there is no universal agreement on the extent of poverty, but a common EU measure is of income below 60% of the median income. A total of 12.9 million people were below this threshold in the UK in 2001. This is a fall of 1 million since 1996/97 but is still almost double the number of 20 years ago (Palmer et al, 2002). People in minority ethnic groups are more likely to be in poverty than members of the white population. For example, Berthoud (1997) found that Bangladeshis and Pakistanis had four times the poverty rate found among white people.

Discourses such as the underclass or social exclusion emphasise the enduring nature of poverty and its transmission from one generation to another. Without denying the existence of this kind of poverty, a discourse of 'new poverty' has emerged (see for example Leisering and Walker, 1998). This discourse sees poverty as an experience which touches a wide range of households, but is one which is often passed through. Leisering and Walker (1998, p 13) argue that "poverty is a phase in people's lives, be it short term, long term or recurrent" and that "poverty is no longer confined to members of the lower classes but reaches well into the middle classes if only as a temporary experience. Social risks are shared by many members of society – the new ecological and technical risks of (late) modernity affect everybody". The flexible labour market is an important element of this discourse because it is held to have increased the risk of episodes of poverty for households from a wide range of occupational and income categories. Some empirical support for the discourse of the new poverty is given by Jarvis and Jenkins (1998) in their analysis of the British Household Panel Survey. They argued that there was a substantial amount of income mobility between the years studied (1991 and 1992). They found that many of the people on low incomes in 1991 no longer had low incomes in 1992 and vice versa. They divided their sample into 'low income stayers', 'escapers' and 'low income entrants'. They conclude that "there is significant turnover amongst the low income population; over a two year period, a significant minority of people experienced low income at some time during at least one of those years" (Jarvis and Jenkins, 1998, p 157). This analysis is supported by data from the British Household Panel Survey between 1991 and 2000 (Palmer et al, 2002) that shows that only 2% of households were below 60% of median income for all those years, but 49% were below the threshold for at least one year.

The triggers for poverty identified by Jarvis and Jenkins (1998) varied considerably with the particular circumstances of the households concerned. Therefore, they argue that the emphasis in public policy should be one of intervention at key trigger points, with policy mechanisms that are sensitive to individual circumstances, and support households to sustain their independence and self-esteem, and to move out of poverty as quickly as possible. The Report of the Commission on Social Justice (Commission on Social Justice, 1994) argues for "an intelligent welfare state which is able to help people negotiate unpredictable changes within both family and workplace. The welfare state must enable people to achieve self-improvement and self-support. It must offer a hand-up, not just a hand-out" (1994, p 8). The Commission proposed the idea of 'investment Britain' (see also Giddens, 1998) in which individuals would be encouraged and supported to invest in their own futures primarily through lifelong education and learning. This is put forward as part of a proactive strategy for the state to provide the conditions for people to be able to cope with uncertainty and risk and to control their own destinies in the rapidly changing world. The concept of 'new poverty' and the remedies suggested for it are closely associated with the flexibility discourse and with the arguments in Chapter One about the incidence of risk in a postmodern world.

The social construction of finance for public rented housing

The provision of new public rented housing has traditionally been subsidised through the availability of capital subsidies from central government. During the 1990s new building by local authorities almost completely ceased and the concentration since then has been on provision by housing associations. Under the financial regime established in 1988, associations are paid a grant that in recent years has covered about half of capital costs. The remainder of the cost has to be met by borrowing from private financial institutions or from the use of internal reserves. The grant rate has decreased over the past ten years, which has created some pressure on rent levels, with rents increasing at a rate much faster than inflation. Therefore, in recent years there have been attempts in the different countries of the United Kingdom to link capital grants to rent levels in order to restrain rent increases.

The reduction in capital grants has been part of a deliberate attempt to move subsidies away from 'bricks and mortar' and towards people through the means-tested Housing Benefit system. The rationale for this is that help is concentrated on those 'who need it most'. At the same time the range of incomes over which some element of Housing Benefit has been paid has been reduced. This has been done by increasing the rate at which benefit has been withdrawn as income increases.

The result is an increase in what has been called the 'poverty trap' facing some households. The impact of the trap varies with the make-up of the household and the rent level, but many households on benefits or with low incomes are faced with marginal tax rates of over 85% (Hills, 1993). Any moves to reduce the problem by cutting the rate of withdrawal of Housing Benefit would increase the number of people in the trap, so there is a trade-off between its depth and breadth. A variant of this trap is the unemployment trap. This is when the difference in net income in employment compared with being out of work is small because of the loss of benefits. There is a concern that this constitutes a disincentive for some households to engage in employment. This problem is reinforced by the design and administrative complexities of Housing Benefit, which create problems for tenants who move in and out of work or who suffer variable earnings.

Assessments of the impact of the poverty and unemployment traps are often based on the assumption that households react solely to financial incentives. The limited research on this topic suggests that the way that the tax and benefits structure works does have some impact on household decisions; but this is only one aspect of often complex decisions (McLaughlin et al, 1989). Other factors that households often take into account include an attachment to traditional gender roles and a frequently strong commitment to work and 'self-sufficiency', even where this is perceived to result in a net income below income-support levels. If households take up employment in these circumstances, they often face money management problems and are vulnerable to disruptions in income, which are an important feature of the flexible labour market discourse. Ford et al (1996) found that a half of their sample made an economic calculation when assessing employment opportunities and based choices on it. A quarter made the calculation but overrode it, and a further quarter made no calculation. They found that, overall, the commitment to work was strong.

Only one study has been undertaken looking specifically at the role of variations in housing costs on household decisions about entering employment (Bradshaw and Millar, 1991). From their study of lone-parent families, Bradshaw and Millar (1991) predicted that a 10% increase in rents and housing benefit would slightly reduce the probability of a lone mother taking up full-time work from 48% to 46%. Much more research is needed before the impact of Housing Benefit and rents policy on the incentive to work can be properly assessed.

Rising rents as a result of the reduction of 'bricks and mortar' subsidies have meant that an increasing number of public sector tenants receive Housing Benefit (just under 60% in 2001). However, for those who do not receive help, rising rents have reinforced the perceived financial benefits of owner occupation. The position of the public rented sector varies considerably in different areas, reflecting different labour market and housing sector conditions. For example, in London there is an overall shortage of housing and house prices are relatively high. As a result there is a demand for public rented housing from those in low-wage occupations who cannot afford owner-occupation. In other areas of the country where economic conditions are less favourable and house prices lower, demand for public sector housing tends to be confined largely to people out of work. In both types of area public renting is the residual tenure for those who cannot afford owner occupation, but the particular groups this applies to vary according to the context.

The implications of the move from 'bricks and mortar' subsidies and the resultant rising rents on the role of the public sector and the situation of tenants has increasingly been recognised at central government level. Therefore, grant levels have not been reduced for a number of years and controls on rents have been introduced. Most attention has focused on proposals for reform of the Housing Benefit system. These proposals are particularly interesting because they illustrate attitudes towards the sector and its tenants.

Housing Benefit provides tenants with a rebate on their rent. The level is determined by the level of the rent as well as the tenant's household circumstances and income. Households eligible for Income Support (the means-tested benefit designed to provide a minimum income for those in poverty) have all of their housing costs met. For incomes above this level the amount of support is reduced by 65 pence for each additional pound of net income. There are detailed regulations that relate to the level of rent eligible because of the lack of any incentive for landlords and tenants to constrain rent levels (for further details of the regulations see Gibb et al, 1999).

From its inception the system has been subject to substantial criticism. Much of this has centred on the administration of the scheme. The desire to tailor the benefit to individual circumstances, together with concerns to prevent fraudulent claims, has meant that the administration of the benefit has always been complex. When it was first implemented, and in subsequent years of major benefit changes, there have been long delays in making payments. This has led to tenants falling into arrears with their rent, not knowing whether they will eventually receive benefit payments. The position faced by landlords has also been difficult. Delays in agreeing entitlement to Housing Benefit have left landlords unsure of their position when tenants get into rent arrears. There have been repeated attempts by central government to simplify the system; but the introduction of regulations designed to reduce the incidence of fraud has made the process more difficult for claimants, landlords and benefit staff.

The difficulties with Housing Benefit are not confined to its administration but are also inherent in its design (Hills, 2001). It has never been clear whether it is primarily an instrument of housing policy or a welfare benefit. As a result of this lack of clarity, responsibility for it at central government level has passed between social security and housing ministries with resultant changes in focus and culture. Should the focus be on the interaction between Housing Benefit and other welfare benefits through factors such as the unemployment or poverty traps, or should it be on the housing sector impacts on, for example, rent levels and incentives for landlords? At various times all have received attention, but have never been tackled in a sustained way. Of course, Housing Benefit has implications for both the social security and housing sectors.

Other criticisms of Housing Benefit relate to its possible impact on household behaviour in addition to the lack of work incentives through the unemployment and poverty traps. It was mentioned earlier that tenants have no incentive to economise on housing costs and could be argued to have the incentive to move 'upmarket' knowing that their costs will be paid. The detailed regulations necessary to counteract this have greatly complicated administration of the benefit. Also, it is argued that households receiving the benefit develop little responsibility towards the payment of their rent as it can meet 100% of rent costs. This effect is alleged to be even more pronounced when landlords have the rent paid directly to them (a measure designed to minimise the likelihood of rent arrears developing). Therefore, for tenants on full benefit there is no direct financial relationship between them and the landlord. It is argued that this can lead to a lack of commitment to the tenancy and a lack of control over one's life. It fits badly with discourses that emphasise the need for independence, flexibility and responsibility. Kemp (1998) has argued that Housing Benefit should meet only a proportion of the rent and all tenants should have to pay some (say 20%). It is argued that this gives tenants a sense of responsibility for the payment of the rent as well as an incentive to 'shop around' for better-value accommodation. Households are argued to have some control over their expenditure priorities, being able to trade off extra expenditure on housing with other household items such as clothes or holidays. Therefore, reform could increase household choice, autonomy and responsibility (Hills, 2001). Critics of these reform proposals point to the higher levels of welfare benefits in countries that have a household contribution to rents, and argue the low level of welfare benefits in Britain would lead to hardship. They are sceptical of the element of choice entailed for households that are on the poverty line and can afford only essentials.

This discussion has highlighted key issues concerning the role of Housing Benefit and the discourses that surround it. The present Housing Benefit system has been heavily criticised because of its incompatibility with the demands of the flexibility discourse. Labour governments since 1997 have seriously considered reform as part of their welfare-to-work strategy, and after a number of failed attempts, a pilot programme was instituted in 2003 in the private rented sector in a number of local areas. The pilot programme moves away from the idea of a benefit that meets actual housing costs. Instead, an allowance scheme has been introduced based on household size and characteristics and average rent levels in the locality. It was hoped that this will radically simplify administration of the benefit while reinforcing household responsibility and control. A number of pilots have also been introduced in the public sector from 2003 with the intention of expanding their scope over time.

The social construction of housing finance for owner-occupation

The institutional structures of private sector housing finance vary considerably between different countries. This simple point serves to show that there is nothing inevitable about the structure or practices of housing finance institutions. It is sometimes assumed that markets in general have a common and predetermined structure that is implicit in their status as markets. However, markets are created and sustained through human agency in different circumstances. A key player in this construction is the state, which creates the legal and institutional framework within which markets operate.

The institutional structure of the British owner-occupied sector has historically been based around the building societies (for a history of the building society experience see Boddy, 1980). They started in the early nineteenth century as self-help societies primarily formed by skilled working class people in order to organise the building and financing of owner-occupied housing. These societies were temporary in that they were disbanded once all the members were housed. They were also based on a direct link between saving and being housed. Both of these features disappeared during the nineteenth century as the sector grew and became subject to government regulation through a series of Acts of parliament. By the late 1980s, building societies had become major financial institutions with a clear role and a close relationship with government.

The state has played a key role in constructing the finance system. This was evident in the early years of the building societies and has been continued up to the present day. It is illuminating to compare the private housing finance sector in the mid-1980s with the sector in the 1990s. This shows how the sector has been radically refashioned largely through government action.

In the mid-1980s there was a very distinctive and internationally unusual institutional pattern that involved the building societies and the government. There was a large number of building societies, although a few of the largest dominated the market. The organisations had a mutual ethos, being owned and controlled by their members who were their depositors or savers and borrowers. However, accountability to the membership was not strongly developed. Essentially the societies were run by their senior management with little control from the membership. The societies were conservative in their operations, generally sticking to tried and tested practices with little innovation. They were risk-averse with stability a major organisational objective. There was a close relationship with government, which regulated their activities through a legislative framework. This had as its cornerstone the protection of borrowers and savers. Therefore, it laid down rules on the financial structure of societies and limited their role to the housing sector. Within this sector the societies were given taxation advantages over other financial institutions, making it difficult for their dominant position to be challenged by, for example, the high-street banks. Competition between societies was gentle and limited in scope. An effective cartel of the large societies set interest rates. Therefore, price competition did not exist and rivalry for customers was never of primary importance and was restricted to general image promotion and competition for prime high-street sites. Coupled with managerial control, this resulted in luxury branches with large marble halls!

Government used the societies as one of the major instruments of macroeconomic policy. Through the Bank of England it controlled the amount of money the societies could lend by stipulating the amount they had to deposit with the central bank. This was one part of a wide range of controls on credit and on financial transactions such as currency exchange, which supplemented interest-rate changes. When it wished to control credit to reduce economic activity and restrain inflation, the Bank of England would restrict the amount of credit the societies could offer and, conversely, would increase credit availability when it wanted to increase economic activity. This resulted in a relatively stable housing sector with credit being expanded when house prices were falling and restricted when prices were increasing. In this way fluctuations in house prices were evened out and this helped to stabilise fluctuations in consumer spending and general economic activity.

The relationship with government was a cosy, corporatist arrangement that suited both parties. The societies received tax advantages and a protected environment in which competition was limited and entry to the sector difficult. The government turned a blind eye to interest rate collusion and in return had an effective tool in the management of the national economy. Consumers had the advantage of a stable housing market, but the risk-averse behaviour of societies, together with the credit controls, meant that the availability of mortgages was limited. There were queues for mortgage lending and the building societies used rationing criteria based on a household's creditworthiness and savings record as well as the location of houses. Housing research studies in the 1960s and 1970s drew attention to the discriminatory behaviour of societies in denying loans to people in areas that were perceived as at risk of house price decline or who, because of their ethnic origin or economic position, were considered to be at risk of not meeting repayment obligations. The 'red lining' of some, usually inner-city, locations was held to be a major factor in the decline of some parts of cities (Boddy, 1980).

In the 1980s a number of factors influenced the government to change the sector. The increasing globalisation of financial capital resulted in pressure from the financial community to lift controls on the sector to allow it to compete with other world financial centres. Banks became increasingly critical of what they saw as the favoured position of building societies and demanded access to the housing sector. This coincided with the election of Conservative governments from 1979 onwards that discarded the traditional Keynesian techniques of economic management, which included the housing stabilisation arrangements, and instead put their faith almost exclusively in control of the money supply to manage the national economy. These Conservative governments were also committed to owner occupation and so perceived the rationing behaviour of societies as restricting the growth of that sector.

Therefore, a new institutional system was constructed during the 1980s by the government. Barriers to entry to the housing finance sector were reduced and, in return, restrictions on building society activities were relaxed and societies given the option of turning themselves into public limited companies along the lines of the existing high-street banks. The system of colluding on the setting of interest rates was outlawed and competition encouraged. The system of credit controls operated by the Bank of England was dismantled as part of a general deregulation of the financial sector. Government relied on the policy instrument of interest rate changes to regulate both the housing sector and the wider economy.

One result of these changes was the entry of new players into the housing finance sector. This mainly consisted of the high-street banks, but also included, during the 1980s, direct lending institutions that did not rely on consumer deposits to provide the funds for mortgage lending. Instead, funds were borrowed directly from the money markets. Competition increased and interest rate variation between lenders appeared. Many societies took advantage of the opportunity to shed their mutual status and become private banks. This change was achieved by 'buying off' the mutual owners through the provision of cash payments for their loss of ownership (see Stephens, 2001).

Although these changes have often been termed 'deregulation', government intervention still exists, albeit of a different kind. The emphasis of government regulation now seems to be to ensure barriers to competition are minimised and consumers are protected from unfair practices. An example of the latter is government action to insist on the provision of certain information to consumers, for example, over the selling of endowment mortgages. The discourses surrounding policy for the private sector are ones of choice, efficiency and consumer protection. Finally, successive governments of both major parties have accompanied deregulation with a withdrawal of subsidy to owner occupation through mortgage interest tax relief (MIRAS). This was achieved in stages as part of a wider tax restructuring and was justified on the basis of restraining house price inflation.

The institutional structures described above provide the framework that shapes the opportunities and choices available to individual households in paying for housing. A household looking for housing is faced with an array of possibilities within the price that they have decided, in the light of lending practices of finance institutions and their own household expenditure decisions, they can afford to pay. Of course, house prices vary in different locations and change over time. One of the unusual features of the British housing lending practices is the overwhelming dominance of variable rate mortgages. This means not only that people are moving house faced with different housing costs at different points in time, but that households staying in the same accommodation may find their housing costs changing as interest rates are varied as an instrument of macroeconomic policy.

The results of the changes are difficult to specify. It is clear that competition has resulted in a wider range of financial products available to consumers and has ended mortgage queues. However, in the new interest rate competition the traditional mutual building societies have consistently undercut the private banks, their rivals. This has not stopped the rush of mutual societies to change their status, or restricted the capture of large parts of the market by the banks. There is also a concern that the new system has resulted in increasing volatility of house prices, which has a destabilising impact on the economy as a whole. This issue will be explored in more detail because of its importance to households. The focus is on the volatility in the late 1980s and early 1990s as this caused considerable problems for many households and shaped views of the sector since (for a review, see Clapham, 1996).

The fluctuations in the housing market in the late 1980s and early 1990s can be gauged by examining mortgage advances for first-time buyers, who tend to be the most vulnerable owner–occupiers. The average monthly repayment cost of a mortgage increased as a proportion of average income from 19.9% in 1985 to 26.9% in 1990. By 2001 it had reduced to 17.1% (Wilcox, 2002). The considerable variation over time can create problems for some owner–occupiers whose mortgage costs increase, particularly if this occurs at a time when they are also experiencing income reductions. The levels of mortgage arrears and repossessions also show considerable variation. It is evident that there is a close relationship between changes in costs and arrears, with the latter following a couple of years behind the former. The time lag makes sense because there will be a period of adjustment by households to changes, and problems will grow over time as some households struggle to cope. There was a steep increase in mortgage costs in the late 1980s that reached a peak in 1990. This reflected economic conditions at the time, with an economic boom in the late 1980s being countered by increases in interest rates. Mortgage arrears rose steeply in 1990 and reached a peak in 1991. Repossessions increased from 19,300 cases in 1985 to 75,540 cases in 1991 (it has since declined to 11,970 cases in 2002; Wilcox, 2003).

It is important to remember that the above figures reflect the number of households in arrears at particular points in time, whereas there is a continuous flow of households moving in and out of arrears. It is estimated that between 1991 and 1993, 20% of all mortgage holders moved into arrears at some point. This represented half a million households. The reasons for the sharp increases in mortgage costs and mortgage arrears at this time shed illuminating light on the changing nature of the British housing finance system and its relationship to the economy.

Rising interest rates designed to slow down the general economy were the immediate cause of the sharp increases in mortgage costs. During the latter part of the 1980s Britain experienced a consumer boom, with GDP growth every year from 1982, reaching a peak of 4.6% in 1987. Real personal disposable income also rose substantially, with a peak of 5.9% in 1988. This coincided with increases in net mortgage lending and in house prices. Both peaked in 1988, with house prices increasing by 22.7% in that year. The number of mortgages outstanding rose by 50% between 1980 and 1990, while the amount of money involved was six times greater despite only a doubling of general prices during this period (Whitehead, 1994, p 233). The large increase in mortgage lending could be explained by the increase in personal disposable incomes, but it seems more than a coincidence that it occurred at the same time as the deregulation of the housing finance system.

During 1988 the government took action to slow down the economy by increasing interest rates. Gross domestic product slowed and actually fell in 1991 and 1992. Mortgage lending also declined and house prices fell in 1991 and 1992. A cyclical pattern of house prices is usual, but the amplitude of the swings was of a level previously unknown. The close relationship between the economic fluctuations and changes in mortgage lending and house prices caused some commentators (including the Treasury) to pin at least some of the blame on to the housing sector. The argument was that the boom was fuelled to a large extent by increasing housing credit. The amount lent on mortgages increased substantially during the 1980s, and rapidly rising house prices encouraged households to withdraw equity to finance consumption. This caught the Treasury by surprise and led to underestimates of monetary growth, in turn leading to an unplanned overheating of the economy.

If the Treasury took some of the blame for the unprecedented overheating and resultant slump, other parties have also been blamed. Households have been accused of being greedy and taking rash decisions by overstretching themselves to take advantage of rising house prices. But most attention has focused on the behaviour of lenders in the new situation created by deregulation. During the 1980s boom, mortgage business increased substantially and this allowed new lenders to enter the newly opened market to challenge the building societies. The proportion of lending by building societies fell from 80% in 1980 to 60% in 1988 at the height of the boom. It had declined further to 53% by 1993 and to 18% by 2001. Banks increased their share from 6% in 1980 to 27% in 1988 and 49% in 1993. This grew to 79% in 2001 as many building societies converted into banks. At the height of the boom in 1988, new centralised lenders had 13% of the market, although this had fallen to almost nothing by 1993 as they rapidly disinvested in the slump. The rapid increase in mortgage business enabled the banks and new direct lenders to enter the market even though the building societies increased their own lending. All participants were concerned to increase their market share, thus leading to a relaxation of lending criteria and substantially increased lending at a time of rapidly rising house prices. It must be remembered that the previous stabilising mechanism operated through the Bank of England had been dismantled as part of deregulation. Therefore, the behaviour of lenders increased instability and there was no government mechanism to offset this. This behaviour by the lenders was encouraged by the traditional practice of insuring the top slice of the loan. When the slump came and lenders found that they did not recover the full cost of loans on some properties after they were repossessed because of mortgage default, it was the insurance companies rather than the lenders that suffered in the short term. When the downturn occurred the lenders did not have the cushion of generally rising house prices, and they responded by tightening lending criteria, which reinforced the downturn. Thus, the previous stabilising mechanism had been replaced by a market-based system that tended to exacerbate rather than diminish fluctuations.

One other contextual factor has been associated with the instability of the housing sector during the late 1980s and early 1990s. The flexibility of the labour market described in Chapter Three resulted in a large number of owner-occupiers losing their employment or experiencing a reduction of income in the economic slump. It is argued that the deregulation of the labour market enabled employers to lay off workers more easily, and the growth in self-employment meant that the economic downturn had a direct influence on employment. The residualisation of the public sector and the growth in owner-occupation meant that many of the people who suffered were owners. State help for people having problems with mortgage payments was small-scale and fell substantially when government realised the potential cost. The justification for this reduction was that it was the responsibility of owners to insure themselves for hardship. This is an interesting issue to which we shall return.

The volatility that occurred in the late 1980s and early 1990s has been followed by a relatively stable period of steadily increasing house prices reflecting the steady economic growth during this period. However, an important question is whether volatility is an endemic part of the institutional structure that will be renewed with changes in general economic conditions. Meen (1995) has argued that financial deregulation left the housing sector more sensitive to interest rate changes. International comparisons have shown that Britain was one of a group of three countries (the others were Finland and Spain) that all experienced rapid house price inflation in the 1980s with similar characteristics (Stephens, 1995). All deregulated in the 1980s, had high rates of owner occupation, and had small private rented sectors. However, these countries are not unique in these characteristics, and the experience of stability in Britain since the early 1990s has calmed fears of inherent and significant instability to some extent. Nevertheless, in 2003 the instability of the housing market was cited by the government as a major reason for the UK not to join the Eurozone and a number of policy prescriptions were put forward to promote stability. These included the wider use of fixed-rate mortgages and new or expanded taxation mechanisms such as stamp duty on housing transactions that could be varied at different stages of the cycle.

Household budgets and housing costs

The ability of people to pay for housing is determined by their income and wealth. In turn this is influenced by a wide variety of factors such as labour market conditions and discourses such as 'flexibility' that frame labour market behaviour. Government intervenes in the distribution of income and wealth through taxation and welfare benefit policies. These interventions are accompanied by discourses that frame them, such as concepts of 'new poverty', which are related to wider discourses such as labour market flexibility. The institutional structures of housing finance mediate between income and wealth on the one hand and housing payments on the other. The housing pathways of households are influenced by the interaction between household decisions and the institutional structures that shape the choices and opportunities. The focus in this section is on the attitudes and behaviour of households faced with these institutional structures.

A relationship would be expected between the income of a household and the amount it spends on housing. In a review of research on household budgets and housing costs, Kempson (1993) argues that the proportion of income devoted to housing costs varies widely with income levels. In a survey of public sector tenants, households in the poorest group paid on average a third of their incomes for housing whereas the richest group paid only one sixth. However, there were variations in the proportion spent on housing between households with similar income levels. These variations were particularly marked for households in the poorest group. Owner-occupiers spent more, on average, than tenants and it seems that households were prepared to pay considerably more in order to enter owner-occupation. In her review of the evidence, Kempson (1993, p 27) concludes that "people with identical incomes and family characteristics chose to spend very different amounts on housing".

How much is spent on housing may be influenced by the way that households handle their finances. Research by Pahl (1989) has identified different patterns of control and management of the household budget; in other words, the way that the common housekeeping budget (as against individual consumption) was determined. Some households pooled their income whereas in others members kept separate bank accounts. In some, the husband controlled the amount allocated to the general household budget, but in others the wife undertook this role. Pahl (1989) identified four patterns for managing how the common household budget was spent. The first is the whole-wage system in which one partner (usually the wife) is responsible for managing all the household expenses, including housing costs. The second is the allowance system whereby typically the husband gives the wife a set amount of money and she is responsible for the day-to-day expenses while he retains the rest of the money and usually pays the larger bills. The third is the pooling system in which both partners have access to all the household money and share responsibility for expenditure. The fourth is the independent management system in which both partners have an income that they maintain separately. Each of them takes on responsibility for different items of expenditure. The form of management determines who pays the housing costs. Overall, in 40% of households it was the man and in 30% the woman, with responsibility being shared in the remainder. It is unclear whether and how the method used to control and manage the household budget influenced the amount a household spent on housing.

Dwellings provide physical shelter and some emotional needs (see Chapter Five), but for some households in owner-occupation, dwellings are also a financial investment. A number of issues are of importance here. The first is the impact of financial investment considerations on the perceptions, attitudes and behaviour of households. The second is the way that households use the wealth accumulated in their housing and the possible realisation of the asset value through equity withdrawal. The third is the impact of this behaviour on the overall distribution of wealth in society and the importance of the inheritance of housing wealth.

It is difficult to assess the importance of financial factors in the decision to become an owner-occupier or to move house. These decisions are made on a wide variety of grounds in which financial issues are intertwined with a large number of other considerations. In Chapter Five the perception that owner-occupation is a secure investment is considered along with the other perceived benefits of the tenure. It has become an accepted part of the lexicon of 'home ownership' that it provides a secure investment for the future or 'something to pass on to the children'. The experience of the housing market decline in the late 1980s and early 1990s seems to have led some households to be more cautious in their behaviour, but has only marginally influenced the general perception of the financial benefits of the tenure, based on the long-term trend of increasing house prices in real terms (Forrest et al, 1999).

The financial benefits of owner-occupation are often contrasted with the allegedly 'lost money' of rental payments that do not result in the acquisition of an asset. Of course, housing is not the only way of acquiring wealth, and households in the rented sectors could conceivably invest the difference between what they pay in rent and the amount they would have to pay on a mortgage. However, there is little evidence that many do this in practice and so the ability to acquire an asset is an important perceived advantage of owner-occupation for many households. Just how important is difficult to assess because of the many different attributes of tenure, such as house and neighbourhood quality and the rights and obligations of occupancy. It is likely that the importance of the investment factor relative to the others may vary between households.

It is just as difficult to disentangle investment issues from others in the decision to move house. Very few households say that they move to a more expensive house in order to build up more equity. Moves are usually made for reasons of changes in employment or family circumstances. However, households may take advantage of the build-up of equity in order to 'move up the housing ladder' even if the main reason for moving is different. They may have in their minds a strategy of house moves that will reflect the ability to build up and reinvest equity and to take out new mortgages. This may be done in order to gain better-quality housing, but it may be done in order to acquire wealth that will be released for spending on other areas. Very little is known about how different households perceive these situations or about their motives.

It was noted earlier that households spend very different proportions of their income on housing. However, it is not clear whether this is related to different attitudes towards wealth acquisition. Do households concerned with building up wealth spend more on housing than households that are primarily motivated by consumption?

The issue of attitudes towards wealth acquisition is also important in decisions on house repair and improvement. To what extent are households motivated to spend money on their properties by concerns over whether the expenditure will add to the asset value of the house? Here again it may be difficult to disentangle the many factors involved. For example, the decision to add an extra room to a house (like a conservatory or loft conversion) may be motivated by a mixture of concerns about current consumption (the increased pleasure from use of the extra space) as well as asset accumulation (it will add to the value or price of the house). It may also be tied in with decisions about whether to improve the present house or to move to another. Again, this may involve a mixture of financial and other considerations. The problem with all of these issues is that the same behaviour may be motivated by different perceptions and attitudes.

The second issue is the way that households use the wealth accumulated in their housing. This wealth may have an important impact on a household in terms of a sense of security and well-being. Therefore, its very existence may influence household attitudes and behaviour even though it remains purely a hypothetical figure until it is realised. It may be thought that the increase in wealth through general house price increases is illusory because any household will have to live somewhere and the prices of other houses they may wish to purchase have also increased. However, housing wealth can be realised in a number of ways. One way is by trading down to a cheaper property and so cashing in some of the value. Even when a household moves to a more expensive house, a larger mortgage may be taken out that allows the deposit to be less than the cash gained from the sale. Another method is by remortgaging an existing house, in other words, borrowing on the basis of the asset value of the house. Forrest and Murie (1995) argue that these forms of equity withdrawal can be seen as ways of rescheduling housing expenditures over the lifetime of the household, as payments can vary considerably over time. Equity withdrawal may also be seen as a way of changing the balance between expenditure on housing and other items such as holidays or daily household living expenses.

Equity withdrawal reflects households making choices in their expenditure. But the scale and unpredictability of the process can create problems in managing overall demand in the economy. The inability to correctly foresee the extent of equity withdrawal in the late 1980s was one of the reasons for the overheating of the economy associated with the boom in house prices. This experience has led economic policy makers to change their models of consumer behaviour, and since 1990 they seem more able to predict and control equity withdrawal through general management of economic tools such as the interest rate.

The third issue is the passing on of housing wealth through inheritance. This increased markedly in the 1980s as the generation of owner-occupiers who entered the tenure in the boom of the 1930s reached the end of their lives. The number of estates in which housing wealth was a major part increased at this time and has continued to increase. There has been much interest in the impact of this phenomenon. The evidence seems to indicate that people inheriting houses do so when they are well into their own housing pathways (the median age is 50) (Forrest and Murie, 1995). They are faced with a number of options. They can sell the house and use the proceeds to pay off their mortgage or to finance non-housing consumption. They could sell both the original (if they are already owner-occupiers) and the inherited houses and move to a more expensive dwelling. The inherited house could be retained and used as the household residence with the original house being sold. Alternatively, the inherited house could be let on the private market. It could also be used as a second or holiday home or retained for the use of children. The wide range of options open to households means that it is difficult to predict the impact of inheritance on the housing system. Much interest has focused on the impact of inheritance of housing wealth on general patterns of inequality. The evidence seems to be that those who benefit most from inheritance are the initially better-off. Therefore, the accumulation of wealth through the ownership of housing is an important factor in the transmission of inequalities in wealth between generations.

The inheritance of housing wealth may be a transitory phenomenon that will decline in importance as households become more aware of it and take it into account in their life plans. For example, there is evidence that some households are cashing in their housing wealth in old age either to finance increased consumption or to increase the quality of life in old age by purchasing care and health services (see Chapter Eight).

In summary, little is known about the reasons for household behaviour in relation to payments for housing. Why do some people spend more on housing than others? How important are financial considerations in housing decisions?

Coping with payment difficulties

It has been shown earlier that rents in the council rented sector increased substantially from 6.9% of average earnings in 1980 to 13.2% in 2001 (Wilcox, 2002). This rise has led to a focus on rent arrears among tenants. The growing emphasis on performance monitoring in housing management has led to a concentration on this area as an indicator of the relative performance of different landlords.

Considerable quantities of advice are available to landlords in dealing with rent arrears (see Harriott and Matthews, 1998; Audit Commission, 2003). Points raised include the necessity of good information systems so that arrears can be spotted at an early stage and appropriate action taken. The importance of welfare benefits advice to tenants is stressed so that tenants can maximise their incomes. Most landlords will provide this advice to tenants or arrange with other agencies for this advice to be available. It is recognised that some households need help in coping with household expenditures on a low income and so advice and training in budgetary skills is also often available. Some organisations such as credit unions have been formed to enable households to save and to gain access to cheap credit. If arrears persist, most landlords have a graduated scale of action, starting with letters requesting that the arrears is paid off and ending with an application to the courts for eviction. In between, the objective of the landlord is usually to agree with the tenant a repayment schedule with regular payments of rent and arrears repayment. As long as any agreement is adhered to a court will be reluctant to evict the household. Households that are evicted for rent arrears can be considered to be intentionally homeless and so may not receive help from local authorities.

Little attention has been focused on the households that experience arrears. Kintrea and Scott (1992) compared a sample of tenants in arrears with a control group not in arrears. They found that tenants in arrears were more likely to have children in the household and were, on average, likely to have smaller incomes. However, many people not in arrears had incomes as low as those in arrears and a similar proportion in the two categories (about 30%) were in full-time employment. In other words, the average differences between the two groups were smaller than the similarities. The group of tenants in arrears experienced a wide variety of circumstances, as did the tenants in the control group. Some tenants were in arrears and others in similar circumstances were not. The predominant research technique used in most studies is the structured interview survey, which seems inadequate to give any real insight into why some households get into arrears and others do not.

Tenants on low incomes are faced with a difficult situation in budgeting for and meeting household expenses. It seems that tenants in arrears have similar views to others about the priority to be attached to different items of expenditure, with tenants in both groups giving the payment of rent a high priority. Interestingly, in the Kintrea and Scott study only 14% of tenants in arrears agreed strongly with the statement that 'people have a moral obligation to pay what they owe', compared with 29% of the control group. Over 70% of tenants in both groups agreed with the statement that 'people only pay what they owe because they are afraid of what could happen if they got caught for avoiding payment'. Clearly, whereas some households would pay expenses such as rent out of a sense of moral obligation, others will primarily look at the sanctions that can be applied to them.

Once in arrears, tenants are forced to respond to the actions of the landlord. Households may ignore any communications, or may seek advice from other parties such as the Citizens' Advice Bureau, or may negotiate with the landlord to pay off the debt in instalments. They may borrow money from family or from loan sharks or may leave the house and disappear in an attempt to avoid the consequences of their debt. Little is known about the perceptions and attitudes of different households in rent arrears and the strategies that they use to cope with the situation.

In contrast, more is known about owner-occupiers who get into arrears with their mortgage; and there has been a particular focus on the experiences in the early 1990s. The extent of mortgage arrears in the early 1990s has already been explored and some of the contextual reasons identified. The immediate cause of difficulty for many households was the sudden changes in interest rates, which increased their monthly payments. Those most at risk were those who bought at the height of the price boom, when lenders were giving loans at high multiples of earnings with high consequent monthly loan repayments. At the same time, many households suffered in the economic downturn from unemployment, small business failure and loss of earnings. Marital breakdown was also a common factor that could result in a sudden change in income (Nettleton et al, 1999).

An interesting aspect of the problem is that the households that encountered problems came from across the income spectrum. It was fluctuations in income and expenditure that caused the problem rather than low income as such (Nettleton et al, 1999).

The huge growth in arrears has placed emphasis on the role of the lenders in dealing with customers in arrears. This was an area that had not received much attention previously, and the lenders were slow to react to the growing problem. The decreasing house prices of the early 1990s removed from many households the primary mechanism for dealing with problems, namely, to sell the house and to move to somewhere cheaper or to rent. Many households found themselves in negative equity, whereby the market value of their house was less than the amount outstanding on their mortgage. Sale would leave households with a debt to the lender that would have to be repaid at some stage. This made it difficult to undertake further borrowing. Dorling and Cornford (1995) estimated that 21% of all people who had bought after 1987 were in negative equity in October 1991. Problems were particularly pronounced for those who had purchased cheaper properties and those in the Greater London area, where house prices declined furthest.

Forrest et al (1994) identified a number of strategies adopted by households that found themselves in negative equity. Some households that were on high and secure incomes tried to buy their way out by paying off a portion of their mortgage and thus reducing their indebtedness. There was a recognition that this involved 'money down the drain'. Some households traded down by moving into a cheaper house, thus reducing the size of their mortgage but often taking their debt with them. Others who were able to access somewhere else to live let their property while waiting for property prices to increase. Many chose to stay put and wait out the crisis in the expectation that prices would rise enough in time to wipe out the negative equity. This strategy often involved delaying moving house and so, in the eyes of some, a delay in moving up the property ladder. Others had to postpone a move that was desired for family or employment reasons, although a few, mainly higher-paid workers, received help from employers to enable them to escape the negative equity and move. Most who stayed put postponed investment in their property by delaying repairs or improvements as this was seen as increasing the money sunk into the house and throwing good money after bad. Interestingly, the experience of negative equity had not changed the desirability of owner-occupation in Forrest et al's sample, but owner-occupiers were less likely to stress the financial benefits of the tenure and more likely to focus on the use value of the dwelling. However, the authors comment that this could change as the market improves.

The difficulty for households in mortgage arrears and in a position of negative equity in selling their house led lenders to emphasise the management of arrears. Most were unprepared for this and lacked both the understanding and the policies and procedures to cope. As a result many lenders found themselves moving quickly to a position of applying for possession of the property of households in arrears and subsequently disposing of the property through auction at a relatively low price. This increased the problems of some households that not only found themselves turned out from their house but were also left with an outstanding debt that was larger than it need have been if the property had been sold at the market price.

The government was forced in the early 1990s to acknowledge that there was a problem and reacted in a number of interesting ways. One of the first actions was to reduce the help given to persons on income support to pay their mortgage interest costs. At first glance this seems surprising, as lenders would usually not take possession action if interest costs were being covered even if no loan repayments were being made. Government action seems to have been partly prompted by the desire to prevent a substantial call on public expenditure. It was also associated with a discourse of responsibility for the problems. Individual households were blamed for taking irresponsible financial decisions and were told it was their responsibility to guard against financial risk. The way to do this was said to be by taking out insurance cover for unemployment or health problems to cover the mortgage payments. This approach enabled the government to paint the difficulties in the early 1990s as a series of individual problems of irresponsible households rather than as a government or institutional failure. This approach to the presence of risk has since been maintained by successive governments, despite evidence that the insurance payments can be large enough to increase barriers to entry to owner-occupation for some households and that more marginal buyers, which are most likely to experience problems, have more difficulty in arranging and being able to afford cover. Of course, this approach suits the lenders, which make commissions on arranging insurance cover while reducing the risks to themselves of default.

The government also urged lenders to improve their practices towards households in arrears. They were encouraged to identify problems earlier, to offer better support and advice to households, and to negotiate recovery agreements to enable households to forestall possession. Also, a mortgage rescue scheme was implemented to enable some housing associations to buy the properties and to let them back to the former owners. In this way households could stay in their home.

There has been relative stability in the owner-occupied sector in Britain since the early 1990s, and the level of mortgage arrears and repossessions has decreased substantially. There were 18,280 cases of repossession in 2001 compared with 75,540 in 1991 (Wilcox, 2002). There is some debate over whether this is because instabilities like those of the early 1990s are a thing of the past. It is argued that prudent management of the national economy together with more 'responsible' behaviour from lenders and households has meant that problems will not occur on the same scale as before. However, the housing sector does seem to have some intrinsic elements of instability, and it remains to be seen whether they can be kept under control.

Problems with mortgage arrears can be very stressful for the households experiencing them. Nettleton et al (1999) found that many people who had been repossessed found the experience one of the most traumatic of their lives. Many people felt a lack of control over their situation. Mortgage debts arose for a variety of reasons, which sometimes occurred together and which in many cases people felt powerless to alter. In some cases wives were left by their husbands and discovered that debts had been left behind. Increases in mortgage payments and service charges were sometimes coupled with reduced earnings in employment or unemployment. Along with the lack of control went uncertainty, with people not knowing what would happen to them and where they would live. The loss of the home brought profound emotional responses in many people. These could be a mixture of anger, bitterness and hurt mixed with feelings of inadequacy and failure. People reported a loss of social status and identity related to assuming the categorical identity of homeless person or renter rather than owner. Self-esteem and confidence was also affected and many people suffered strained personal relationships and poor health.

Despite the reported lack of control, households pursued many actions both to attempt to save their home and to mitigate the consequences of losing their home (Burrows and Nettleton, 2000). Many continued a dialogue with their lenders, keeping them informed of the situation and attempting to negotiate reduced payments. This strategy sometimes worked for a limited period of time, but many lenders lost patience as time wore on. Croft (2004) argues that the capacity of households to act to ameliorate their situation varies at different stages of their debt trajectory. At certain points some lenders cease to listen to the households' point of view. Lenders also tended to categorise debtors into 'can't pay' and 'won't pay' groups and to act differently to households placed in each classification. She also points to many households' lack of information about the available options.

Households tried to find practical solutions to their difficulties in a wide range of ways. Burrows and Nettleton (2000) give examples of households borrowing money from family members or friends. Some decided to use 'last resort' lenders that made loans at high rates of interest, which provided short-term relief but compounded the financial problems in the medium term. Some households looked at ways of supplementing their income by working longer hours or taking in a lodger, or tried to reduce their expenditures. Despite the perilous position in which many households in mortgage arrears found themselves, and the lack of control over their circumstances that many felt, they still actively pursued strategies to cope with their situation and to improve their position. However, not all households pursued positive strategies. Some tried to ignore their problems, hoping something would turn up.

Even among those who pursued a positive strategy, many were not successful and had to cope with the loss of their home and the practical and emotional problems that it brought. They were then confronted with a different set of circumstances as they attempted to rebuild their lives in often difficult circumstances. They were faced with trying to find somewhere to live and mitigating the impact on important areas of their lives such as children's schooling. Finding somewhere to live often involved negotiations with local authority housing departments and other landlords. The loss of a home meant that household routines were often severely disrupted and had to be re-established in often difficult circumstances. Loss of the home was usually associated with a low income as well as possibly a large outstanding debt that lenders could insist on being repaid. The change of lifestyle and categorical identity involved often challenged people's self-esteem and ontological identity, and created scars that people carried for the rest of their lives. Croft (2004) argues that debt problems can have a long-term impact on a household's housing pathway because of its impact on the future behaviour of housing finance institutions (through 'blacklisting') as well as on the behaviour of the households themselves.

Conclusion

The chapter has sought to describe the institutional structure of housing finance in the UK and the discourses that are associated with it. Changes in the structure have been associated with the wider discourse of globalisation that has emphasised the necessity of freedom of movement of capital. This has led to the deregulation of private housing finance and the reliance of government on interest rates to attempt to stabilise housing market activity and reduce fluctuations in house prices. The influence of the 'flexible labour market' discourse can also be seen. For example, the incidence of mortgage arrears in the early 1990s showed that employment insecurity affected households across the income distribution. Pressure to reform Housing Benefit arises from its perceived contradiction with the 'flexibility' discourse. For example, the existence of poverty and unemployment traps, and the difficulty of households in claiming benefit when their income fluctuates or they move in and out of employment, are features that are perceived to hinder flexibility. The flexibility discourse emphasises people's responsibility to make their own lives by investing in their education and skills and making their own economic decisions. Mention was made in Chapter Three of the iconic 'portfolio worker'. This sense of responsibility is being applied to housing through the expectation that owner-occupiers should insure themselves against risk rather than rely on state financial help. A further example is the concern about

Housing Benefit paying all of a household's housing costs (often direct to the landlord) which is held to militate against the household taking responsibility for its own payments.

Much is known about how households behave in these situations in the aggregate, but little is known about differences in behaviour and their causes. Decisions about paying for housing are usually tied up with many other aspects of life. How do households decide what to spend on housing in relation to other items of family expenditure? How important are investment considerations in the decision to buy a house? Research is required to fill these gaps in our knowledge.

The discussion of household financial decision making on housing, and the strategies that households pursue to deal with financial crises, shows the importance of a pathways approach that examines interactions between households and the institutional structure. It is argued that analysis of the causes and impact of, for example, mortgage arrears needs to look at both the level of structure and individual agency. Households react in a variety of ways to the circumstances that confront them. However, the scope of agency is defined by structural factors. In other words, households may have more leeway at certain points in their pathways, and success in achieving their goals is by no means assured. For example, a household may adopt imaginative and constructive strategies to deal with a problem of mortgage arrears, but may still lose its home if the finance institution decides to seek possession for its own reasons. The pathways approach draws attention to the interactions between structural and agency dimensions and places them at the centre of the analysis.

FIVE

Houses and homes

This chapter focuses on a key theme of the book which is the importance, for housing research and policy, of the meanings attached to houses. It is argued that meanings exist at many levels. Individual households hold meanings towards their houses, but these are influenced by wider meaning structures associated with discourses of family, home, and tenure. Also, it is argued that meanings towards a house will be associated with other aspects of living and lifestyle.

House and home are two key concepts in the analysis of housing pathways. It was argued in Chapter One that many analytical approaches tend to treat houses as 'units of accommodation' that can be described by a number of 'objective' physical attributes such as size, amenities, repair condition or form (that is, detached house or flat). Much government housing policy is concerned with laying down physical standards for houses, which is usually justified either on the grounds of safeguarding the stock for future generations or as a public health measure. These standards can also be used as measures of the quality of the housing stock and targets set to meet goals for improvement. A house provides physical shelter for households and can be seen as a 'machine for living in'. Indeed, this is the way that it is perceived by many academics, policy makers and professionals solely concerned with the physical fabric of the dwelling. But a house is far more than this, as it is the setting or locale for certain social practices that we may call 'home life'. It is the setting for some of our most important, emotional and intimate relations and behaviour. But it is not a neutral setting. A house carries meanings that arise out of, and in turn influence the use of, the physical structure. As Arias (1993, p 1) argues:

> Use gives meaning to housing, and at the same time meaning guides how housing is used. How housing is used and what it means to those who reside in it ... and to those who do not have a house to reside, are probably the two most important topics to housing policy, planning or design in any cultural context around the world.

A distinction is often made between the terms 'house' and 'home'. Dovey (1985, p 33) sees the difference as follows:

> Although a house is an object, part of the environment, home is best conceived of as a kind of relationship between people and their environment. It is an emotionally based and meaningful relationship between dwellers and their dwelling places.

The relationship between dwellers and their houses is influenced by the relationships that people have in the setting of the house. These are related to social constructions of appropriate behaviour, which were discussed in Chapter Two. The key element here is the concept of the family. Home and family are two closely related concepts that are often combined into the one picture of a normative lifestyle. Housing plays major practical and symbolic roles that can serve to support or undermine the concept of the traditional family.

The chapter begins with a discussion of the physical fabric of the house and the policy instruments that have been developed to effect government policy to impose minimum standards. The rationale for this intervention is critically assessed and its limitations are explored. This is done through a discussion of different conceptions of housing quality. The main argument of this section is that it is impossible and undesirable to deal satisfactorily with the physical condition of housing independently of the use to which the house is put and the meanings it has for those living there.

The chapter continues by exploring some of these meanings. First, it focuses on the design of housing, looking at the forces that shape the form that housing takes. Different design conceptions and their impact on the built form are described and their underlying assumptions of the meaning and use of housing are made explicit. Designs encapsulate specific views of the nature of social relationships within the house and are related to societal structures of class and gender. These are often expressed through symbols and related discourses that link designs to the political arena.

The next section focuses on the concept of 'home' and looks at arguments that home is becoming more important to people in postmodern society. The section reviews the existing research on the meaning of home. Links are made between discourses of home and those of family and family life at different stages of the life course. Much of the existing literature on home focuses on the influence of tenure and the supposed importance of owner-occupation, or 'home ownership' as it is often labelled. The assertion that the experience of home is qualitatively different in different tenures is assessed. There is then a short section on the concept of homelessness. This analysis casts light on the meaning of home and shows the importance of both individual meanings and the wider discourses that influence them. Finally, the future directions for research are identified.

Houses

There are many different kinds of houses (see Goodchild, 1997, for a classification), which may vary in terms of their perceived quality. Perceptions of quality may differ over time as expectations change, may be culturally specific and may vary by class, gender or lifestyle. The dimensions of quality may include the size, internal layout, external appearance or location of the house. Goodchild (1997) uses the term 'habitability' to describe the extent to which the house supports human life or health. This is most often defined in the negative sense of the absence of harmful living organisms (such as moulds or infectious bacteria) or materials (such as asbestos, noise or atmospheric pollution). Goodchild (1997) draws a distinction between this concept of habitability, which concerns the impact of the environment on the human body, and what he terms socio-cultural aspects of quality, which concern the relationship between the house and the user's way of life. However this distinction is highly problematic because of the strong links between the two dimensions. Many common diseases are strongly related to lifestyle, and susceptibility to disease may differ substantially between individuals. In most forms of disease the body and the mind are closely related.

Government intervention in the quality of housing has tended to ignore this problem and to be solely confined to habitability in the narrow sense used by Goodchild. Therefore the emphasis has been on defining an objective minimum standard that all houses should meet. The origins of this approach lie in the public health concerns of the nineteenth century, when the twin emphases on unfitness and overcrowding emerged. There have been a number of statutory definitions of unfitness, which have varied over time and between different countries in Britain. The kinds of issues covered have included freedom from dampness; adequate natural lighting and ventilation; facilities for cooking and waste disposal; piped supply of wholesome water; drainage and sanitation; hot and cold water; wash basin, bath or shower; heating; and structural stability and adequate repair. Some of these elements can be judged objectively but many cannot. The definitions often contain words such as 'satisfactory' and 'adequate'. The overall test to be applied is whether any defect renders the house 'not reasonably suitable for occupation', with the primary consideration being that of 'safeguarding the health and safety of any occupants', and discomfort, inconvenience and inefficiency being secondary although relevant considerations. In 1996 around 7% of dwellings in the UK were considered to be unfit and this figure had declined to 4.2% in 2001 (ODPM, 2003b). Poor conditions were over-represented in the private rented sector. People living in unfit housing tended to be either at the start or in the later stages of their housing pathways and to have a lower than average income. Minority ethnic households were also over-represented.

Overcrowding has also been covered by statutory provisions since the late nineteenth century. Two guidelines are used here. The first is that the size of the property should be adequate for the number of people living in the dwelling (there are schedules of appropriate sizes for different numbers of people). The second is that adults of opposite sexes not living together as man and wife, and children over 10 years of age of opposite sexes, should not sleep in the same room. These standards arose partly out of a desire by reformers to inhibit the spread of infectious diseases and partly to discourage incest. The arbitrary nature of the space standards is underlined by the fact that a different and more generous standard is used in government social surveys such as the Survey of English Housing and the General Household Survey. According to the definition in the Survey of English Housing, 2.4% of households were overcrowded in 2003/04 (ODPM, 2004).

Standards for new private sector housing are laid down in building regulations and in voluntary standards adopted by the industry. The statutory regulations are more narrowly drawn than in other countries and make only passing reference to issues such as space standards or disabled access.

This discussion of the statutory standards relating to unfit housing raises a number of important issues. Although it is difficult to disagree with the concept of minimum standards of house conditions and amenities, there are many problems of implementation. The standards are arbitrary and difficult to define precisely, which accounts for the repeated use of terms such as 'adequate' and 'satisfactory'. Interpretations differ between individual surveyors and according to the use to which assessments are to be put. For example, there is evidence that surveyors tend to use a stricter definition of unfitness when assessing for enforcement action than for eligibility for grant aid (Goodchild, 1997, p 85).

But even if the standard could be defined precisely and variation in interpretation removed, the standard would still be arbitrary. Although justified on health grounds, evidence of the deleterious effects of housing that is sub-standard on this particular definition is very limited. For example, Myers et al (1996) argue that research in the US has never shown a consistent relationship between overcrowding and poor health. They argue that the pattern of overcrowding is associated with the distribution of newly arrived Asian and Hispanic households that may not perceive that statutory levels of overcrowding are harmful or unacceptable. Myers et al (1996) conclude that any standard of overcrowding is a form of ethnic imperialism, imposing the views of the majority on the minority. Walmsley (1988) argues that it is not overcrowding per se that is a health hazard but the powerlessness to deal with it by households if they perceive it to be a problem.

The evidence for a direct link between sub-standard housing and health is limited to specific issues such as the impact of dampness and mould growth on respiratory problems, particularly in children (see Lowry, 1991; Marsh et al, 1999). Any other health justification must either rely on the precautionary principle that it is better to be safe even if no evidence exists, or rest on the significance of poor conditions in interaction with a wide range of other factors such as low income, stress and lack of control or self-esteem. Byrne et al (1986) found that the self-reported health status of tenants living in unpopular or difficult-to-let housing was worse than that of tenants living in identical house types in more popular areas. This could be explained by the lack of choice available to less healthy tenants, resulting in their concentration in the less popular areas; on the other hand, it could be that their perception of their situation was crucial in influencing their health status. The latter view is supported by research by Woodin et al (1996), which showed that the rehousing of tenants from an unpopular estate led to an increased sense of well-being and a reduction in demand for medical services. They argued that the higher morale of tenants meant that they were better able to deal with problems. The importance of such factors in influencing health was stressed by Macintyre et al (2000), who found that the most important factors in predicting health and psychological outcomes were age, self-esteem and income. Poor neighbourhood conditions predicted more health outcomes than poor dwelling conditions. "In some respects, better housing conditions were associated with poorer mental health, so that having more consumer durables and a house that was worth more than others in the surrounding area were predictive of anxiety" (Macintyre et al, 2000, p 12). They also found a relationship between health and housing tenure, with households in public rented housing enjoying poorer health, but this could mainly be explained by differences in age and income. However, the condition of the dwelling and area, and the psycho-social benefits of protection, autonomy and prestige (more often associated with owner-occupation) were important in explaining the relationship between housing tenure and mental health.

All this evidence points to the importance of the perception by the household of the house in influencing health rather than any objective characteristics of the building. This view is reinforced by the lack of a consistent relationship between household views of the quality of houses and the defined standards. One well-documented example of this is the slum clearance campaigns of the 1960s when unfitness standards were used by professionals and politicians to suggest widespread clearance of whole areas of housing even though most residents wanted to stay where they were (see for example Gower Davies, 1972). A survey of people living in a clearance area in Birmingham showed that a majority of people saw the quality of their house in a more favourable light than professional surveyors, and considered the condition of their home to be acceptable (Heywood and Naz, 1990).

A more recent example is an assessment of a pilot project to test the use of an objective indicator of house quality by the DETR (2000). The measure used was found to be reliable in that it was interpreted consistently by surveyors. However, the measure was found to have no relation to the way households rated the quality of their houses. This did not prevent the assessors of the pilot lauding it as a major success and suggesting the measure should be widely used!

The analysis of resident satisfaction surveys carried out in tandem with house condition surveys gives some interesting results. First, many households who live in housing classified as unfit are satisfied with their house. This is particularly true of older people, who are in general more likely to live in unfit housing but who are more likely to be satisfied with their house. In other words, the level of satisfaction depends on the expectations, situation and position in the housing pathway of the household rather than primarily on the house itself. Second, studies that have attempted to correlate the physical features of houses and the satisfaction of residents have found unclear and often conflicting results. This could be because the analysis has usually focused on universal findings. It is possible and indeed likely that people will appreciate different elements of their house depending on their attitudes and lifestyle.

The position of houses in multiple occupation (HMOs) is another occupancy path. They argue that, typically, a household moves into a dwelling and in the early stages carries out substantial amounts of work to remedy defects and to achieve an acceptable level of comfort and aesthetic appearance. Further investment may follow on a lesser scale, but the amount of work declines until the household moves, when new occupants repeat the process. They argue that, as long as there is a frequent turnover of occupancy, repairs are dealt with in a reasonable fashion. Newly-formed young households may be willing to devote considerable time and resources to repairs and improvements if they have the financial resources. Households with young children may be less inclined to invest in major repairs because of the cost and disruption involved, but may be more willing to invest in improvements to increase comfort. Older people may be reluctant to undertake any cosmetic or repair work because of low income, the disruption and a declining Do It Yourself (DIY) capacity. They identify four situations where repair and maintenance is likely to be problematic. The first is where a household, especially an older one, remains in a house for a long period of time. The second is where a young household is unable to afford repair work. The third is where insecure employment reduces the confidence of the household and decreases its capacity to afford repairs. The fourth is where relationship instability and an increasing propensity to live alone undermine the capacity to finance repairs. Leather et al (1999) argue that each of these situations is likely to increase in the future. This approach is a useful one because it considers the dynamics of the maintenance process and ties it in with the situation of the household. However, the approach assumes universal attitudes towards the physical condition of the house by households at different stages of the life course. Only a limited set of variables is considered and there is no link to differences in lifestyle and attitudes. We have seen in Chapter Four that households with similar income levels vary considerably in the amount they spend on housing; and later in this chapter we shall see that households differ in the way that they view 'home'. Therefore, it is not surprising that there are differences in the way households consider the maintenance and repair of their dwelling, which the application of a pathways approach would make explicit.

The attitude of households to the maintenance of their house is often considered to be a major problem because many are said not to spend money on vital repairs (see Leather and Mackintosh, 1997; Leather, 2000). A number of policy directions are put forward to remedy this. The first is for the state to take responsibility for the condition of the private housing stock by providing grants to households to undertake repairs. This has been the predominant approach in the UK since the 1960s, but has declined in importance since the 1980s as the amount of money devoted to the programme has been reduced and many statutory obligations removed. This has been associated with a discourse that has emphasised the responsibility of individual households. Mechanisms have been devised to encourage and support households in undertaking repair and improvement. The most widespread and successful has been the Care and Repair network of agencies for older people, which provide information, technical help and advice on funding options to older owner-occupiers. The final approach is to change the workings of the housing market by increasing the knowledge on the part of purchasers of house condition in the hope that this is reflected more sensitively in house prices. This final approach fits well with discourses of responsibility and choice, and seems to be the present government's preferred option. The assumption is that households paying a lower price for a house in poor condition would be able to afford the resources to remedy defects. At the same time it is hoped owners would become more aware of the costs of ownership, thus changing their preparation for repair costs whether through insurance or a greater propensity to borrow against the equity. Leather and Mackintosh (1997, p 154) look forward to a time when:

> It would be as important to plan to meet housing repair costs in old age as to receive an adequate pension. Houses would come to be seen as liabilities as well as assets. Owners would be persuaded to see housing equity as a resource for repair and improvement work rather than as a source of wealth to be utilised for consumption purposes or passed on through inheritance.

The attempt to change attitudes would have more chance of success if it were based on an understanding of why households hold the attitudes they do and how they relate to other areas of their lives. Clearly there is a disjunction between the perceptions and attitudes of households towards their housing and those of professionals and policy commentators.

The main argument of this section is that the impact of the physical fabric of a house on its occupants is mediated by their attitudes towards the house and the meaning it has for them. As a consequence it is difficult to justify more than a minimal use of so-called objective indicators of housing quality that need to be interpreted in the light of household perceptions. It has been shown that there is not a consistent relationship between household views of the quality of houses and their physical standards. Housing mainly impacts on the health of the occupants where they feel a lack of control over their circumstances and low self-esteem and status. Houses are liable to fall into disrepair where households do not have, or are not prepared to devote, the resources necessary for their upkeep. The physical fabric of a house cannot be considered in isolation from the meanings and perceptions held by the occupants.

House design

Attention to the physical attributes of a house is not restricted to its condition and amenities but also focuses on its external appearance and internal layout – what may be called its design. As can be seen from a walk through any city, there are many different styles of house design. Fashions have changed over time and there are cultural differences – for example, not all European cities look the same. This section examines the factors that shape house design and its impact on households.

Lang (1993) distinguishes between rationalist and empiricist approaches to house design. Rationalism involves the application of logical reasoning from the designer. The emphasis in rationalism is on the efficient functioning of a house according to a set of principles of how people should live, and an aesthetic dimension based on the work of influential artists. Rationalism is, therefore, often utopian. It reflects an architect's view of the perfect world and of appropriate human behaviour. Rationalist designs have often involved a radical break from past practice. The most influential example of rationalist thinking is that of Le Corbusier (1960), with his radical designs of 'streets in the sky' and houses as 'machines for modern living', which led to the building of high-rise blocks of flats in many cities. Lang (1993, p 58) is very dismissive of the rationalist tradition: "Designs based on the designer's logical reasoning of how people should behave, what social organisations should exist, and the tastes that people should possess have been poorly related to how people wish to live and the meanings that they wish the environment to hold for them".

As Burnett (1986, p 267) argues: "People did not want 'a machine for living' so much as 'a vehicle for living out a fantasy'".

The alternative approach is the empirical one, which attempts to design on the basis of what people who are to use the house want. Lang (1993) argues that in practice this has often meant that casual observation by an architect of what has seemed to work in the past leads to conservative and traditional designs. However, there is a growing emphasis on the systematic appraisal of household needs and desires through research or by using techniques such as 'planning for real', which allow households to design the houses themselves under the guidance of professionals.

Brindley (1999) points to the distinction between the two approaches in the modernist architecture of high-rise and deck-access public sector housing built in the 1960s and 1970s. The internal layout of the flats was closely regulated by the state through space standards and design criteria implemented after the Parker Morris report in 1961. This guidance was based on an analysis of the preferences and needs of households and was conservative, being based on what had been shown to be popular. In contrast, architects were given free rein to innovate on the external design and arrangement of the flats, which led to radical designs that were a complete break with traditional house forms. Brindley argues that subsequent research on this form of housing has shown that households in general were happy with the insides of their dwellings but were unhappy with the exteriors, leading in some cases to unpopularity and demolition.

In practice it is more difficult to make the distinction between the two approaches because all designers have some degree of predisposition towards certain views of appropriate behaviour and design – it is just that some are more willing to compromise and to take on board the views of households. What this discussion draws attention to is the implicit meanings that designs have, both to those who design them and to those who live in them (as well as to those who view them from the outside). These meanings may be related to the behaviour thought appropriate to the space within the house or to the way the occupants are or wish to be viewed by outsiders. These meanings may be related to wider social structures. An example is the design of the kitchen reflecting certain societal views of the role of women in the home. Another example is the symbolism attached to the garden suburb form of design in the inter-war years linked to the political slogan 'Homes fit for heroes to live in'. The meaning of design will be explored by examining some design ideas in British housing.

Design in public rented housing

In public rented housing the provision of public subsidy has enabled the government to intervene in issues of design through the formulation of design guidance to local authorities and housing associations. Design has varied substantially over time, reflecting different political priorities of who should be housed and associated symbolic meanings. Immediately following the First World War the Tudor Walters report endorsed the ideas of the garden city movement, and many council estates were built at low densities and along tree-lined avenues. The political slogan 'Homes fit for heroes to live in' was associated with houses of a symbolic form of design aimed at the 'aristocracy of labour', the skilled working class that the government was keen to win over as a bulwark against socialism. A large housing programme came to be seen as a symbolic centrepiece and a visible demonstration of commitment to a social reform programme.

The adopted house design instigated by architects Unwin and Parker was a direct reaction to the Victorian bylaw house. This had a narrow frontage that resulted in a lack of light and a strong distinction between what Goffman (1971) has termed the 'front' and 'back' regions. The front region is a place of display to the outside world and a projection of identity. The front parlour was the public area where guests were entertained and the status of the household displayed. It was a large room with decorative ornamentation. The hall was an important room that served as a 'holding space' for visitors and to protect the family in space and time from intruders (Burnett, 1986). At the same time it was a display area that announced to the visitor certain things about the taste and social status of the household.

The back region was the arena for more personal and intimate activities where public display could be prevented. This was centred on a smaller family room and the kitchen or scullery (which was usually in a back extension) where the woman of the house (or, in more affluent households, the servants) worked. Home was not simply a place for a relaxed presentation of a real self away from public gaze in the back regions but also a place for the display of social virtues in the front region. Hepworth (1999, p 19) argues that this reflects the Victorian concept of home as a boundary against deviance – as a "place of constant struggle to maintain privacy, security and respectability in a dangerous world".

Burnett (1986, p 99) describes the many functions the middle-class Victorian home had to fulfil:

> ... to comfort and purify, to give relief and privacy from the cares of the world, to rear its members in an appropriate set of Christian values, and, above all, perhaps, to proclaim by its ordered arrangements, polite behaviour, cleanliness, tidiness and distinctive taste, that its members belonged to

a class of substance, culture and respectability. The house itself was to be the visible expression of these values.

The long thin profile of the Victorian house was replaced in garden city designs by a squarer profile that allowed more light to enter and enabled all the rooms to be of a more equal size. Taking their inspiration from the Arts and Crafts movement, Unwin and Parker proposed simplicity and honesty of materials and construction rather than ostentatious display. They disapproved of one room being reserved for display, and some local authorities dispensed with the front parlour altogether, to the annoyance of many tenants (see Swenarton, 1981). They wished to make the kitchen-living room a family room in which all manner of tasks could be undertaken. Roberts (1991, p 32) argues that this design was based on clear ideas about appropriate family roles and behaviour.

> The layout of the garden city, with its clear separation between work and home and its single-family housing let at a rent which only a skilled manual worker could afford, reinforced trends of women's dependency on men and the cultivation of an ideal family of a working man with dependent wife and child. The internal layout of the houses introduced a new way of regarding domestic work by dignifying it as part of family living rather than designing spaces so that all was kept from public view.

The aim of this example is to show the links between house design and political symbolism and social institutions such as the family. Ravetz and Turkington (1995) note that the Tudor Walters Committee saw the use of different rooms as a moral issue. Family life takes place in the home and so the design of the house reflects and is sometimes designed to stimulate certain conceptions of family life. The physical design and layout of a house carries meaning at a number of levels. As we shall see later, it also carries meaning for the household living in it, which may seek to alter the physical appearance or internal layout in order to change or reinforce that meaning.

The public funding and control of public rented housing means has often made it the subject of political symbolism and architectural vogue. The 'peoples' house' of the 1950s and the prefabricated and high-rise building of the 1960s and 1970s are other examples. The latter saw the modernist architectural ideas of Le Corbusier and others united with a political symbolism of modernisation and the 'white heat of technology' (see Dunleavy, 1981). Ravetz (2001, p 5) has argued that "the concept and material embodiment of council housing did not spring from working class culture.... The whole operation was a culture transfer amounting to a cultural colonization: a vision forged by one section of society for application to another, to whom it might be more or less acceptable and appropriate".

An example of the imposition of cultural values is the widespread provision of flatted accommodation in the public sector. Ravetz and Turkington (1995) argue that flats have a shorter history than the house, and have been seen as alien to the English (and Welsh) scene. This contrasts with experience in many European countries as well as in Scotland, which have a longer tradition of flat living. A minority form of provision in England, flats have rarely been the adopted form of the middle classes and have been associated with negative images such as the barrack-like blocks built for the working classes in the nineteenth century by the model dwelling companies. This negative image existed even before the provision of mass high-rise blocks of flats in the 1960s. Ravetz and Turkington (1995, p 57) argue:

> The essence of the problem of council flats was that, unlike the English house, their use by families was not rooted in a long evolutionary process. In addition they were the products of monolithic and large-scale design which gave little scope for the users to modify through their ordinary domestic behaviour.

Cole and Furbey (1994, p 112) argue that the imposition of design standards and the prohibition of alterations to the outside of dwellings through tenancy agreements has removed from tenants the power to impose their own meaning, symbolism and control upon their homes and project their own sense of identity to the world.

> The spatial segregation and architectural distinctiveness of many estates, most notably the post-war flatted developments, involved the powerful imposition of producers' meanings and symbolism on working class households. Such architecture announces to society the 'differentness' of the scheme's residents, underlining the marginal status of many inner-city households and prompting the question, in the context of concern about 'problem housing estates', as to why people should be

expected to care for the symbols of their own social inferiority.

At present the design of new public rented housing through housing associations is tightly controlled by the government agencies that provide the funding and regulate the sector. For example, the National Assembly in Wales has a pattern book that lays out minimum room sizes and other aspects of design. One aim of this seems to be to reduce costs by reducing the need for the involvement of design professionals for each development. The current trend in design in the public sector seems to be to mirror as far as possible the private sector in order to overcome any social stigma directed at a sector that caters largely for the poorest in society.

Design in the private sector

Design in the private sector has been less radical than the public sector. Ball (1983) argues that speculative builders face conflicting pressures on design. On the one hand appropriate and popular design can enhance the value and marketability of a development. On the other hand it is an expensive activity that can influence the building costs. These conflicting pressures have led to the adoption, by most speculative builders, of a limited number of common structural forms of house (one for each segment or price band in the market), with individuality of design being limited to superficial external detailing and finish. Even then there will be only a limited number of variations, which may be standard across the builder's sphere of operations. The styles are usually chosen to reflect traditional designs; for example, mock Tudor was popular in the inter-war period and neo-Georgian in the 1970s. Today's style is more eclectic with a number of different traditions apparent. Individuality is usually attempted through breaking up a uniform site layout by, for example, stepped configurations and the widespread use of detached houses even when the space between houses is very small. Variations in colour and in finishing materials are also used. Construction costs are kept to a minimum through the universal use of a rectangular house shape with no protrusions from any of the walls except for a non-structural 'lean-to' such as an entrance porch. Space standards tend to be small when compared, for example, with public rented housing built under the Parker Morris standards in the1970s. Carmona et al (2003) argue that there has been persistent criticism of the design of the standard product, which they call the 'speculative house'. The essence of the criticism is the conservatism of the design and its lack of connectivity with a particular site or location. This is said to militate against the creation of a 'sense of place' in new developments. House-builders respond by arguing that they are producing what the consumer wants as evidenced by past sales and the high level of consumer satisfaction with the product (Carmona et al, 2003).

One reason for the conformity of new housing is the importance to the developer of managing risk. Standard designs both reduce costs and maximise the chances of consumer acceptability. To increase marketability developers usually have a particular market segment in mind and use 'show houses' that use internal decoration, furniture and facilities to create a 'look' that is intended to fit with a desired lifestyle (Chapman, 1999a). New houses are sometimes sold with kitchen and other facilities such as furniture and house equipment as part of a marketing package.

The importance attached by speculative builders to the external appearance of the house seems to be justified in the light of research in the US. Nasar (1993) tested pictures of six house designs on a sample of people drawn from two cities in the US. The houses were the same basic size and height, like speculatively built housing in Britain, varying only in exterior finish and detailing. There were systematic differences in the popularity of the designs and the way they were rated. The designs also had different symbolic meanings. Respondents were asked to imagine that they had a flat tyre on a street and to say which style of home they would feel most comfortable approaching for help. Also, designs were ranked on the basis of the perceived status of occupants. There were some differences in class and gender reactions to the designs, but these were not strong. The precise results of this study may not be generalisable to other cultural settings, but they do serve to emphasise the importance of the appearance of a house to residents who associate different meanings to building styles. Developers are clearly aware of this and design and market their products accordingly.

There are a number of interesting current trends in the internal layout of houses. One concerns the number of bathrooms. The desirability of a second bathroom/toilet is said by builders to be important even in relatively small houses, and an en-suite bathroom is considered especially desirable. Chapman (1999a) found that in luxury houses the provision of three bathrooms was common. Bathrooms had changed from functional rooms that one spent little time in to a "place of self-indulgence and body celebration" (Chapman, 1999a, p

53). This reflects the growing importance of the pampering of the body as part of a lifestyle choice.

During the 1970s and 1980s the distinction between the parlour and the family living room largely disappeared in favour of one large living area. Madigan and Munro (1999) argue that this led to extra work for women because of the lack of a distinction between the front and back regions. The large space was multi-functional, being both a place for the family to relax away from the gaze of the world and somewhere to receive visitors and to display domestic standards and taste. This creates a dilemma for women "who strive to maintain the high standards of cleanliness and tidiness required of a public room while making everyone else feel comfortable and relaxed" (Madigan and Munro, 1999, p 69). Many women resolved the dilemma by internalising high standards of tidiness, which resulted in more work for them.

However, during the 1990s the trend to a large multi-functional room was reversed with more emphasis on the differentiation of living space. The increasing use of houses for work has added to the demand for a work area or study. Chapman (1999a) states that in show homes this room is decorated in a masculine style. It is portrayed as a "definitive masculine space to raise men's expectation of renewed status in the family and the opportunity of splendid isolation" (Chapman, 1999a, p 53). The differentiation of internal space has followed a change in the ideal of family life in the postmodern individualist era. As Chapman (1999a, p 52) argues: "there has been a shift from the notion that 'collective' family life leads to happiness to one which asserts that 'individual self-fulfilment for all members of the family is vital'". One of the main beneficiaries of this approach has been children. In their sample of families, Madigan and Munro (1999) found that the ideal that all children should have a room of their own was generally accepted. This room was to be multi-functional, combining a sleeping and a sitting area with place for clothes storage, study and play. Many children's bedrooms were generously equipped with electrical equipment such as computers, televisions and sound systems. This reflects the growing status of children in the family as well as the growing use of the home as a place of leisure. Sending the children out to play for the day was not considered to be desirable or safe.

Perhaps the most important change has occurred in the kitchen. Craik (1989) charts the change from the large multi-purpose and sociable kitchen of the Victorian era to the small private specialised room of the 1940s and 1950s and back to the large multi-purpose room of the present. The differences between the Victorian model and that of today relate to the place of the kitchen in relation to the rest of the house. The Victorian kitchen was isolated, especially from the formal rooms. Hepworth (1999) argues that the aim was to conceal the internal machinery of the household from public view. The present-day kitchen is more likely to be at the centre of the life in the house, with easy access to and visual surveillance over other areas. But like the Victorian model it has become a place of many functions, whether eating, socialising, playing or working as well as cooking and washing. The increasing use of the kitchen as a public room has resulted in the provision in some upmarket properties of a utility room with an additional sink and space for a washing machine (Chapman, 1999a). The outlook of the kitchen has been the subject of some differences of opinion. Denby (1941) argued that the kitchen should look out over the street to reduce the isolation of women who, as housewives, may feel isolated from the wider society. However, in practice most kitchens are designed to overlook the rear garden rather than the street. Surveillance of a family space of play and recreation is considered more important than community integration.

According to Craik (1989, p 57), these changes reflect the changing expectations of the role of women and their place and power in the home and family.

> In short the kitchen has become the metaphor for family life, not just in terms of specialised function but in terms of articulating domestic patterns in general. The kitchen is now a specialised room for food preparation as well as the key social space in a house. As such it is designed to integrate with other spaces in the house and with other occupants.

There have been numerous criticisms of present standards of house design. The limited number of design variations is said to have led to monotony of appearance. Munro and Madigan (1989) have argued that the average floor space of new housing has declined and many new houses are too small. This is creating an inflexibility that does not accommodate the needs of all members of a household or for the increasing incidence of home working. The growth in numbers of non-traditional family households has not been recognised because of the concentration on meeting the needs of traditional families. Finally, there has been much criticism of the ability of older or disabled people to access new housing and of the inadequacy of internal layouts and space standards to meet the needs of people with mobility problems. Many people are disabled at some time in their lives and many of the specific layout requirements such as barrier-free access and wide internal circulation spaces are as useful for others such as adults with young children in pushchairs. Nevertheless, private developers have shown a reluctance to include relevant design modifications as a standard feature of their houses or to exploit any particular market niche. Developers have resisted suggestions of including accessibility standards such as 'lifetime homes' into the statutory regulatory framework, arguing that changes would increase costs. Given the importance of the symbolic meaning of housing, they may also not welcome features that may create a less 'homely' or traditional appearance. The reluctance of developers to cater for disabled people is a manifestation of the marginal status of disabled people in society. The built environment of the house is the physical manifestation of economic and social exclusion.

Concern with the physical design of speculatively built housing is one of the factors that has led to the growth of self-provided housing. Clapham et al (1993, p 1355) define this as follows:

> Self-provision is used here as a relatively wide term to cover instances where households are involved in the production of their house rather than buying it ready-built from a speculative builder or on the second hand market. This involvement may take the form of building all or part of the dwelling themselves (self-building); or of acting as promoters by bringing together the elements of land, design and construction while not being closely involved in these processes (self-promotion); or of being actively involved in planning and managing the construction process (self-development). Self-provision may be carried out collectively as in a co-operative or housing association self-build project, or individually by one household.

In a survey of individual self-providers in Scotland, Clapham et al (1993) found that the most popular reason for pursuing this form of provision related to the reduced costs that ensued. In addition, 40% of self-providers cited dissatisfaction with the characteristics of the houses available in the market as being important. There were concerns about the lack of choice and about the size and number of rooms and of the quality of materials used. Overall, satisfaction with self-provision was high. When asked about the advantages, 80% said that it helped them get what they wanted in a house while 62% cited cheaper costs.

House design is an important influence on the meanings that households attach to their houses. The appearance and layout of houses carry symbolic messages about the life lived within, both to household members and to visitors. These messages are related to wider social constructions of family life, gender roles and lifestyles. Housing developers are aware of the importance of these meanings because of their impact on their ability to sell their product. Therefore, much attention is given to understanding the perceptions of prospective purchasers and to the use of appearance and style both in the house itself and in associated marketing material. Not all perceptions are given equal weight; and the built environment of the house will mirror the distribution of power within the society as, for example, in the relative neglect of the demands and needs of disabled people.

Homes

So far we have concentrated on the importance of the physical structure of the house, and the meanings households have towards this is an important element of the feeling of home. But homes are more than this. They are also the locale for many social practices, including the most intimate, which are often given the label of family life. "If society has grown more 'family oriented' the family itself has identified more and more squarely with its physical location, the home. 'Home' and 'family' are now virtually interchangeable terms" (Oakley, 1976, p 65).

The main dimensions of family life were discussed in Chapter Two. The importance of the socialisation of children and the maintenance of a stable and loving relationship between adults of different sexes (preferably in a state of marriage) was shown to be an important element of traditional ideologies of the family. We have seen above that the home is also the place where the practical servicing of this unit takes place through housework and where the adults (although primarily the male breadwinner) enjoy the relaxation and leisure to be able to maintain their roles in the outside world. As the 'warm bath' image of family life is pervasive, so too is the 'warm bath' image of the home as the place of privacy and security that acts as a base for recuperation before forays into the public sphere of the outside world.

Home is the setting for our most intimate relationships and feelings. Gurney (1996) argues for a focus on the emotional element of home, stating that the emotional discourses of family, intimacy and love are the most significant rationalisations drawn upon in making sense of home. Home is constructed through 'emotional labour' involved in the creation and sustenance of our most intimate personal relationships.

Privacy is an important element of intimate functions and

relationships and can be reinforced or challenged by house design. The spread of noise between dwellings, for example, may be an important factor in the ease with which intimate acts are undertaken. Ability to control access to the home or parts of the home is important in allowing these intimate relationships and feelings to flourish. A married couple's bedroom is an example of where outsiders and other members of the family may be refused entry.

The perceived importance of this role of home and family has led some sociologists to stress its vital importance to the functioning of society as a whole. Functionalist sociologists have long argued for the value of the traditional family and home life in sustaining a well-functioning society. But other sociologists concur. For example, Giddens (1984) emphasises the home as the prime locale for the creation and sustenance of what he calls 'ontological security', which he defines as "Confidence or trust that the natural or social worlds are as they appear to be, including the basic existential parameters of self and social identity" (Giddens, 1984, p 375). According to Giddens, globalisation and the increasing pace and impersonality of postmodern life (what he calls time-space distantiation) have led to a sense of rootlessness and meaninglessness. People lack a sense of belonging and a sense of purpose in their lives, which is leading to a search for a sense of identity and belonging in the private sphere of the home (see Chapter One for a fuller exposition of this view). We will return to this argument later when we evaluate the proposition that life is becoming more home-centred. However, its importance here is to reinforce the view held by functionalist sociologists of the importance of home life to society in general.

Saunders (1990, p 263) argues;

> The home is one of the core institutions of modern British society. It is the place where we are reared when we are young and in which we tenaciously try to remain when we grow old and frail. In the years in between, home is a place which we 'make' for ourselves, for the definition of maturity in our culture is bound up with the movement out of the parental home into one of our own. It is also the place where we spend most of our lives. We usually start each day from home and end the day by returning to it. It is the fixed place in our lives, a place of familiar routine.

The importance of home in society is also expressed through the importance attached to it in the common use of popular homilies and aphorisms. Examples include 'Home is where the heart is', 'an Englishman's home is his castle', and 'there's no place like home'. These express different elements of home as the place for deep emotions, for privacy and control, and for security and personal identity.

Gurney (1996) makes the valuable point that the meaning of 'home' may not be restricted to a particular setting but may encapsulate elements that are emotional and transportable. This is an important point to which we will return. Nevertheless, it is clear that the house is the major setting for the meaning of home. It is important here to be clear about what is meant by a locale or setting of social practices. What is meant is that the house is more than just a neutral physical location, but itself influences, and in turn is influenced by, the social interactions within it. We have seen how the physical nature of the house influences the meanings that people have towards it. The physical structure, then, is implicated in and is part of the concept of home and the social interactions that it entails. The feelings and emotions of home may be expressed through changes to the physical fabric of the house. For example, the growth of Do-It-Yourself (DIY) activity in the home is well documented. Some households change the room layout, facilities or decor of the house to make certain social interactions within it easier. This could involve changing walls to combine or separate rooms or changing their size or altering the facilities in rooms to facilitate particular activities such as putting up bookshelves to turn a spare bedroom into a study or workplace.

Much DIY activity is to change the decor of the house. There has been a large increase in this activity supported by an industry of magazines, television programmes and DIY stores. The internal appearance of the house is seen as a form of identity and self-expression. It can complement or reinforce particular lifestyles or be an expression of them. DIY can function as an outlet for creativity and as a form of relaxation. Allan and Crow (1989, p 10) argue that "The significance of the project of creating an appropriate environment in which domestic life can take place has grown to the point at which it stands alongside paid work and bringing up a family as a major life interest".

Craik draws attention to the growing importance attached by households to decorating styles in the kitchen. She identifies four general styles: modern, traditional, oriental, and country, which she argues denote, respectively: adventure and ambition; family, ritual and security; simplicity, sophistication and aestheticism; and homespun qualities, the natural. She argues that:

> Such styles combine the 'reflection' of personality with
> the 'projection' of a public image. These tend to play on
> nostalgia for past periods, project future utopias or construct
> an ideal image of family life. Style and fashion
> overdetermine use and tradition. Interior design has replaced
> household management as the focus of domestic ideology.
> (Craik, 1989, p 59)

Hunt (1989) also sees the importance of style in the home as an important expression of the skills of the home maker (usually a woman) and so is a symbol of her status and an indicator of her own self-worth. Pride in the home rests in part in its being clean and tidy, but also the appearance of the home is an expression of taste. Hunt (1989) points to class differences in taste based on the materials used and the colour schemes adopted. It is likely that there are also differences of gender, age and culture. These differences may be seen within the same house if members of the household have 'their own' space. For example, the decor in 'his' den or study may be different from that of 'her' kitchen. Age differences may be shown by the personalisation of children's bedrooms. The decor is used as a way of asserting independence from parents and a development of taste and identity. It may be coupled with humorous signs for the outside of the door urging adults to keep out and proclaiming the identity of the occupant. Posters of pop or film stars, a 'wild' decor and deliberate disarray may be used to communicate an emerging sense of self-identity and to signal control over that space.

Possessions may add to the personalisation of space in that they can enhance our feeling of being in control of our environment, increase our self-confidence, provide us with feelings of security, and allow us to communicate our identity to ourselves and others (Altman and Werner, 1985).

> Home contains the most special objects; those that were
> selected by the person to attend to regularly or to have
> close at hand that create permanence in the intimate life of
> a person and therefore that are most involved in making
> up his or her identity. Thus household objects constitute
> an ecology of signs that reflects as well as shapes the pattern
> of the owner's self. (Csikszentmihalyi and Rochberg-
> Halton, 1981, p 17)

Possessions may also provide memories of previous episodes in one's lives and of loved ones who may have left or died. The importance of possessions and privacy in the home is shown by the impact of burglary on its victims. Chapman (1999b) argues that burglary leads to disruption of the order of the household and a sense of invasion and pollution as well as the loss of treasured objects. It can lead to a striking impact on an individual's deeply rooted sense of security and place.

Gurney (1996) speaks of the home as a kind of psychic warehouse in which memories are added in layers and stored. Meanings of the home can change over time as new experiences happen and memories re-emerge or fade. Since we live out much of our lives in our homes, it is understandable that we become attached to the home as a symbol of our bibliography, an expression of self, and a source of security (Altman and Werner, 1985).

There have been a number of attempts to bring together all of the elements of home. Somerville (1992) divides the meaning of home into six categories. These are: shelter; hearth (by which is meant feelings of physical warmth and cosiness); heart (loving and affectionate relationships); privacy (power to exclude others and prohibit surveillance); abode (place to call home); and roots (individual's source of identity and meaningfulness). In similar fashion, Gurney (1996) derives 12 categories from empirical work with a sample of owner-occupiers. He asked his respondents to say what made the difference between house and home. The results are set out in Table 5.1.

The importance of emotional factors relating to family relationships is apparent. Other important factors were privacy, relaxation, comfort and safety. Other categories are concerned with autonomy, personalisation and creativity, and display (what Gurney classifies as 'front-region').

An important category of responses was what Gurney called negative/instrumental. Here he has put together a number of responses that either do not recognise the difference between house and home and stress the physical elements of the house, or else do not consider where they are living as home. Also, a number of negative responses question the positive image of home. References to a millstone, source of worry, debt, and hard work show that some people either do not recognise or are not experiencing in their present circumstances these positive elements. Interestingly, in Gurney's sample almost all these responses were from men. In Chapter Two it was stressed that family life did not always conform to the positive ideal of the traditional image; and it is important to recognise that the same is true of home. Home is a place of work as well as leisure, can be the scene of violence,

Table 5.1: Discourses of home: patterns in responses to the St George postal survey

Discourse	Words used by respondents
Emotions	*Family, relatives, marriage, relationships, children, security (emotional stability), 'where the heart is'*
Back-region	*Return to, come back to, private, privacy, refuge, alone, peace, peaceful, quiet, haven, solitude, be on your own, be yourself*
Negative/ instrumental	*Roof over your head, millstone, debt, worry, just a place to eat and sleep, my real home is my parent's home, I can't relax here, it doesn't make any difference if you own, housework, hard work*
Relaxation	*Relax, relaxation, unwind, take things easy, rest, put your feet up*
Comfort	*Comfort, comfortable, cosy, warm*
Safety	*Feel safe, safety, security (physical)*
Ownership	*Pride, achievement, investment for our future and for our children's future, worked hard for it, it belongs to me/us, feel differently about it if you own, security (financial)*
Personalisation	*Place to design, your own tastes, belongings, furniture*
Autonomy	*You can do what you want, your own rules, freedom, you can say what you want, 'a man's home is his castle', your own world*
Front-region	*Invite people in, entertain, neighbours, community, Bristol*
'What you make it'	*Home is what you make (of) it*
Other	*Words that did not clearly fall into discourses above, such as security (ambiguous), everything, very important, garden, a base*

Words in *italics* are responses to the question, 'Some people say that the words house and home mean quite different things. What does your home mean to you?'

Source: Adapted from Gurney (1996)

abuse and emotional trauma, and brings with it financial and other responsibilities such as for upkeep or repair. Goldsack (1999) argues that the privacy of the home has seriously worsened the likelihood and severity of domestic violence. Women were reluctant to break the norms of privacy by speaking about abuse, and public agencies were reluctant to intrude on what was perceived as the private sphere.

Ownership is one of Gurney's categories, in which he includes responses that mentioned pride and a sense of achievement as well as the financial benefits of owner-occupation. The academic and often the policy discussions about home have often associated home with the tenure of owner-occupation, and we will turn to this in the next section.

Gurney examined gender differences in the meaning of home in his sample and found no clear pattern. It seems that the differences between individuals were greater than any systematic gender differences. But the issue of gender differences should remain open. Gurney found that women mentioned more responses than men and relates this to the greater length of time they spend in the home and the greater number of roles that they play. It is likely their experience of home is more complex and contradictory than that of men.

The separation of home and work started with the Industrial Revolution, but it was noted in Chapter Three that the trend is being reversed, with up to a quarter of people in Britain now working from home for at least some of the time. Bulos and Chaker (1995, p 227) argue that this may alter their perception and attitude towards home: "homeworking constitutes a physical, interactional and personal disruption to homefullness". Homeworkers may experience isolation and find difficulty in separating their work and private lives. Attempts to juggle work and family schedules may become more difficult, especially for women with family responsibilities. On the other hand homeworking may strengthen attachment to the home because of the time spent there. Households may be able to reconcile the different uses of the house through the management of time or space. If the space is available a room may be devoted solely to work or have this use for certain times of the day.

There are likely to be cultural differences in the meaning of home. For example, religion may influence the attitude towards a home and its use. Harrison (2001) notes that a view held by some Muslims that 'home is my heaven' would imply a particular set of physical arrangements and a particular ordering of family and community life. Fog Olwig (1999) shows that Nevisians (inhabitants of Nevis, a Caribbean island), living in Britain have a multiple attachment to home and can eventually come to feel at home in several places, moving frequently between their several homes. The continuing emotional and practical attachment to their homes and families in Nevis was exemplified by the sending of money to contribute towards the family living expenses and the furnishing of the home for display. Therefore, they drew a distinction between home as a sense of belonging and home as the place where everyday life is lived. The concept of home in Nevis was strongly influenced by the British colonial experience and shared ideas of respectability and the importance of display in front regions. However, one of the key spaces in the Nevisian house was the fenced-in yard, where many domestic activities took place and children played. It was the place of many childhood memories and provided privacy and a separation from surrounding houses. In Britain, many Nevisians could afford only to live in flatted accommodation, where some facilities were shared. Even though the space and facilities were superior to those in Nevis, households did not see it this way because of the lack of privacy.

Much of the research on the meaning of home has been focused on traditional families of married or cohabiting couples with children. In Gurney's sample, replies to his questionnaire were received from only 13 single-person households out of 209. Given the changes in household make-up identified in Chapter Four, this is an important gap in knowledge.

Hardey (1989) examines the meaning of home among single parents. He found that they held similar attitudes to couples, which he explains in terms of their acceptance of the prevalent ideology of home. However, the experience of single parents, although varying considerably, did not always mirror the ideal picture. Many suffered from a lack of money and had to bear the pressures this brought in terms of a poor standard of accommodation unsuited to their lifestyle. Some had a punishing domestic routine coping with the tasks of child care, housekeeping and often employment, that is, combining the traditional male and female family roles. Those who had previously been part of a couple household had had to remake their home, usually in different accommodation, and to rework their family routines. Many stressed the autonomy that their situation brought them and enjoyed being in control of their home and not having to compromise with another adult. Nevertheless, it was recognised that a future partnership with a man would involve a reversion to the traditional gender roles, and they differed in the perceived desirability of this. In some people the autonomy brought with it a feeling of isolation and of being confined within the home, particularly when their routines left them little time or opportunity to explore leisure or other activities outside the home. There could also be problems of ensuring 'adult space' within the home for privacy and the expression of an identity other than that of mother. In Hardey's sample this was sometimes done by designating one room as a 'work room' that children were discouraged from entering. In some instances children's toys were kept to a minimum in the main living room so that it could be easily converted to adult space when the children went to bed. Many lone parents were less able or willing to spend time on the creative aspects of home because of the pressures on them. Interestingly, Hardey found that some single parents pursued shared living arrangements in order to cope better with their lives.

The research on home has tended to neglect non-traditional living arrangements such as HMOs, or cooperative living, or young people sharing a flat or living in a hostel. Young people are a relatively neglected group and may have different needs and demands from those at other points of the life course (see Chapter Seven).

More attention has been given to the meaning of home for older people, and we shall return to this in Chapter Eight. It has already been observed that older people tend to be more satisfied with their house even though on average they tend to live in worse accommodation than other age groups. Some older people may be more restricted to the home than others because of physical disabilities and mobility problems. They may, in Allan and Crow's (1989) terms, consider home to be a cage rather than a castle. It is commonly assumed that older people are less inclined to move than younger people, partly because of the stress of moving but also because their home is a store of memories and valued possessions. The family home established for child rearing is for most people such a powerful communicator of identity that its loss with the onset of old age or divorce may be as great a threat to self-identity as the loss of a human relationship (Altman and Werner, 1985).

Older people may have had to reconstitute their home on a number of occasions. Rising mobility may mean that home has been made in a number of locations. In later life, the growing up and leaving home of children is a major transition. Mason (1989) argues that parents hold norms of the desirability and appropriate timing for children to leave home, which is regarded as an important and vital stage in the development of adulthood. There are signs that this norm may be changing as there is evidence that some young people are now staying longer in the parental home. Nevertheless, it is still widely assumed that adult children will set up their home elsewhere, although parents felt that 'there is always a home for them here'. The parental home was seen as a refuge for children to return to temporarily in times of trouble. Children were often given keys to the parental home and allowed to drop in unannounced and 'to make themselves at home' in a way that parents did not expect in their children's houses.

The departure of children from the family home means a transition in the meaning of the home for parents. Mason (1989) found that many regarded this positively and valued the increased autonomy that it entailed, but there were often adjustments to be made in the relationships between couples as the focus of the home changed. Retirement also can constitute a major change in the meaning of home. Retired people tend to spend more time in the home, as would be expected, but people 'negotiated' their retirement transition in different ways with the people around them. Retirement may be a gradual transition rather than a one-off event, with people working part-time or doing voluntary work. It may involve a move of house in a search for security and peace in a 'last home'.

> Taken together, the two factors of ageing and retirement, and the reconstitution of the membership of the home, contributed to an emerging ideal image of the home: it was to be about relaxation, leisure, or at least non-work, it was to be secure, safe, comfortable, and 'ours', and to provide an environment conducive to a gentle process of ageing. Not only was it to be *an* environment, but *the* pivotal environment for the ageing couple, and for their newly special relationship – whether that be ostensibly good or bad. (Mason, 1989, p 116)

Gender roles in this situation may be renegotiated. The man's additional time in the home could lead to a change in the traditional role of the woman as 'homemaker', but Mason reports that many women resisted this as an encroachment on their territory.

In this section the existing literature on the meaning of home has been examined. This is a very large and rich literature, which has illuminated many of the different elements of the meaning that home can have for different people. 'Homemaking' often can involve substantial investment in decorating styles and the arrangement of possessions to personalise space or to reflect or project an individual's or household's personality. The feeling of home can be attached to a number of places or to no particular place at all, and may vary according to different cultural values. It may also vary for different kinds of households and at different points of the life course. The meaning of home is continually made and remade through negotiation within and outside the household, and may change as household circumstances alter.

Before looking at future directions in examining the meaning of home it is necessary to consider the impact of tenure. Perhaps surprisingly, much of the existing research has focused on the importance of tenure in the construction of meaning.

Home and tenure

Tenures are social and legal institutions that are socially constructed and vary over time and between countries and cultures. Tenure defines the social relationships in the ownership and use of housing, and can mirror social relationships in the society at large. For example, the state ownership and control of public rented housing can be seen as reflecting socialist relations, whereas private renting or owner-occupation may be seen as reflecting the social relations of market-based capitalism. This has meant that tenures have been at the forefront of political debate on housing and have been seen as carrying meanings that resonate beyond the housing field. In Britain most political debate has focused on owner-occupation, which has grown significantly from 50% of dwellings in 1971 to 69% in 2000, reflecting strong political support from all major political parties. As Allan and Crow (1989) point out, the meaning of having a 'home of one's own' has changed over the twentieth century, from meaning living in a self-contained dwelling to being an owner-occupier. Although 'homes fit for heroes' in 1918 were council houses, it seems unlikely that it would be the same today. Government support for owner-occupation is seen in financial and policy instruments such as the 'right to buy', which increase access to the tenure and create and sustain financial incentives.

The policy mechanisms are embedded in a discourse that describes owner-occupation as the normal and natural tenure. This is shown in government policy documents that project the tenure as successful, growing and popular. It is said to be flexible; facilitates mobility; is the best form of housing for the majority; is popular; gives pride of ownership; gives the valued freedom to decorate and undertake internal modifications and to create the living environment; and brings financial advantages in old age. Renting is usually relegated to a minority, residual status confined to those who do not share the dream of ownership or cannot aspire to that level. The term 'social housing' came into common usage from the 1990s in Britain. The implicit meaning in the term is obvious: it is, in Margaret Thatcher's terminology, 'for social cases' and therefore not for the 'normal'. Overall, in the dominant political and policy discourse the natural and preferred state of owner-occupation is contrasted with the problematic nature of renting and its association with social problems and crime. It is an example of what Gurney (1999) calls the 'normalising discourse' of owner-occupation.

Research by Gurney and others shows that that discourse reflects attitudes widely held in the population at large. Ford and Burrows (1999) report widespread support for owner-occupation in the British

Social Attitudes Survey. Support was at its highest in 1989, when house prices were increasing fast, but fell in the early 1990s after the housing market slump. Nevertheless, support had increased again by 1998, although people seemed to be more cautious, being more aware of risks from fluctuating house prices. Research on the housing perceptions of children (Rowlands and Gurney, 2001) shows the importance of owner-occupation as part of a status 'package' that children aspire to. "You've got the job, you get the family, have a house, get a car. You want to be a higher class than what you are now" (young person quoted by Rowlands and Gurney, 2001, p 125). Rented housing was perceived as giving a negative image and signifying low social status. Owner-occupation was perceived as a symbol of success.

The question of the existence of different meanings of home between residents of different tenures has been a key issue in housing research. Saunders (1990) argues that owner-occupation resulted in increased feelings of control and autonomy and ontological security. On the basis of a survey of owner-occupiers and council tenants in three towns in England, Saunders argues that owners are more likely to see home as a place of relaxation and comfort and to equate it with personal possessions. Tenants were more likely to equate home with friends and neighbours. Interviews with council tenants who had bought their homes are reported to have shown that ownership affected the way that people felt about their homes. For example, one respondent said, 'When you own you can do a lot more with it and make it more homely because it's yours. You don't bother too much when it's rented.' From this limited evidence Saunders (1990, p 273) concludes:

> Such findings suggest that the meanings which people
> derive from and invest in their homes may be influenced
> by whether or not they own them. It stems from the tenants'
> answers that people may find it difficult to establish a sense
> of belonging in a house which they do not own.

Ownership is seen as having these effects because it allows people greater choice over where they live and more control over their living conditions. Saunders accepts that the tenancy agreement of most tenants enables them to decorate and change their living arrangements to a substantial degree, but argues that it is significant that many tenants do less work in their houses than owner-occupiers and wait for the landlord to undertake improvements and repairs.

Saunders's conclusions have been heavily criticised (see for example Forrest et al, 1991). The evidence for his conclusions is not as strong as is claimed. For example, twice as many owners as tenants reported feelings of comfort and relaxation and equated home with personal possessions, but these meanings were still reported by a substantial number of council tenants. Sixty-four per cent of owners said they had strong feelings of attachment to their home, but 40% of tenants did as well. In other words, the relationship between tenure and these variables is not absolute as one would expect if tenure was the key causal factor. Saunders is also selective in his use of evidence. For example, just as many tenants as owners said home was a place one owned or worked for. More tenants than owners said home was for family, love and children, and belonging to a neighbourhood. By the logic used by Saunders, this would be interpreted as council tenancy resulting in a better family life and better relations with one's neighbours!

The problem with any comparison between tenures is that tenure is related to many differences of income, age and social status, and therefore it is difficult to isolate tenure as an explanatory variable. In addition, there are substantial variations within tenures in social, economic and physical conditions that may make overall generalisations meaningless. Also, one possible explanation of Saunders's findings is that people with particular attitudes gravitate towards particular tenures rather than the tenures creating the differences. In other words, council tenants may not be thwarted in their quest for rest and relaxation in their home, but are not looking for it. Finally, even if Saunders is correct in his conclusions, it may be the difference in social status of the tenures that is the important factor reflected in the document outlined above, not as he claims, the inherent characteristics of the tenures themselves.

In Gurney's research on owner-occupiers, some had a negative view of public renting and many did not consider entering the tenure, saying 'It didn't enter our heads'. Aphorisms such as 'Money down the drain' were used (Gurney, 1996). In a recent review of tenant attitudes towards public rented housing in Wales, Murie et al (2001) conclude that most tenants reported an aspiration for owner-occupation, and their support for continued renting was associated with a lack of belief that owner-occupation was a feasible option for them. Nevertheless, there was strong support for public renting and little support for private renting, which was regarded as providing poor value for money with little security of tenure. A similar picture emerges from the British Social Attitudes Survey (Kemp, 2000). Interestingly, people who had experience of council housing either as tenants themselves or as children of tenants were more positive towards the tenure than those with no experience.

The overall support for public renting from tenants did not mean that they were not highly critical of their landlords. There were specific criticisms of repair services, but general criticisms related particularly to the perceived failure of landlords to listen to tenants or to take notice of their views. Residents felt powerless to affect what was happening on their estates. The theme of powerlessness runs through much research on the attitudes of tenants (Centre for Housing Research, 1989; Saunders, 1990; Bines et al, 1993; Cairncross et al, 1997). Although most tenants reported in surveys that they were satisfied with their landlord, many seemed to feel a sense of inferiority from their status as public sector tenant, which was reinforced by their interaction with their landlord. One tenant interviewed in Cairncross et al (1997, pp 105-6) sums up his feelings as follows:

> My view is why should the working class still be classed as the skivvies? Why should we have to live like this, the middle classes don't.... I can honestly say I don't see why I should have to go to the council when every time I want something doing in my house, say to them, right if you don't get out and do it I'm going to see my solicitor, because that's the only way I get them to move. They look at me as though I am the dirt of the world and why should we be still classed like that. That was years ago the workhouses. We're not workhouse people, we are the backbone of the country as far as I am concerned and we should be given our rights, as people, as human beings, not be cheated and trod upon.

Public sector tenants and owner-occupiers were united in their negative attitudes towards private renting. Some interesting research has been undertaken on the meaning of home held by private renters (Knight, 2002). Knight divided his sample of private renters into five groups. The first group was labelled the impatient would-be home-owners, being made up of people who wanted to be owner-occupiers as soon as they could manage it. The second group was fatalistic would-be home-owners. Households in this group were often in receipt of social security benefits and most had rented from the public sector before becoming private renters. In general they were unhappy with their present accommodation and wanted to become owner-occupiers but thought they were unlikely to ever achieve this. The third group was pragmatic endurers. These were students or other young people who felt that private renting suited them at present but planned to become owner-occupiers eventually. The fourth group was procrastinators, who wanted to be owner-occupiers and had the money to afford to be owners, but who valued keeping their options open and did not want to make the long-term commitment to owner-occupation yet. The fifth group was contented nesters, who were contented and comfortable in their private rented homes and anticipated remaining there for a long time. Knight (2002) found that the groups had different attitudes towards issues such as the desire to decorate and personalise the rented house. Households in these groups seemed to have similar views of the meaning of home and to recognise that the constraints of living in private rented accommodation compared with being owner-occupiers meant that not all elements of home (such as privacy, a feeling of being settled, and a sense of ownership) could be achieved. For some, these disadvantages were offset by the flexibility that renting offered.

Research on the meaning of home has been overly concerned with generalisation, searching for universal meanings whether within or across tenures. The research on private renters is evidence of a more fruitful approach examining differences between individuals in the meaning of home and the relationships between this and other aspects of their lives. Gurney (1996) identified five typologies of owners. The first were what he calls Lexic-owners. These were households that had a strong ideological attachment to ownership and tended to express this in common-sense aphorisms such as 'if it's yours, you take more care of it'. The second group were pragmatic owners. They were concerned with what ownership brought to their lives in terms of practical benefits. They were prepared to do essential repairs to the house, but did not wish to get involved in the self-actualisation of DIY activities. Ownership was seen as a valuable tool in accessing good schools for children, and was perceived to bestow financial benefits. The third group were labelled by Gurney as petty tycoons. They regarded ownership as a financial investment and were concerned with movements in house prices. The paradox identified by Gurney is that most of this group of owners were on the margins of the tenure. The fourth group were called by Gurney extrinsic owners. Ownership was seen as an achievement that was part of display to others. This group took substantial interest and pride in the garden and the decor of the house and had often undertaken substantial improvement work. This group tended to be without children often because they had left home. The fifth group was labelled conflictual. Here there was no clear household view of ownership because it was a source of conflict and ongoing negotiation between the household members.

The typologies identified by Gurney were based on a small number of households in one location. However, the approach seems to be an important way of breaking out of the simplistic search for generalisation that has characterised much of the work on meaning of home. The typologies can be refined and extended across tenures. The way forward in looking at the meaning of home is to examine tenure as one among many factors that could influence the meaning people hold towards their housing as well as seeing tenure as one expression of this meaning.

The meaning of homelessness

So far the discussion has been focused on people with homes, but it sheds some light on definitions of 'homelessness'. Jacobs et al (1999) show that homelessness is a social construction that has been the subject of conflicting interpretations. They distinguish between 'minimalist' and 'maximalist' definitions. The minimalist definition treats homelessness as being without shelter. The terms 'rooflessness' or 'rough sleepers' have been coined to reflect this view. This definition tends to lead to only those sleeping in the streets or outdoors being considered to be truly homeless. The maximalist definition stresses that being homeless is being without a *home*, with all that entails in terms of security, privacy, warmth and so on. This definition could include those living in temporary accommodation, such as bed and breakfast, or institutional forms of accommodation, such as hostels, which are not suitable for permanent living and do not generate a feeling of being at home. It could also include people living in suitable accommodation but being under stress because of, for example, harassment from a landlord or violence from a partner.

Public policy is the result of political conflict over these definitions and has varied over time. Jacobs et al (1999) argue that the particular definitions tend to be associated with discourses of the causes of homelessness. The minimalist definition tends to be associated with a view that the personal failings of homeless people themselves are responsible. The maximalist definition is associated with the view that the causes of homelessness are many and varied, and stresses the failures of public policy in explaining why people are not able to cope.

In her research on young homeless people, Fitzpatrick (1999) found that they stressed safety and security in their view of the meaning of home, perhaps not surprisingly given their position. They also thought it involved feeling cosy and being surrounded by their own possessions. The importance of family was stressed, with homelessness being equated with being unloved. Privacy and being in a 'decent' place were also mentioned. For many, traditional forms of accommodation for homeless people such as hostels or shared living arrangements did not come within the bounds of their definition. Hutson (1999) argues that many forms of accommodation and support for homeless people are based on professional definitions of 'need' that conform with the interests of the professionals in claiming special expertise rather than with needs as defined by the homeless people themselves. Some homeless people viewed hostels as frightening and hostile places where they felt threatened. According to a survey by Randall and Brown (1996), 40% of rough sleepers would not accept a place in a hostel if it were offered. Fitzpatrick (1999) identified many people who would not avail themselves of services in the centre of the city because they felt unsafe venturing outside what they defined as their own area. An interesting phenomenon is emerging in Britain whereby some homeless people are choosing to sleep rough on the streets rather than accept the accommodation and support that is available for them. For them the streets provide more elements of 'home' than the hostel accommodation they are offered.

Hutson (1999) argues that this is because such temporary accommodation is almost universally regarded by young people as unsafe. The fear of violence and of the consequences of drug taking are common. Such views are also commonly held of shared accommodation. Although physical conditions are better than in hostels, concern is expressed by many people about sharing with unknown people who may be taking drugs and leading chaotic lifestyles. Hutson argues that repeated surveys have shown that young homeless people want self-contained, unfurnished flats rather than hostels or shared housing. She reports one young person as saying of their flat "It's more like home here. It's the freedom.... I've my own time, my own space, not people telling me, you know. It's quiet and peaceful" (quoted in Hutson, 1999, p 215).

The discussion of homelessness shows the importance of the concept of home in shaping public policy. It also shows that some physical conditions, which may be officially considered to be home, may not be considered so by the people for whom it may be designed.

Conclusion

Houses are physical structures with characteristics that influence the health, well-being and lifestyle of people who live in them. Poor housing, whether due to design or condition, can lead to discomfort and ill health, and government policies have been designed and implemented to deal with this. But this is only part of the story. Houses also carry meanings for the people who live in them and for others. There is no universal and objective way of measuring poor housing conditions because people's perception of them and reaction to them differs. Houses are also homes. Home is a physical structure and space – a house – but also a locale for social practices and relationships and a setting for the most intimate and private emotions. Its meaning is produced and reproduced by individuals in the course of their lives, but the production of meaning is influenced by normative discourses and ideologies of family, home and tenure. The traditional ideal of the structure and nature of family life is related to an ideal of home as a place of privacy, security and relaxation. To this can be added an ideology of ownership that stresses the importance of private ownership – 'a home of your own' – to the achievement of the goal of a rewarding family life. These ideologies are strong but not all-encompassing, as they are contested by some households. Different meanings of home have been identified that differ from, and sometimes conflict with, the dominant ideology.

An understanding of all the dimensions of home is essential for an understanding of housing and for the design of housing policy. Much housing research treats houses as units that can be reduced to a limited number of quantifiable, objective characteristics. This chapter has shown that houses are rich with meanings that influence, and are influenced by, the way people act in them and towards them. Without understanding these processes, our understanding of the housing field is very limited. Policy mechanisms that are designed around the concept of houses as meaningless physical structures are bound to falter when confronted with the rich and complex webs of meaning around homes. It was this limited policy conception that led in the 1960s to the widespread clearance of houses that people wanted to live in because they breached some professionally defined physical standard. Today it is resulting in the waste of public resources in changing the physical layout of popular properties that do not conform to rigidly defined space standards.

Many households change, adapt and decorate their houses to make themselves feel at home and as part of their lifestyle choice. The ability to do this varies depending on factors such as financial resources and tenure position. Some households are unwilling to accept the restrictions on their choices imposed by the design decisions of private developers, and are designing and building their own houses. The importance of control over one's housing circumstances is a key theme throughout this discussion. Lack of control and a feeling of low status and powerlessness seem to be key factors in poor health. Increasing choice and control may be an important theme of future housing policy.

If this chapter has stressed the importance of an understanding of the meaning of home, it has also shown the limits of our current knowledge. Much research in this area has been partial in its scope and preoccupied with single issues such as physical design or tenure. It has succeeded mostly in defining the parameters of the issue through the search for universal meanings, but only limited progress has been made in illuminating differences and patterns. More research is needed that examines different meanings of home and their relationship to lifestyles and housing pathways. The differences in the meaning of home have not been linked to other aspects of life such as attitudes towards family life, work, money or the use of time. Only when these links are made will we be in a position to understand the position that home has in people's lives and how housing circumstances contribute to personal identity and the search for self-fulfilment.

SIX

Neighbourhoods and communities

This chapter argues that concern with the meaning of a house and home does not stop at the front door. The house derives meaning from its setting as well as its own characteristics. Feelings about the house will be influenced by the perceived physical and social environment outside the front door. Also, the social relationships of family, which are primarily associated with home, are also played out in other settings. Family relationships may span a number of homes and considerable distances, and the location of a house will influence the frequency and ease of contact. At the same time, social relationships are formed with friends and neighbours; they may take place in a number of settings including the home and its immediate environs as well as in accessible leisure facilities such as pubs or restaurants. People need to leave the home to service their lives within it, whether to go to school, work or the supermarket. Access to these facilities will be influenced by the location of the house. Also, lifestyles may influence the location of housing that is sought. The estate agents' adage that the three most important factors in selling a house are 'location, location and location' shows that its importance is widely recognised.

As in Chapter Five, the starting point is the physical environment, in this case of the neighbourhood. Therefore, the chapter begins with a consideration of the design of public spaces between houses, including the street layout. It is argued that physical design carries implicit meanings at different levels from the political to the individual. These meanings often symbolise particular views of lifestyle. Examples are given of 'homes fit for heroes' and modernist high-rise housing, introduced in Chapter Five. In the latter case it is argued that the designs carried different meanings for the architects and those living in them, which in some cases led to unpopularity. Underlying many design discourses is a belief that physical design has a direct and predictable impact on behaviour; a current example of this is concern with 'designing out crime'. It is argued that this is a very simplistic proposition, which assumes a universality of meaning that may not always exist.

The chapter continues with a discussion of the meanings of

neighbourhood and community, focusing on the discourses that have dominated discussion. The chapter reviews the popular discourse that people are becoming more home-centred and adopting more 'privatised' lifestyles, with the increased individualism leading to a decline of a sense of community. The central argument of the chapter is that lifestyle changes are occurring, but not in the rather simplistic and universal way usually assumed in the 'decline of community' discourse. It is argued that the meaning of neighbourhoods is increasingly differentiated and important to the lifestyle and identity of those who choose to live in them.

The implications of different meanings and changing lifestyles for different spatial environments are then examined. The first example is of so-called disadvantaged or deprived neighbourhoods, which are related in policy discourse to concepts of 'social exclusion' and 'underclass'. The impact of these discourses on the definitions of policy problems and solutions is discussed. Concepts such as community development and a 'balanced' community, that are used in professional and political discourse in relation to remedies for the perceived ills of these neighbourhoods, are examined. The second example is of inner-city neighbourhoods that are perceived to need regeneration through an 'urban renaissance'. In these two examples the importance of discourse and meaning and their link to lifestyle and identity are emphasised.

Neighbourhood design

The physical design of the neighbourhood is one of the factors that will symbolise and articulate meaning.

> More than just conglomerations of houses and families, neighbourhoods carry many meanings and uses which are especially noticeable when communities are compared cross-culturally. In some nations, neighbourhoods are natural extensions of home, with the public and private lives meshing and becoming almost one. Houses are designed with open, fluidly connected courtyards while streets and public places provide a theater of activity leaving little space left for privacy. In areas of other nations, neighbourhoods consist of sprawling homes separated by tree-lined streets through which dwellers drive cars into and out of two-car garages without having to leave the sanctuary of the auto or home. Guards may even prevent

undesirables from entering these neighbourhoods, thereby further insulating an individual from the possible discomfort of unplanned human contact. Clues to a society's vision of family, community and social responsibility are apparent from an examination of the spatial attributes of its neighbourhoods. (Yen, 1993, p 237)

Britain clearly corresponds more closely to the 'private' model of neighbourhoods articulated by Yen. Houses are mostly grouped on a street rather than a courtyard pattern, and public space is usually restricted to road access. Nevertheless, there have been changes in the dominant approaches to neighbourhood design over time.

'Homes fit for heroes' were designed as country cottages to reward the returning troops and the skilled war workers with a vision of a rural England in the suburbs. This was based on the assumption that "every Englishman was, or felt he was, a disinherited country gentleman" (Burnett, 1986, p 255) and reflected the first moves towards the suburbs by the middle classes in the late Victorian era. The design of individual houses (discussed in Chapter Five) was in tune with the design of the neighbourhood and generated similar meanings. Cottages were set along tree-lined avenues and crescents with wide grass verges that created an atmosphere of space, greenery and peace. Public open spaces were designed to emulate the greens of village communities. This was a deliberate contrast to the predominant Victorian urban model of the narrow-fronted terraced houses that were separated from the narrow pavement only by small front gardens or sometimes opened directly onto the pavement. Public space was restricted to public parks. Nevertheless, in the garden suburb model the public space was there to provide a backdrop rather than to be used for communal activity or interaction.

In the 1930s the private sector suburban developments were laid out in a similar way to the garden suburbs in the public sector, but there was less emphasis on public space. Ball (1983) argues that private developers put little emphasis on public space because it was not saleable and could cause problems of maintenance in the longer term. Therefore, it was in their interest to maximise returns by including as much of the space as possible in individual plots as is consistent with the image of the scheme they were trying to project. In practice this meant that open space was more likely to be private garden than public space.

Burnett (1986) argues that this emphasis on private space reflected a continuation of the Victorian emphasis on home as a place of retreat distanced from the physical and social perils of urban life. Gardens surrounded by walls and hedges provided social distance by deterring visitors and prohibiting casual and unwanted contact. The suburbs represented "the collective attempt to lead a private life" (Burnett, 1986, p 256) based on the domestic ethos centred on the family and household activities around the children, gardening, home improvement and home-bound leisure activities.

During the 1960s and 1970s there was a reaction against suburban privacy by the architects of the modern movement. They sought to use the built form to change behaviour, and their preferred form was high-rise building, which symbolised technology and mass-production. Within these designs they sought to incorporate design features that would produce desired forms of interaction. Although Le Corbusier (1960) envisaged substantial public facilities within the blocks, these were rarely provided in practice. The most influential idea was Le Corbusier's (1960) 'streets in the sky', which were meant to improve contact between neighbours by recreating a vibrant street life away from the dangers of road traffic. Of course, the experience of schemes designed in this way showed that people were not influenced in the way envisaged by the architects, and the 'streets in the sky' became threatening places. Ravetz and Turkington (1995) describe them as hard to maintain, poorly illuminated, cold, draughty and menacing places where the prudent did not linger. They usually provided little possibility of supervision as they were not overlooked by windows. At the same time, the important buffer space between the home and the public domain, traditionally provided by the front garden, was absent.

Jephcott (1971) argued that this environment was particularly unsuitable for families with small children because of the limited areas for play either outside or inside the flats, in the corridors and landings, and the difficulties of surveillance when children played on the ground. Instead of a vibrant street life, Jephcott argues that many women found flat life profoundly depressing with none of the areas such as yards, gardens or doorsteps that help to encourage social interaction. In addition, women were not encouraged to do things that house dwellers took for granted, such as hanging out washing, as this was held to spoil the simple lines of the design.

High-rise housing required a large amount of space around blocks to allow daylight. This space was often left landscaped without particular use. Even when the housing was not high-rise, mass production techniques could result in vast areas of unused public space. For example, the large peripheral housing schemes built in Glasgow were tenements constructed from prefabricated units assembled on site by crane. The productive use of the cranes in long runs dominated the layout, which tended to be in long rows of tenements all facing the same way and a large distance apart to facilitate the manoeuvring of the cranes. The result was a high-density dwelling form in a low-density environment with large areas of unused open space. The street had tenements fronting on to only one side, with the other being dead frontage as it provided only access to rear communal gardens which themselves were ambiguous space. The lack of upkeep of these gardens and their fences added to the difficulties in defining space.

Brindley (1999, p 39) argues that the modern movement was "an attempt to provide a dramatically improved, functional environment which would sustain the way of life of an urban working class, based on families and communities with a strong collective life". But, as we shall see later, that collective life was itself changing and anyway was destroyed, to a large extent, by the activity of slum clearance, which cleared the ground for modernist buildings. Modernist design led to collectivist buildings in an increasingly privatised era.

The 'Radburn' layout of separation between pedestrians and cars, which was used in many new town developments, also contributed to the move away from the traditional street layout of Victorian times. Ravetz and Turkington (1995) describe common 'Radburn-type' layouts whereby houses were arranged in short rows accessed by public footpaths both front and back. The car was consigned to a garage court or block that might be located out of sight of, and a short distance from, the house, providing scope for children and others to use them for play and other purposes without supervision. Cars could not be brought up to the front door as this no longer faced a 'proper' street. Often it was difficult to tell the front from the back of houses, and layouts were often considered to be confusing. Residents were condemned to "endure high density living while being surrounded by plentiful open spaces of uncertain and possibly sinister functions" (Ravetz and Turkington, 1995, p 37). Such layouts were never used by private developers and so added to the visual difference of council housing.

These changes brought a strong reaction in design terms and perhaps have been instrumental in setting the current image of public space as a threat. The first contribution to this approach was from Jacobs (1965). She argued that cities were being killed by the threat of crime posed by unused and unsupervised public places. She argued that the safest streets were those where the buildings were oriented to allow surveillance by residents and where there was a sufficient number of pedestrians to provide 'eyes on the street'.

Newman (1972) developed the concept of defensible space that has dominated the design of neighbourhoods since the 1970s. The ideas revolved around the clear definition of space between public and private and the minimisation of public space. This meant the provision of clearly defined private gardens with fences and gates. Houses with gardens were preferred to flats because they minimised communal space. But where flats were necessary they could be made safer by designing entrances and communal areas in order to limit access to as few people as possible. Surveillance of space was promoted through the siting of windows and doors and the banishing of high fences or large bushes that would break sight lines. The preferred street layout was the cul-de-sac, which, it was argued, enabled strangers to be easily spotted. Access points were to be cut to a minimum to reduce escape routes. Features such as overhead walkways and rear footpaths or lanes were to be removed where they existed.

An extreme version of the defensible space idea was put forward by Coleman (1985). She undertook a statistical analysis of existing estates, correlating indicators of malaise (litter, graffiti, vandalism, presence of excrement, and family breakdown leading to children being placed in care) with various design features. The ones most associated with malaise were the number of dwellings per entrance; dwellings per block; storeys per block; spatial organisation (the extent of non-private space); and the existence of overhead walkways. From this analysis she devised a checklist of undesirable design features which, she argued, could be applied to any estate. When the analysis was applied to some estates in a government-funded programme, design changes did not result in a reduction in crime.

Coleman's work was notable for its strong environmental determinism. As well as the social malaise indicators she used, she argued that:

> There are also many other forms of stress and trauma, including crime, fear, anxiety, marital breakdown, and physical and mental disorders that would largely be avoidable in more socially stabilising environments. Designs which have this disadvantaging effect are an iniquitous imposition upon people who cannot cope with them, especially as there is every reason to believe that most of them could cope perfectly well with life in more traditional houses. (Coleman, 1985, p 3)

The concept of defensible space, as articulated by Coleman and Newman, has now passed into design orthodoxy in Britain. From the wider considerations of estate layout to the detailed design of houses, the concepts of definition of space, the maximisation of private space, and surveillance are now the conventional wisdom. The phrase 'designing out crime' sums up both the primary design preoccupation and the faith in design as an appropriate way to tackle what is clearly perceived as a threatening neighbourhood. Design is also being used to challenge the dominance of vehicular traffic in streets through the creation of 'Home Zones' (Biddulph, 2001). The aim is to make the streets into more than just a through passage and storage space for cars, by encouraging people to use the street for other activities such as children's play or socialising.

Despite the apparent consensus, there is disagreement stemming from the differences between the ideas of Jacobs and Newman. Whereas Newman sought to restrict entry to public areas so that strangers could be identified, Jacobs stressed the importance of a vibrant and busy street life to deter bad behaviour by providing 'eyes on the street'. Jacobs' approach has led some designers to emphasise the integration of estates into the traditional street layout to encourage use (see Hillier et al, 1987). This distinction between integration and exclusion is a very interesting and important one, to which we will return.

Despite their differences, the two approaches share the view that the neighbourhood has become a threatening place that needs surveillance to contain anti-social behaviour. The increasing fear of crime seems to indicate that this view is shared by the population at large. Visual cues such as the existence of graffiti, vandalism, litter and dilapidated or empty buildings can reinforce this view. So can the use of streets by people perceived as undesirable or threatening, such as groups of young people. Campbell (1993) argues that, in many areas, the streets have been taken over by young males who create a threatening environment for others. She argues that residents' associations, usually run by middle-aged women, are engaged in a campaign to 'reclaim the streets' for others in order to reduce the perceived threat.

The design of the neighbourhood has symbolic importance at many different levels. The example of 'homes fit for heroes' shows the importance of political symbolism reflecting what is seen as the appropriate environment for a 'desirable lifestyle'. Implicit views of the nature of the neighbourhood inform design thinking. The current view seems to be that the neighbourhood is a hostile and threatening place that has to be designed in such a way as to increase surveillance and minimise threat. Underlying this view of the neighbourhood as a threat is a discourse that stresses the changing nature of interaction in the neighbourhood and, in particular, the view that households are increasingly becoming home–centred and having much less local social interaction. It is to this discourse that we now turn.

Neighbourhood discourses

Academic and policy discussion of neighbourhoods and public perception has been dominated by what may be termed the 'decline of community' discourse. This discourse has a number of elements that all emphasise a reduction of local social interaction and sense of community.

One element of the discourse is the argument that lifestyles are becoming more home-centred, which started with what has become known as the 'affluent worker' study by Goldthorpe et al (1969). The authors examined a group of car workers in Luton and found that they had instrumental attitudes towards their work, which was seen as primarily providing the resources for the better enjoyment of home life. There was little identification with the workplace in terms of loyalty to employer or to colleagues, and workers tended to go home at the end of the day and not to socialise much with workmates. Geographical mobility meant that most workers did not have friends or kin in the locality and so became almost entirely focused on the home and the immediate family. Most workers and their wives were happy with this situation and had left kinship and friendship ties in search of financial reward. As Goldthorpe et al argue, "primacy was clearly given to material well being, the social cohesiveness and the autonomy of the conjugal family over against the demands or attractions of wider kinship and community ties" (Goldthorpe et al, 1969, p 108).

This so called 'privatised' lifestyle was contrasted with traditional working class communities such as those described by Young and Willmott (1957) in their study of Bethnal Green. They reported a strong orientation towards work among men. This generated a strong sense of workplace solidarity that spilled over into leisure time, when men sought the company of workmates. Women were tied to the home because of the heavy duties of housekeeping before modern appliances were available. There was said to be a strong sense of solidarity here too, with women helping each other out in times of need and sharing tasks such as supervising children's play in the street. There was little geographical mobility and so wider kinship networks were common and extensive. Men and women lived quite separate lives with men focusing on the work relationships and women on family and the home.

When Holme (1985) restudied Bethnal Green in the 1980s she found little evidence of the communal life described by Young and Willmott.

> One striking difference was how home-centred most Bethnal Green families had become... the corollary in Bethnal Green to this new home centredness was the emptiness of the streets and corridors and staircases in the housing estates...no longer could it be said that people in Bethnal Green were (in Young and Willmott's words) 'vigorously at home in the streets'. (Holme, 1985, p 45)

There has been much debate about the growth of privatism, with some authors arguing that it existed well before the 1960s and indeed was there for Young and Willmott to see even in Bethnal Green. But there is little doubt that home is the centre of most people's lives, as Chapter Five showed. Most homes are now comfortable and full of labour saving devices and leisure facilities. Time, effort and resources are spent on making the home environment amenable, as the growth of the DIY industries and home-style magazines and television programmes show. However, the fact that many households today spend a lot of time in the home and value, it does not necessarily mean that they do not indulge in or value relationships and links outside the home.

The growth of privatism has been linked to the so-called decline of community. This is a strong theme in urban writing going back as far as the work of Wirth (1938), who argued that urban society was characterised by impersonal, superficial and transitory social relations.

> The distinctive features of the urban mode of life have often been described sociologically as the substitution of secondary for primary contacts, the weakening of bonds of kinship, and the declining social significance of the family, the disappearance of the neighbourhood, and the undermining of the traditional basis of solidarity. (Wirth, 1938, p 76)

We have already shown in Chapter Two that Wirth is wrong in his contention that family life is weakening. The nuclear family is alive and kicking, and wider kinship contacts are intact even though geographical mobility may have changed their nature.

> Contact with kin, particularly between parents and grown up children themselves married, is maintained by the motor car and telephone. In times of need, one can travel to the other, but day-to-day local contact has more typically been replaced by week-to-week contact from a distance. (Bulmer, 1987, p 55)

However, the changes in the nature of the family and the household point to one reason why the nature of neighbourhoods and communities is changing. Willmott (1986) argues that there are three major ties: of kinship, friendship and locality-based community. In Bethnal Green and many other traditional working class communities the three ties were all linked to the locality. People worked, enjoyed leisure with friends, interacted with the extended family and enjoyed neighbourly relations in the same neighbourhood. In other words, the locality was the scene of overlapping networks. This is far less likely to occur today, with increased geographical mobility that means that some families may live far apart and friends are more likely to be made through work and leisure activities rather than in the neighbourhood.

Neighbours can be defined as people who live near to one another. They may be people who live next door, or who live in the same street or block, or in a wider area or 'neighbourhood'. Willmott (1986) argues that people perceive the term 'neighbour' in different spatial terms, with some referring only to those who live next to them and others to people living varying distances away. Many people embrace all these levels and so use the term 'neighbour' in a number of ways. Neighbours can be friends. In this case friendship tends to subsume the neighbour relationship.

Willmott (1986) argues that contact between neighbours is high. In a sample in 1982, two thirds of people said that they spoke to one or more neighbours every day and 40% said that they visited the home of a neighbour weekly or more often. However, in the same survey 20% of people said they had experienced some kind of problems with their neighbours over the last two years. The most commonly reported problems were noise, pets and the behaviour of children. The risk of problems led people to stress the need for 'good neighbours' to be aware of concerns of privacy as well as to be friendly and helpful.

The dilemma is clear enough. People want to get on with their neighbours. If they can do so life is pleasanter and less stressful than it would otherwise be. Neighbours will also be able to do useful small services for each other as needed. People want, however, to preserve the privacy of family life, and to admit others to their homes only as a matter of choice. Most neighbours recognise all this, but some may not. If the neighbours turn out to be inquisitive, over-enthusiastic about entering the homes of others, inclined to gossip, liable to stir up trouble, the relationship will turn sour. (Willmott, 1986, p 56)

The kind of help most commonly given and received by neighbours was looking after keys, plants or pets, borrowing food, or shopping. But other functions, such as helping with house maintenance or repairs, help during illness, or looking after children were undertaken in some cases. Willmott argues that there is an ebb and flow of interaction with neighbours over the life cycle. High interaction tends to occur at stages when more of life is undertaken within the neighbourhood, such as in childhood, early parenthood and old age. More interaction is undertaken by those confined to the local area, whether because they are housewives or because they do not have access to transport. Interestingly, middle class people tend to have higher rates of interaction than working class people. A number of factors may be leading to changes in the nature and extent of neighbourhood ties. First, household change is resulting in more of the household types that do not tend to engage as much in neighbourly activity, such as single people and childless couples. Second, the number of people who are limited to the local area is declining as more women engage in work and more households have access to a car.

In a study of a Swedish residential area, Henning and Lieberg (1996) stress the importance of weak ties (Granovetter, 1973) in the neighbourhood compared with the strong ties that were commonly wider in geographical spread. Nevertheless they argue that 'The significance of weak ties was underlined by the inhabitants who stated that these contacts meant a "feeling of home", "security" and "practical as well as social support"' (Henning and Lieberg, 1996, p 22). They also stress that these weak neighbourhood ties are particularly important for vulnerable and marginal groups.

Based on research in the US, Guest and Wierzbicki (1999) argue that there has been a decline in neighbouring over the last three decades, but it has not been dramatic. The more marked trend has been an increase in socialising outside the neighbourhood, which is becoming more separated from forms of local interaction. Despite the concern about the privatism of lifestyles, it is clear that neighbour relations are still important to many people. Forrest and Kearns (2001) argue that the quality of neighbouring is an important element in people's ability to cope in disadvantaged neighbourhoods. In more affluent areas, however, "*neighbourhood* may be rather more important than *neighbouring* – people may 'buy into' neighbourhoods as physical environments rather than necessarily anticipate or practice a great degree of local social interaction" (Forrest and Kearns, 2001, p 2130).

The discussion of the growth in privatism and the decline of neighbouring is linked to a discourse that describes a growing lack of local 'community'. Rather like the concepts of family and home, community has come to have a normative meaning that is common in everyday and in political discourse. MacIver and Page (1961, p 9) define a community as "an area of social living marked by some degree of social coherence. The bases of community are locality and community sentiment". It may be that these two elements are linked with high rates of social interaction between people reflecting a high degree of community sentiment, but it may not necessarily be so. As Clapham and Kintrea (1995, p 264) argue, "Community does not consist of a specific pattern of social interaction, but is a feeling of solidarity or inter-dependence. Therefore community cannot be measured by outsiders as it only exists in the sense that it has meaning to those who are part of it".

In research on community-based housing associations in Glasgow, Clapham and Kintrea (1995) explored the meaning that community had for the residents. Many older people had been brought up in the older, inner-city tenements, many of which had been demolished through slum clearance. They had fond memories of their early lives and of the places in which they lived at that time.

> I was born and bred in Glasgow – George Street – but the city of Glasgow's changed ... it had terrific community spirit. I'll never forget that. I think people were ... for example, you knew the name of every policeman, you knew your neighbours. I can always remember my mother taking an illness and the neighbours would step in. They took over. (Clapham and Kintrea, 1995, p 272)

Others specifically related community to village life. They wanted to "get back to the old village style thing, communities". "I'd love to see like a wee village night, everybody knew each other and they were very supportive to each other" (p 273).

One tenant summed up the general attitude towards the desired community. "People being neighbourly and being able to walk down the street unafraid. People looking out for each other" (p 272).

There was a general feeling that community spirit had declined. "People are just isolating themselves, staying in the house. Television is like a religion" (p 273). "I think maybe it's a generation gap.... That everyone's changing.... I don't think you'll get it like it used to be years and years ago – there was always someone on hand to help you if something went wrong". "In the old days children would be reprimanded by adults for bad behaviour such as graffiti, but nowadays people are frightened" (p 275).

The feeling of a lack of control and influence over behaviour in public places was widely shared. The tenants reported here had formed a housing cooperative in an effort to deal with some of these problems. It was generally felt that this had succeeded in changing identification with and attitudes towards the neighbourhood. "I think the area's improved, the tenants are going to have a lot more pride in the place and therefore they're not going to stand for what they've put up with till now".

The tenants reported here were middle-aged or older and had largely lived and been brought up in an inner-city area of a city renowned for its history of working class solidarity and militancy. The attitudes they reported were similar to those uncovered in the 'community studies' of the 1960s and 1970s epitomised by Young and Willmott's study of Bethnal Green. The question is whether their ideas are widely shared by new generations and by people of other class and locality backgrounds.

Scase (1999) argues that traditional communities, as experienced by the Glasgow tenants and the Bethnal Green residents, have been destroyed by economic and social change.

> Economic change has brought about the destruction of traditional household, neighbourhood and community relations. In the past the old industrial towns consisted of social networks which functioned as modes of integration and informal social control. These, with their routines, duties and obligations offered life-style certainty and security. They gave individuals identity and status, derived from their roles as neighbours, friends, family members and local residents. (Scase, 1999, p 49)

It has been argued that the decline of community discourse is made up of different strands that emphasise a growing privatism of lifestyles, a reduction of social interaction in the neighbourhood, and a declining community sentiment. The discourse has dominated academic and policy discussions on neighbourhoods and is reflected in popular perceptions and attitudes. At the policy level there have been attempts to recreate the lost communities, particularly in some policy towards deprived neighbourhoods, as we shall see later. However, another discourse is emerging that would argue that such attempts are doomed to failure because of the changing nature of perceptions of neighbourhood and the increasing importance of the search for identity and lifestyle choice.

Lifestyle and identity

Scase (1999) sees traditional communities being replaced by more diversified localities. Some would consist of people with choice pursuing active lifestyles that to a large extent transcended the locality. Scase argues that mobility and the growing use of information technologies will enable people to interact with a broader geographical network of friends and acquaintances, but will not negate the importance of neighbourhood. Lifestyles will shape the availability of local facilities such as schools, shops and leisure facilities, and the 'image' of areas will influence their appeal.

In an echo of the views of Giddens, Scase (1999, p 54) argues that community will increasingly have a 'psychological' dimension: "In an uncertain world where jobs are insecure and futures are unpredictable, living in a risk society reinforces the importance of community in a symbolic sense. Individuals obtain a sense of 'place', of attachment to the communities in which they live". He argues that this will be true even if highly mobile and affluent people do not make use of local facilities. The most important factor will be the status or 'brand' of the community, which will be strongly influenced by the local media that can promulgate images and symbols with which people can identify and 'buy into'. Forrest and Kearns (2001, p 2130) argue: "In a sense, the neighbourhood becomes an extension of the home for social purposes and hence extremely important in identity terms: 'location matters' and the neighbourhood becomes part of our statement about who we are".

Scase argues that neighbourhoods will be increasingly segregated by demographics and lifestyles as well as income and occupation. Older people will continue to move to areas that match their lifestyles and provide facilities for hobbies, socialising and shopping. He argues that the growth of single-person households among the young and the middle aged will be concentrated in the inner cities. Housing developers will focus on their leisure, health and personal security needs, and facilities such as fast food outlets, delicatessens, wine bars, clubs and 24-hour stores will be concentrated here. These areas will contain the most 'cosmopolitan and fashionable' lifestyles and be the primary areas for 'experimentation and innovation' of lifestyles.

Those with 'more traditional' lifestyles and family patterns will live in the outer suburbs where the provision of quality schooling, education and childcare will be concentrated. Other neighbourhoods will consist of people socially, culturally and economically excluded who are constrained into locality-based lifestyles, dependent on the quality of local facilities.

The picture painted by Scase is a very interesting one. However accurate the predictions prove to be, it opens up a debate about the nature of neighbourhood in a complex and useful way that recognises the importance of the meanings and perceptions of households. The link between locality and lifestyles raises the possibility that people will view their neighbourhood in different ways depending on their income, gender, life cycle stage, age and lifestyle. In their study of three gentrified neighbourhoods in London, Butler and Robson (2001) found that there were differences in the images of neighbourhoods that reflected the attitudes of the residents. One area attracted people because of its cultural diversity, another because of its social networks and schools, and the third because of its social and recreational facilities. These differences were reflected in the attachment which residents had to the area and their expectations of what a 'good' neighbourhood was. Therefore, the factors that give the neighbourhood meaning will also vary considerably, but they are unlikely often to reflect the traditional view of community articulated by the Glasgow tenants.

The different discourses on neighbourhood can be illustrated by looking at two forms of neighbourhood that have dominated policy debates. The first is the 'deprived neighbourhood' that contains a high proportion of households on low incomes. The second is the 'inner city' that is said to be increasingly abandoned by households choosing to live elsewhere and therefore in need of 'regeneration'. Below, the discourses underlying the policy debates in these two types of neighbourhood are described, and the way policy problems and solutions are defined is examined. In each example the importance of identity and lifestyles and their relationship to the image of a neighbourhood is stressed.

Deprived neighbourhoods and the discourse of social exclusion

Of the different kinds of neighbourhoods identified by Scase, the one that has most consistently featured in policy debates is what is usually today called a deprived area or socially excluded neighbourhood. There has been a long-standing concern in housing and general public policy with neighbourhoods that have a concentration of poor people living in them. This can be traced back to the earliest slum clearance of the nineteenth century, which aimed to open up the slums and disperse the residents. The policy discourse of the time stressed the need to break up concentrations of poor people in order to remove the breeding grounds of disease and crime (Gauldie, 1974). Over the following years the policy emphasis on deprived areas has waxed and waned and the definition of the policy problem with its associated set of policy prescriptions has been contested, with different conceptions becoming dominant at different times (for a review, see Lawless, 1989). Nevertheless, the concern with such areas has been an enduring one.

In recent decades two particular discourses have dominated policy debates. The first is the concept of an underclass, which was dominant in the 1980s and early 1990s, to be replaced by the concept of social exclusion, favoured by the incoming Labour government in 1997. Both stress the importance of the neighbourhood in the causality and alleviation of poverty or deprivation.

The concept of an underclass was popularised by Charles Murray (1989) and has two main roots. The first is in the work of Oscar Lewis in South America, where he coined the term 'culture of poverty' (Lewis, 1966). The argument was that the concentration of poor people in particular neighbourhoods led to the emergence of cultural norms different from those of society as a whole. This counter-culture could be self-sustaining through socialisation processes of parenting and the following of the role models provided by local leaders. These durable cultural norms served to reinforce the poverty of neighbourhood residents by cutting them off from the norms of society as a whole, and reinforcing behaviour that the wider society deemed inappropriate. This thesis has some parallels with the idea of a cycle of deprivation put forward by Keith Joseph and other politicians in Britain (Rutter and Madge, 1976).

The second root is the concern expressed by Murray and others about the decline of the traditional family (see Chapter Two). Murray argued that the rise of illegitimate births and family breakdown led to poor parenting and the lack of appropriate role models for children.

In turn this led to rising crime rates; juvenile delinquency and hooliganism; drug abuse; educational failure; a dependency culture; and idleness. He argued that single parents, young people, the long-term unemployed and 'recidivists' constituted an 'underclass' that held different cultural norms from mainstream society and was cut off from it. The remedy was seen to lie in the encouragement and strengthening of the traditional family and the reform of welfare programmes which undermined this.

There is a third root that is usually implied rather than explicitly stated. In the US urban poverty is often synonymous with membership of a minority ethnic group and residence in a 'ghetto'. The discourse of 'ghetto' implies a clear separation from society, with alternative cultural norms thriving behind impervious physical and social boundaries. In Britain there is a high degree of residential segregation of minority ethnic households. Harrison (2001) points to the interplay of household choice and constraint that has resulted in this pattern. Some minority ethnic households may wish to live close to family members or others with whom they share a cultural background. Some may feel safer from racial harassment in a segregated neighbourhood. Others may be constrained to live in a particular neighbourhood because of low income or the constraints that stem from differential access to finance for house purchase. Some of these segregated areas overlap with the categorisation of deprived neighbourhoods. Therefore, policies towards deprived neighbourhoods have usually had an implicit or explicit racial element.

Advocates of the concept of social exclusion accept that a group of people exists that is cut off from the wider society. However, in seeking to explain the phenomenon, they emphasise the importance of what is done to the people and families concerned, as well as their behaviour. Despite its importance in political debate, the meaning of the term 'social exclusion' is far from clear. For example, one report from the Chartered Institute of Housing (1998) gives six different definitions of the term and does not choose between them, rather implying that social exclusion is taken to include, in some way, all of them. The difficulty in reaching a consensus on the definition of social exclusion shows that it is a contested concept that holds different meanings. Nevertheless, there are a number of consistent emphases. The first is the recognition that social exclusion means more than just material poverty. In this the concept is similar to the idea of multiple deprivation that preceded it in political debate. There is no agreed definition of the factors involved, but the Social Exclusion Unit (2000) has defined a number of indices of deprived neighbourhoods, namely: poor housing conditions; high crime; unemployment; community breakdown; poor health; educational underachievement; and inadequate public transport and local services. It is often accepted that, since the precise mix of problems will vary, in tackling social exclusion the primary need is said to be to discover its manifestation in each individual case.

The second major element in social exclusion is the implied causality of the problems. In contrast to the concept of an underclass, there is more concern with what is done to the excluded as well as with their attitudes and behaviour. Nevertheless, this is only a difference of emphasis. Underclass theorists stress the failures of the welfare state in creating a dependency culture. Social exclusion, too, focuses on the importance of the incentive to work, but also stresses the breakdowns in the nature and coverage of state services in creating and reinforcing exclusion. The targeting of state services on the problems of exclusion is alleged to be a positive help. The concern of underclass theorists with the personal behaviour and attitudes of the poor is also shared by theorists of social exclusion. Ameliorative state action is often mixed with punitive action against those who transgress against societal norms.

The third element is the reference to what people are excluded from. This is usually defined as 'normal citizenship' or 'mainstream life'. The problem arises in defining exactly what this is when life chances and lifestyles vary so widely. Nevertheless, there are strong links here with the postmodern emphasis on the importance of 'lifestyle choice' in today's society. Social exclusion can be seen as the inability to make the choices that most people are able to take in their everyday lives. These may be choices about the consumption of food or clothes or services, or about how to live and where to live.

The fourth element of social exclusion is a concern with the lack of power in the political and decision-making processes. Here the rhetoric of 'citizenship' is often used. Attention is focused on the excluded people's lack of control over their lives and over the actions of public services that affect them. The term 'empowerment' is often used in discussion of appropriate strategies to improve citizenship and combat social exclusion.

The concept of citizenship was first popularised by Marshall (1950) and is concerned with social and civil rights and obligations. However, advocates of citizenship vary in the emphasis they assign to civil as against social rights, or in the appropriate balance between individual and collective rights. Debate has also centred on the nature and practicability of rights and the processes whereby rights are acquired or bestowed. Most recent debate, however, has focused on the appropriate balance between rights and obligations. Marshall was at pains to point out that rights had to be seen in relation to the corresponding duties and obligations, but advocates of citizenship have often concentrated on the extension of rights. Etzioni (1995) challenged this emphasis in arguing for what he calls communitarianism. Etzioni argues that many current social problems arise because of excessive individualism and an over-concentration on social rights compared with social obligations. He argues for a moratorium on the creation of new social rights, which he claims have been devalued, and a new emphasis on shared moral responsibilities. People should not wait for their lives to be made better through social rights given by the state, but should actively take responsibility themselves.

> People have a moral responsibility to help themselves as best they can ... the laying of a claim to participate actively in advancing their lives on those who are disadvantaged ... rather than to lie back and be compensated ... is based, first of all, on a concept of human dignity. There is ... something deeply degrading about being dependent on others. It is respectful of human dignity to encourage people to control their fate the best they can. (Etzioni, 1995, p 144)

Therefore, the differences between the discourses of 'underclass' and 'social exclusion' are ones of emphasis, with both focusing on the attitudes and behaviour of poor people as well as the actions of the state. Social exclusion is a particularly difficult discourse to define precisely because of its broad scope and often contradictory elements.

The policy prescriptions for dealing with social exclusion have had a dual focus. Particular problems have been highlighted such as rough sleeping and truancy, but the primary emphasis has been on neighbourhoods where social exclusion has been seen to be concentrated. This follows a trend started with the so-called rediscovery of poverty in the 1960s to emphasise the spatial dimensions of poverty. There followed a plethora of programmes and policies to regenerate poor neighbourhoods that stretch back to the Urban Programme and the Community Development Projects of the late 1960s and 1970s.

Why is the problem of poverty usually seen as the problem of poor neighbourhoods? It has been pointed out (Holtermann, 1975) that the majority of poor people do not live in poor neighbourhoods. However, it is the concentration of poor people that is held to be problematic. The underclass discourse would emphasise the need to prevent alternative cultures emerging with their concomitant threats to order. The social exclusion discourse would include this element, but would also emphasise the impact on the local environment, reputation and services of a concentration of poor people with little political or economic power. There are also arguments that it is easier to tackle the interrelated nature of disadvantage at a local level where the relevant agencies can work together and with local people to focus on the individual problems of that area. It should also be pointed out that selective area-based approaches (which are often demonstration projects) are cheaper than an overall increase in income for poor people and have a high political visibility.

There are other arguments for the neighbourhood focus. Skifter Anderson (2002) argues that deprived neighbourhoods do not just reflect the spatial distribution of poverty but have a downward dynamic of their own. He argues that deprived neighbourhoods become locked into spirals of social conflict, lack of care for the dwellings and immediate environment, and stigmatisation, which reflect back on the behavioural norms of residents. He argues that the image and problems of the neighbourhood often influence the self-identity and self-understanding of residents. This is reinforced by the actions of outsiders who have a negative view of the neighbourhood and stigmatise those who live in it. Following Rijpers and Meets (1998), the image of a neighbourhood can be divided into the internal image (that held by residents); the external image (that held by outsiders); and the self-reflecting image (what insiders think outsiders think of the neighbourhood). Dean and Hastings (2000) show that each of these images can be fragmented. For example, they show that in three deprived neighbourhoods, residents put different emphases on the negative and positive aspects of the neighbourhood, with some accepting and agreeing with what they perceive as the negative external image of the area and wishing to leave. Others challenge the negative image and stress the positive aspects of the area. The negative images are said to be held by external agencies such as estate agents, government agencies, employers and the local media as well as prospective residents. "As counterparts to one another, neighbourhoods seem to acquire their identity through an on-going commentary between themselves and this continuous dialogue between different groups and agencies shapes the cognitive map of the city and establishes good and bad reputations" (Forrest and Kearns, 2001, p 2135).

There is little research on the factors that influence these negative images; they seem to be independent of personal experience as many people have not been to the area or met the residents. An important question is the extent and nature of the links between these images and general discourses of 'underclass' or 'social exclusion'. It is recognised that a negative image can influence the opportunities and constraints that residents face, for example in the lack of job opportunities open to them because of discrimination. However, both Dean and Hastings (2000) and Skifter Anderson (2002) speculate on the impact that negative images and the behaviour of outsiders have on the attitudes and behaviour of the residents themselves. Some residents seem to accept and adopt the dominant perspective. In terms of structuration (see Chapter One) they reproduce the social structure through restructuration. Others challenge the negative image and attempt to destructure. Whether they are successful will depend on the power games involved.

Strategies to regenerate socially excluded neighbourhoods have tackled a wide range of issues. There has been a focus on design by adopting the ideas of defensible space and attempting to 'design out crime'. This has sometimes included changing the house type by replacing flats with houses.

Other strategies have focused on the management of these areas, which, because of the social polarisation of public sector housing, have tended to be in that tenure. Power (1987) has argued for locally based housing management that focuses on the needs of the local area through local lettings policies to stabilise the population mix and reduce the number of empty properties. This is combined with local housing management policies that focus on strict adherence to the terms of tenancy and effective action to deal with anti-social behaviour. There is a focus on the local environment by attempts to reduce vandalism and to eradicate graffiti and other unsightly nuisances.

These, particularly housing, responses are often linked with programmes to improve other opportunities, through economic development (whether through skills training or job creation); educational attainment; health status (through healthy-living campaigns or the improvement of primary health care); and crime prevention initiatives. The government is supporting the idea of neighbourhood managers to bring together different agencies to provide an integrated neighbourhood strategy.

Linked with the above is usually an attempt to engage the 'local community' with the strategy through, for example, the creation of decision-making fora in which local people are represented. This may be linked with the support of 'community groups' and 'community activities'. It is also associated with what is called 'community capacity building'. This seems to mean providing support (whether material, training, knowledge, access or confidence building) to enable local people to build and maintain local organisations and to engage with the regeneration process.

The term 'community' in the previous paragraph was put in quotation marks because it is used glibly in social exclusion and regeneration discourse. But as we have already seen, it is a term with a contested meaning and so its use here raises a number of important questions. Do communities exist in socially excluded neighbourhoods? The research reviewed earlier would suggest that communities in the traditional sense no longer exist because of social changes in families and lifestyles. What then is meant by 'community' here? Is it possible to create a traditional community in the present day where one does not exist? Why is it necessary when areas containing more affluent people seem to exist without it? Giddens argues that an improved community can be achieved without trying to recreate the 'lost' traditional working class community. "'Community' doesn't imply trying to recapture lost forms of social solidarity; it refers to practical means of furthering the social and material refurbishment of neighbourhoods, towns and larger local areas" (Giddens, 1998, p 79).

The idea of 'new communities' identified by Willmott (1986) is relevant here. Willmott identifies what he calls 'new communities' that depend on the organisational skills and willingness of people to construct and maintain local networks. This is more likely to occur in middle class neighbourhoods where these skills exist and is likely to be focused around shared local concerns. These can occur either where an outside threat exists, such as of crime or some form of unwelcome development, or where there is a shared interest in local facilities such as schools, or organisations such as amenity societies or community or parish councils. Much community development activity in areas of social exclusion is devoted to improving the organisational skills of residents and creating and developing the organisations to pursue local concerns, whether play schools, community businesses or any other form of economic, social or political function.

A recent concept that encapsulates this approach is that of social capital.

> By analogy to physical capital and human capital, social capital refers to the norms and networks of civil society that lubricate co-operative action among both citizens and their institutions. Without adequate supplies of social capital – that is, without civic engagement, healthy community

institutions, norms of mutual reciprocity, and trust – social institutions falter. (Putnam, 1998, p v)

Putnam argues that there is a decline in the stock of social capital in present-day US and that this applies in particular to poor neighbourhoods that lack the necessary resources of self-help, mutuality and trust that are essential for their regeneration (Forrest, 2000). Forrest and Kearns (2001) divide social capital into a number of elements. These include: a sense of belonging; a feeling of safety; trust in co-residents and local organisations; the existence of collective norms of behaviour and values; support networks and reciprocity (people helping one another); associational activity with a common purpose; participation in community activities; and empowerment (people feel they have a voice that is listened to).

Which aspects of social capital are necessary for an 'effective' community? A report submitted to the Scottish Social Inclusion Network stresses only a few of these elements: "Communities function well where individuals have a sense of belonging to, and responsibility for, the community and for others who are part of it" (Scottish Office Strategy Action Team, 1999, p 7).

A sense of belonging may arise from, and be sustained by, local organisational activity. People are more likely to take a pride in, and responsibility for, something that they have had a part in creating. But a sense of belonging may exist without local organisational activity. This explains why many middle class neighbourhoods are popular and considered to be successful even though people hide behind their garden fences. People may still identify with their neighbourhood and take a pride in it. This idea is associated with Scase's focus on the importance of the status or 'brand' of the neighbourhood. However, this may be more difficult in poor neighbourhoods where facilities are poor and people live there because they have no other choice.

Another element in the attempts to regenerate socially excluded neighbourhoods has been the desire to create 'balanced' communities. Forrest (2000) charts concern with a balanced community back to the design of new towns in the 1950s and 1960s. Here the ideal was to design neighbourhoods of mixed social groups living together and on a scale that would lead to the cost-effective provision of facilities such as shops and schools within the neighbourhood. Balance meant an element of self-containment as well as a mix of social groups.

In terms of socially excluded neighbourhoods, recent concern has mainly been with bringing in more affluent households because of the perceived benefits they would bring in terms of increased status, stability, more social capital, and increased purchasing power, resulting in better facilities. As Forrest (2000) points out, the concern to create mixed neighbourhoods has existed even though most successful 'traditional communities' were very homogenous in their social mix, and concentrations of minority ethnic groups may constitute what he terms "highly supportive neighbourhoods of choice" (Forrest, 2000, p 209).

Because of the polarisation of tenure in Britain, the creation of social mix in socially excluded neighbourhoods means, in practice, the introduction of owner-occupation into predominantly public housing estates where sales to sitting tenants through the 'right to buy' have been lower. In addition, attempts to prevent social exclusion have resulted in a growing number of mixed-tenure new estates often developed through the planning powers of local authorities to negotiate quotas of public rented housing as a planning gain from private developers. Jupp (1999) documents the strong government support for mixed-tenure developments that is reflected in planning guidance to local authorities. Research on existing mixed-tenure communities shows that not all the perceived advantages are achieved (see Jupp, 1999 and Atkinson and Kintrea, 1998). Owner-occupiers tended to spend most of their time outside the estate and to have few local contacts. This contrasted with tenants who, probably because of the greater likelihood of unemployment and the constraints of lack of money and lower car ownership, tended to spend most of their time on the estate and to have more ties with others in the same situation. The relative scarcity of close contacts between individuals in the two groups means that the potential for tenants to become more socially included through access to the wider social networks of owners was slight. However, Jupp (1999) reports that contact was higher where developments were mixed on a street level, because most local contacts were with close neighbours. Residents in these streets were also more likely to be positive about the impact of mixing on the estate, and the potential for the public rented housing to develop a negative image was less. In one or two estates, problems of vandalism, noise and the behaviour of children developed into broader social tensions, which polarised neighbourhoods. Jupp (1999, p 11) argues for the development of mixed tenure streets but concludes that "The hope that the current models of mixed tenure estates will foster widespread mutual support between people from different economic groups, considerably broaden understanding between groups and or introduce role models into an area appears largely misplaced".

In summary, much policy attention has been focused on

neighbourhoods with a concentration of poor people. The definition of the problem has varied, with different discourses of 'underclass' and 'social exclusion' current. Policy prescriptions for dealing with the problems of these areas have varied from physical design solutions to the creation of mixed tenure neighbourhoods. The current focus is on a wider spectrum of policy mechanisms tailored to meet the needs of local areas and led by local people. The experience of past attempts to deal with the problems of poor neighbourhoods is not encouraging. Many of the areas singled out for attention from the 1960s onwards are still unpopular places to live, with poor reputations and images. Even if individual households are helped, they tend to leave the area to be replaced by others with no other choice.

Atkinson and Kintrea (2002) criticise the focus of social exclusion policy on the deprived neighbourhoods themselves and argue that the key issue is the linking of the area to the rest of the city, which involves tackling the negative image that was highlighted earlier. The community-based approach runs the danger of reinforcing inward-looking attitudes that reinforce the exclusion of the residents. This section has shown the importance of discourses in shaping the way that neighbourhoods are perceived by policy makers in terms of the assessment of the causation of problems and appropriate strategies to cope with them. It has also highlighted the importance of the image of neighbourhoods both to those who live there and to others.

Inner cities and the 'urban renaissance'

One of the types of neighbourhoods identified by Scase (1999) was the 'inner city', which he said would be inhabited by the growing number of new, young, single-person households that would be attracted by areas with an image of enabling a 'cosmopolitan and fashionable' lifestyle. Such areas clearly exist in some of Britain's cities, but there has been a general concern about the continued viability of many inner-city and traditional urban areas.

Champion (1999) shows that urban areas are subject to large migration flows that are changing their character. The precise nature of these flows and their magnitude varies between conurbations, with London standing out as unique. Overall the population of the eight largest conurbations, including London, grew between 1991 and 1997, although at a slower rate than the rest of the UK. Despite this overall picture half of them lost population over this period. The population totals hide large flows of people in different directions. In general there is an 'urban exodus' disproportionately made up of affluent middle-aged families out of the cities, and the inner cities in particular, to the surrounding areas. At the same time there is an inflow of generally younger single people into the cities, and the inner cities in particular, both from the rest of the UK and from overseas. London's uniqueness is partly due to its ability to retain a higher proportion of professional families than other conurbations, and its position as the primary destination of immigration from overseas. This immigration, which is present in all cities to differing degrees, is skewed towards young professional people and those coming to Britain to study. As Champion (1999, p 76) argues,

> International migration is strongly selective on age and citizenship, with the net effect being strongly in favour of 16-24 year olds and people from the New Commonwealth and 'other foreign' (not Commonwealth or EU) countries thus providing a strong boost to these conurbations' youthfulness and cultural diversity.

The result of these trends for inner-city neighbourhoods is the over-representation of older, poorer people unable or unwilling to join the 'urban exodus' and young professional newcomers from the UK or overseas. Lee and Murie (1999) point to the high incidence of social deprivation in many inner-city areas. Although particularly associated with public rented estates, there is also a concentration of deprivation in some private rented and poor-condition owner-occupied areas. The proportion of empty properties in all tenures, particularly in northern cities, has led some commentators to talk about neighbourhood abandonment (see Keenan et al, 1999).

The changing demographic pattern has been associated with a poor neighbourhood environment. Lee and Murie (1999) show that the perception of neighbourhood problems is as acute in some lower-value owner-occupied areas as it is in public rented estates. The problems most often mentioned were crime, dogs, lack of leisure facilities, high levels of vandalism, and litter and rubbish in the streets. In their analysis of the 'geography of misery' Burrows and Rhodes (1998) identified six types of neighbourhood in which problems are perceived by the residents to be most acute. These are: inner-city public sector estates; deprived industrial areas; deprived city areas; industrial areas; lower-status owner-occupation; and metropolitan professional.

There has been considerable political concern about the perceived problems of cities and inner-urban areas in particular. In Britain, the government set up an Urban Task Force to examine the problem, which recommended an 'urban renaissance'. The 'urban exodus of professional households was said to be a reaction to the poor public facilities (such as schools and leisure) and crime and environmental problems of inner-city areas. It was leading to the slow death of the cities and was not environmentally sustainable because of problems caused by the residential development of surrounding rural areas and long commuting journeys causing increased car traffic and pollution. The report called for the restriction of development of greenfield sites and measures to increase the reuse of brownfield land. It also called for measures to improve the quality of life in urban areas in order to stem the outflow of people.

Urban design was given a key place in the 'urban renaissance'. The aim was to create "compact developments with a mix of uses, better public transport and a density which supports local services and fosters a strong sense of community and public safety" (Urban Task Force, 1999, p 3). These ideas mirror those popularised in the US by the 'new urbanism' movement and in Britain by adherents of 'urban villages'. Their shared aim is to create urban neighbourhoods that are balanced by including a mix of income groups, and self-contained, with a mix of uses in order to meet environmental standards by reducing car usage and promoting cycling and walking. Density is to be high enough to be able to sustain facilities as well as by populating public areas and providing 'eyes on the street'. Bohl (2000, p 763) describes the key element of new urbanism as being planning around neighbourhoods:

> The neighbourhood is limited to an area approximating a 5- to 10-minute walk from center to edge, ensuring that all neighbourhood facilities are within convenient walking distance of residents. Within the neighbourhood are a variety of housing types and land uses, a mix of shops, services, and civic uses capable of satisfying many of the residents' daily needs. Streets are designed for pedestrian use, with generous sidewalks, street trees, and on-street parking to provide a buffer from street traffic and make walking a safer and more appealing option. Buildings are generally low- to mid-rise, set close together, and built close to the street to promote pedestrian use and help define neighbourhood public space in the form of streets, squares and plazas. Small parks and civic institutions are given

prominent sites and dispersed throughout the neighbourhood.

It remains to be seen how successful these design solutions will be. They have been criticised as a new form of environmental determinism, but the Urban Task Force report (1999), for example, puts forward a raft of economic and social measures that are meant to be implemented in tandem with the design solutions. One criticism is that it is not clear who is to be attracted to these areas. It seems unlikely that the professional family households who are creating the urban exodus will be prepared to forgo the pleasures and facilities of the affluent suburbs. Further attraction of the growing number of single-person households may stabilise population loss, but is unlikely to create the mixed community and the public life that is desired to reduce problems in the neighbourhood environment.

Conclusion

This chapter has shown the importance of the setting of the house in both reflecting and shaping patterns of life. The physical neighbourhood influences and is influenced by patterns of social interaction between family, friends and neighbours. There is evidence that these patterns are changing due to changing household and family structures and lifestyles. Whereas in traditional working–class communities in the 1950s the three kinds of ties overlapped in the neighbourhood, this is increasingly unlikely due to increased mobility and changed leisure and employment patterns. There is a widespread feeling that a sense of community has been lost. Neighbourhood activity is largely confined to middle class areas where the organisational skills exist to enable action to be taken on local issues, usually focused around a single issue such as the state of a local school or the desire to prevent a new development. As a consequence, the neighbourhood is increasingly viewed as a threatening place, and physical design practices reflect this with an emphasis on privacy, surveillance and designing out crime.

Nevertheless, the meaning and image of a neighbourhood are still important factors for many households and it is argued that neighbourhoods are becoming increasingly differentiated in terms of their meaning and associated lifestyles. Two types of neighbourhood were examined. The first was areas of social exclusion where the lack of a sense of community is considered to be particularly important in the dominant discourse that frames public policy towards the areas.

The links between the discourses of community and family were explored. In particular, the discourse of 'the underclass' is based on the perceived decline of the traditional family. Many of the policy prescriptions for social exclusion are based on the idea of recreating lost communities by improving social capital in the areas through changes in local social interaction. Another strand of policy is beginning to emerge that focuses more on the meaning that areas have for their residents and for outsiders. This discourse looks outside the neighbourhood as well as inside it, and looks for the factors that lead to unpopularity and a poor image.

The second area to be examined was the inner city, which is at the centre of concerns to create sustainable cities. Much of the policy discourse here has focused on the physical environment in an attempt to create an infrastructure that fits with certain design principles. However, there has been an assumption that physical design will alter household preferences and behaviour, with little concern for the meanings of inner-city neighbourhoods. The result is a blanket policy that is not grounded in the perceptions, attitudes and meanings of the households that are expected to want to live there.

The chapter has shown that family, home and community are related concepts with linked discourses. The terms carry meanings that resonate with policy makers and with households as they pursue their housing pathways. It has been argued that a house derives important meaning from its setting in its physical and social environment. When one considers housing pathways it is necessary to conceive of the house as both a home and a part of a neighbourhood.

SEVEN

Early pathways

Previous chapters have sought to elucidate the pathways approach through a disaggregated analysis of the different elements that constitute pathways and the meaning these particular factors have for households. Chapters Seven and Eight further explore the pathways approach by focusing on particular parts or stages in a household's pathway in a more holistic way. This chapter considers the early stages of a pathway by focusing on young people leaving home and their early experiences as a household. Chapter Eight covers the pathways of households in later life. Of course, these are only illustrations of the full extent of pathways and by no means cover all the different stages of any pathway.

The chapter aims to show the dynamic nature of pathways over time and some of the processes involved such as leaving home or becoming homeless. It attempts to show how some of the factors considered in previous chapters interact in the early stages of a housing pathway. Also, the chapter reviews existing applications of a pathways approach and uses this analysis to suggest ways in which research on housing pathways could be fruitfully taken forward.

The chapter begins with a discussion of the discourses that surround the process of leaving home. These discourses include those of 'the family' and 'labour flexibility', which have been discussed fully elsewhere in the book, as well as discourses of 'youth'. It is argued that these discourses frame the actions of individuals and are embedded in social norms and public policies. The following section examines the process of leaving home, looking at the different factors that trigger the process and the stages that young people move through. Some of the living arrangements or destinations of young people when they leave home, such as shared living, are described. The general theme of the section is the diversity of experience among young people in all aspects of the process and particularly in the ability to sustain independent living. In a few cases the problems are such that young people may become homeless, and this is the focus of the rest of the chapter. The first part of this section looks at the discourses of homelessness that are embedded in public policy. The second part examines the experiences of young homeless people through the framework of the pathways approach. Homelessness is used as an example to show how a pathways approach could be used as an aid to understanding housing circumstances.

Leaving the parental home

The process of leaving home and establishing an independent household has usually been seen as part of a 'transition' from childhood to adulthood. This occurs in a number of areas. Coles (1995) suggests that there are three interrelated transitions made by young people: from school to further education and employment; a domestic transition from family of origin to family of destination; and a housing transition involving a move to residence away from the parental (or surrogate parental) home. These three transitions are interrelated because experiences in one dimension will have an impact on the others. For example, problems in the move from school to work may result in financial hardship, which will make the domestic and housing transitions more difficult. Also, problems in the housing transition may hinder attempts to find work.

Leaving the parental home is seen as a common part of the move from dependent childhood to independent citizenship. It is generally expected that children when they grow up will leave the home in which they were raised and eventually establish homes of their own in which to raise a new generation of children (Jones, 1995). The existence of this expectation shows that the process of leaving home is surrounded by societal norms and values that influence the choices individuals make. People who do not meet these norms can be the subject of sanctions ranging from low public esteem or stigma to public policy sanctions such as the withholding of social security benefits. The norms involve the appropriate timing, process and reasons for leaving home and are related to general conceptions of the nature and form of family life.

The social expectations have changed over time, corresponding to the economic imperatives of the labour market. Jones (1995) notes that in the pre-industrial era it was common for young people to leave home at an early age to become a servant or apprentice and to live in the employer's household. This intermediate, dependent status continued until marriage and the creation of an independent household, which came later as adult status and economic independence was gained. Therefore, the transition from dependence in the parental household to independence in a new household could be protracted.

In the period following the Second World War, leaving home became synonymous with marriage and economic independence. This led to more condensed transitions between the parental home and an independent household. As Jones (1995) notes, especially during the 1950s and 1960s young people typically left home, married and started families within a short space of time. The average age of marriage declined during this period and the general availability of employment and relative affluence meant that financial independence was possible at an earlier age than previously. This period was the 'golden age' of the 'traditional family' and it has left a mark on some present discourses of family life and related norms of legitimate leaving-home processes.

As the need for skilled workers has grown, so the length of time at school has increased, and the proportion of young people who enter further and higher education has grown substantially. This has led to an extended period in which young people are financially dependent on the family and the state. The links between the different elements of transition have also become more complex. As we saw in Chapter Two, many young people leave home before getting married or establishing a household with a partner. More young people are leaving home for work or further education reasons or just to experience a period of independence between the parental home and the partnership home. As Beck (1992) points out, the ideal household form for the current stage of postmodern society is the single person because the requirements of the flexible labour market revolve around the ideal type of the detached, geographically mobile and temporally available worker. Therefore, young people who give emphasis to their career often have expectations of substantial geographical mobility that may influence their household choices.

These changes are leading to different definitions of adulthood. In the 1960s this was associated with marriage, which defined the transition from parental home to new household and from dependence to independence. In recent decades this link has been broken, but with no clear point at which adulthood is attained taking its place. This is partly because the links between the three transitions mentioned earlier have been loosened, with the school-to-work transition, the domestic transition to a new partner household, and the move to a new residence often occurring at different times, sometimes a long way apart. The period of transition between childhood and adulthood has become more complex, more ambiguous and longer. This intermediate period is what is often called 'youth'. Furlong and Cartmell (1997, p 41) define youth as follows: "Youth is ... a period of social semi-dependency which forms a bridge between the total dependence of childhood and the independence of adulthood".

As we shall see, this period of semi-dependency can be protracted, can be difficult for some young people to accomplish and is characterised by continual negotiations and renegotiations of duties and obligations between young persons and those on whom they are dependent, such as parents and the state.

Traditionally, independence has been associated with marriage and sometimes even the birth of children. However, as we saw in Chapter Two, the birth rate is declining and marriage is becoming less popular and occurring later. There is a growth in the number of young people living on their own or sharing with others. These changes are sometimes characterised as a challenge to 'traditional family values' and this has led to some public policies designed to discourage the trends.

It is generally considered (Coles, 1995; Jones, 1995; Furlong and Cartmel, 1997) that state policy over recent decades has made the transition to adulthood more difficult and protracted. For example, Income Support payments were withdrawn in 1988 from young people under 18, who instead were expected to take part in employment training schemes. Entitlement to Housing Benefit for those under the age of 26 was restricted in the private sector to the cost of a single room rather than a self-contained dwelling. The rationale for these changes was to remove what were seen by the government as financial incentives to encourage young people to move out of the parental home (Furlong and Cartmel, 1997). Underlying this move was a belief that the place for dependent young people was in the parental home and the primary responsibility for them rested with parents. Support for young people leaving home was seen by the government as undermining the 'traditional' family and constituted unwarranted state involvement in the responsibilities of families (see Chapter Two).

Jones (1995) argues that this view led to a conception of the varying legitimacy of the different reasons for leaving home and an idealised view of the process. Legitimate leaving home was held to be the product of choice rather than being forced on the younger person; was the result of discussion and agreement between the parents and the young person; and should occur only where it was economically viable. Leaving home processes that do not conform to this ideal are considered to be deviant and 'premature'. Public policy is structured to remove any incentive for 'premature' departures from the parental home. As we shall see, many young people leave home for reasons and in ways that are not perceived as legitimate, and as a consequence of a lack of parental and state support, find the process problematic.

Heath (1999) criticises the emphasis on the constraining impact of public policy on leaving home and points to factors that are leading some young people to choose to remain at home for longer. One is the increasing participation of women in the labour market, which enables parents to be better able to afford to support young people financially in the home. The increasing flexibility of the labour market for young people means that they may prefer the security of the parental home in the early stages of their employment pathway when jobs may be insecure. The increasing desire and need for further education to enhance employment prospects may have increased the likelihood of young people choosing to stay at home. The changing financial support for students may both have reduced the financial autonomy of students and encouraged them to study closer to home. Heath (1999) also points to changes in the parental home that may make staying at home more attractive for young people. One is the increasing space within many homes and increasing standards of comfort. Another may be changes in parental attitudes that may allow young people greater freedom and privacy than previous cohorts enjoyed.

Despite the policy emphasis and changing social attitudes towards delaying leaving home, there is some evidence that the median age of first leaving home for men is declining, while for women it is remaining stable but at an earlier age than men (Heath, 1999). However, the proportions of both young men and women who live in the parental home at any one time have increased over the last 20 years, reflecting the increasing likelihood of returning to the family home after having first left. Berrington and Murphy (1994) show that 53% of 22-year-old men were living with their parents in 1981 and this figure had risen to 59% in 1991. By the age of 30 most young people had left the parental home, but the proportion that remained increased from 10% of men in 1981 to 15% in 1991 and from 4% of women in 1981 to 6% in 1991. Heath (1999) shows that this pattern of longer residence in the parental home is common across European countries and in the US.

There are differences in the propensity of different groups of young people to leave the parental home. The children of middle class parents are more likely to leave home early, often in order to study, but are more likely to return later. In contrast, children of working class parents tend to leave later but not return. Stepchildren tend to leave home earlier than children who live with both their natural parents. The more siblings a child has, the earlier he or she is likely to leave home. There are also ethnic differences with black young men more likely to leave home early than Asian or white men. White young women are more likely to be living away from the parental home in their early to mid-twenties than their Asian or black peers (for a review of these trends, see Heath, 1999).

Of course, these are average trends and they hide substantial variations in individual circumstances. If there is one key point that emerges from this review it is the growing differentiation in leaving home processes reflecting the individualisation of postmodern society.

Of course, for young people to leave home they need to find somewhere else to live. The availability of appropriate housing is one of the factors that will influence the desire and ability to leave home. Public policy towards access to housing for young people will be influenced by the discourses of family and flexible employment. These discourses are also likely to influence the attitudes and behaviour of young people themselves.

The majority of young people view owner-occupation as their preferred tenure. Ford (1999) shows that in 1989 the overall percentage of people saying they would want to be living in owner-occupation was 83%, whereas for people aged 16-25 it was 95%. In 1996, the overall figure was 79%, but the figure for young people was 84%. Despite the drop in the figures between 1989 and 1996, young people were more likely than the population as a whole to see themselves in owner-occupation. The differences in attitudes over time are also matched by differences in the proportion of young people entering the sector. Ford (1999) concludes that young people have less positive attitudes to owner-occupation than a decade ago and are more cautious in their desire to enter the sector.

Part of the explanation for the caution is the experience of young people in the housing market in the 1990s. During some of this time there was a recession in the housing system, with falling house prices and growing problems of negative equity, mortgage arrears and repossessions (see Chapter Four). Young people suffered more than most from these problems. Because they were more likely to be recent entrants they were more likely to have bought at the peak of house prices at the height of the boom. Therefore, when the slump came they were more likely to move into negative equity. Also, being more recent buyers, their mortgage costs were a larger proportion of their income than for others, and so were hit harder by increases in interest rates imposed by the government to choke off the boom. The consequences were higher rates of mortgage arrears and repossessions than for the population as a whole. In the minds of many younger people this has increased their conception of the owner-occupied sector as being risky.

Other factors have increased the perception of risk among young people. The flexible labour market (see Chapter Three) with its expectations of job and geographical mobility has also influenced the perception of younger people. Demographic and cultural factors are also important. The decreasing incidence of marriage and the short duration of many cohabitation arrangements have led to more emphasis on flexibility. The growing number of single-person households means that house purchase has increasingly to be afforded on only one income rather than two, although younger people may pursue strategies such as sharing or taking in lodgers to deal with this. The changing finance of further and higher education is resulting in many students graduating with large outstanding loans that may hinder their entry to owner-occupation. Institutional policies such as the proportion of the purchase price covered by a mortgage and the income-repayment ratio have changed over time, reflecting different housing market conditions. Also, the propensity of developers to build houses for different segments of the market will influence the number of new, suitable properties that will be available to young people in places where they want to live, and at prices they can afford.

Less is known about the attitudes of young people towards the private rented sector, even though 60% of single people aged 16-25 are in this sector (Rugg and Burrows, 1999). Among the four roles of the private rented sector identified by Bovaird et al (1985) was short-term housing for the young and mobile, and housing of last resort for those unable to secure accommodation in other sectors. As Rugg (1999) argues, both of these uses are particularly associated with young people. Short-term housing may occur immediately on leaving home or at other times of household change such as the end of a relationship. It may occur because of geographical mobility or because of a need to save for entry to owner-occupation. However, some young people are choosing to stay longer in private renting. Some young people enjoy sharing as a way both of saving on housing expenses and of enjoying a communal lifestyle. Kenyon and Heath's (2001) sample of young people sharing were keen to point out that their housing conditions were good and to distinguish their position from student housing, which they saw as being in much worse condition.

Ford et al (2002) argue that the attitudes of young people towards the private rented sector depend on whether it is a chosen stepping stone to owner-occupation or housing of last (or only) resort. The residual part of the private rented sector is associated in particular with young single people on low incomes who are excluded from the two main tenures of owner-occupation and public renting. Of course, low income may exclude someone from owner-occupation because of difficulty in obtaining mortgage finance. As we shall see later, young single people may also be excluded from public sector rented housing because of the allocation policies and procedures, or may be excluded from the sector because of a history of rent arrears.

Poorer tenants in private rented housing are supported by the payment of Housing Benefit (see Chapter Four). Changes to limit what were perceived as financial incentives for young people to leave home, by restricting the availability of Housing Benefit for those under 26 to what became known as the 'single room rent', have reduced young people's access to the tenure (Rugg, 1999). The assumption was that young people would share accommodation and would not be supported to live in single-person households in self-contained accommodation.

Access to private renting is generally regarded as providing few obstacles than other tenures, but this could be a misleading picture. On entering a rented dwelling tenants are generally expected to pay a month's rent in advance as well as a returnable deposit. This can be a considerable sum of money for some households, and schemes have been established by public and voluntary agencies to provide bonds or guarantees to aid access.

Anderson (1999) shows that young people, and young single people in particular, have to surmount substantial barriers to enter the public rented sector. For example, many local authorities do not offer tenancies to people below the age of 18 and many needs-based systems fail to reflect the housing situation of young people by, for example, not giving points for residence in a hostel. Young people are handicapped by the scarcity of smaller public sector houses and the propensity of many landlords to reserve those which are available for older people. There has been a traditional bias towards families in allocation policies and discrimination against single people, as policies have been influenced by the discourse of the traditional family (see Chapter Two). Until recently this has also been reflected in statutory homelessness policies (Evans, 1999).

Young people are also often thought to be 'problem tenants' and landlords report that young people often experienced tenancy 'failures' because of rent arrears, 'anti-social' behaviour, or not being able to manage on their own (Anderson, 1999). Some landlords have reacted to this by arranging for support to be provided or letting furnished tenancies.

In summary, young people leaving home have to overcome substantial barriers to entry to all of the housing tenures. These are partly created by public policy, but are also influenced by the flexible labour market and associated perceptions of risk. Young people vary in their ability and the resources at their disposal to overcome these obstacles. The process of entry to one of the tenures consists of a complex series of interactions between the young people and other actors such as private landlords, estate agents and building society staff or local authority allocations officers (see Clapham and Kintrea, 1986) in which the outcome will be dependent on both structural factors and individual agency.

The leaving home process

Leaving home has often been seen as one part of a transition from young person to adult. The drawback of the idea of 'transition' is that it tends to imply a movement from one fixed state to another. In practice leaving home is a gradual process that can begin in early childhood when parts of the house may be claimed by children and attempts made by them to exert control over actions within the space. The process of leaving home may continue for an extended period after residence in a new household. It is difficult to define when someone has 'left home' even when someone has left the parental home to take residence for at least some of the time in another dwelling. People may consider their new dwelling to be a temporary expedient or may live in two houses by continuing to spend time in the family home. Residence away may be punctuated by spells back in the parental home. As we saw in Chapter Two, family ties can be strong and contacts within families extensive. The parental home may still be considered to be 'home' or at least to encapsulate some aspects of home for extended periods.

Also, the destination on leaving the parental home may vary considerably and may involve shared living or living alone. Although most young people do intend eventually to form a couple household, many can spend considerable time in other household forms before reaching this point. To treat these household forms as merely transitional underplays their growing importance.

The parental home is the place where most young people learn the skills and knowledge needed for adult life in an independent household. This may involve specific skills such as meal preparation or household budgeting as well as more general issues about the conduct of household life. Of course, young people may vary considerably in the extent to which they are exposed to role models in these areas or absorb the lessons from their experiences. Some young people, such as those living in institutional care, may not be exposed to these experiences and may be at a real disadvantage when having to cope on their own unless formal means of imparting these independent living skills are available. Also, the preparedness of young people is likely to depend on the age they leave home. Therefore, all other things being equal, it is likely that someone leaving home at 14 is less likely to have the appropriate skills than one leaving home at 18.

The process of acquiring the necessary skills for independent living often does not stop when the young person moves out of the parental home. Parents can provide substantial support, whether emotional or practical. This may involve providing advice on household tasks or financial support. As we shall see, the family home provides a source of security and a sense of belonging to some people long after they have ceased to live there. Where such support is not available from parents it may be provided through the state or voluntary organisations. It may take the form of hostels or other forms of supported living arrangements such as foyers or floating support schemes that provide help in 'ordinary' housing. The help may take the form of assistance with daily living skills; access to appropriate employment and training; help with social skills; or practical help through the provision of furniture or the guarantee of a deposit for private rented housing. The aim of this provision is usually to aid the transition to independent living.

Young people will also be exposed to their parents' views about appropriate housing situations. Along with their own experiences in the family accommodation and messages absorbed from the mass media, they are likely to influence the development of their own views or preferences of appropriate housing. Rowlands and Gurney (2001) show how young people have developed clear views of the type of housing they desired by the age of 16 through what they call a housing socialisation process. These views tended to follow societal norms of desired tenure and house types. Thus, young people wanted to be owner-occupiers and to live in houses rather than flats. Housing was seen as being part of a lifestyle 'package' that was associated with high social status. This package consisted of a 'good' job, family, car and an owner-occupied house. Council housing was associated with social failure and low status. Rowlands and Gurney (2001) note that the aspirations of young people were not matched with a detailed knowledge of the options likely to be open to them or their ability to access them. They conclude by arguing for more education on housing options for young people.

As argued earlier, the process of leaving home can be traced back to childhood life in the parental home. Chapter Five showed that many young people negotiate their own space within the home, usually their own bedroom, and attempt to enforce their own control over this space and to express their own identity through decoration and the display of possessions. This process of negotiation generally continues throughout the time the young person spends in the parental home. Jones (1995) notes that many young people are ambivalent about whether they stay at home, as are their parents. Being at home may provide the young person with 'home comforts' and a friendly and caring environment. At the same time, it may result in less autonomy and control over their lives and a more dependent status, resulting in a delay in achieving the adult status of independence in their own and others' eyes. Parents may desire to keep the young people dependent on them in the home in order not to 'lose' them. Perhaps at the same time, parents may desire to live a 'quieter life' and to be able to enjoy more space and time for their own desired activities. However, Jones (1995) warns against any simple generalisation because the issues involved are complex and interlinked, involving trade-offs by both parents and young people between competing and sometimes contradictory feelings, and practical costs and benefits.

In general, Jones (1995) argues that parents employ strategies of control and their children employ counter-strategies of resistance until the growing emancipation of the young person results in renegotiation and a more equal and reciprocal arrangement can be made. A key element in this can be the payment of 'dig money' or payment by young people towards their keep. This can represent a justification for staying in the parental home and a way of retaining a degree of independence and status within the household. Young people may feel it gives them a 'right' to enjoy the facilities of the home and the services of their parents while giving them a negotiating counter. However, many young people, especially those who are unemployed, have few financial resources and so find it difficult to be able to contribute to the household in this way. An alternative contribution is help with housework, which is more commonly expected of girls than boys. Smith et al (1998) found that parents' willingness to provide a home to young people was conditional on their observing an informal contract specifying reasonable behaviour.

All this suggests an ordered and civilised process of discussion and negotiation between young people and their parents; and this is what takes place in many cases. However, it must be remembered that some family relations are characterised by conflict and sometimes even violence. In these circumstances remaining at home may be difficult and painful for the young person and the process of leaving home may be a fraught and challenging process. Hutson and Jenkins (1989) carried out a study in south Wales of unemployed young people living at home. They found family conflict to be widespread and the presence of an unemployed young person could result in difficulties for the rest of the household in terms of lack of privacy and overcrowding, affecting younger children. Where young people had found employment, this resulted in greater income for the household and avoided conflict, especially with the employed person being out of the house and away from other family members for substantial parts of the day.

'Families' take many shapes and forms, as was noted in Chapter Two, and so the negotiation process may take on different forms and result in different outcomes. Of course, not every young person lives in a 'family'. For example, some young people live in institutions such as children's homes. As we shall see later, there has been a particular problem in leaving home for this group of young people and as a result they are more likely to experience homelessness.

The reasons for leaving home can be divided into 'pull' and 'push' factors. The 'pull' factors are the positive and socially sanctioned reasons that include setting up home with a partner; taking up a job; or taking up training or education. An increasingly common reason is the desire for independence and the opportunity to pursue a desired lifestyle without the constraints of parents and before the experience of 'settling down' with a partner and raising children. "... independent living – either alone or with unrelated others – is seen by young adults to provide the requisite freedom from parental supervision and the space in which to develop intimate relationships on one's own terms, yet without the responsibilities and potential conflict which often attend cohabitation or marriage" (Heath, 1999, p 555).

This is socially sanctioned as long as the young person is financially independent. The 'push' factors are the non-socially sanctioned reasons, such as family conflict or overcrowded or inadequate housing in the parental home. The relative importance or severity of these factors will vary considerably between different young people. Also, more than one may be involved. For example, getting a job may give a young person the opportunity to escape family conflict. In general, the more important the 'push' factors, the more likely the early housing pathway is to be problematic and the young person to experience homelessness. Also, the more important the 'push' factors, the more likely a young person is to leave home 'prematurely' at an early age and so to lack appropriate skills.

The reasons for leaving home also influence the speed with which leaving home occurs. Young people leaving home because of marriage or entering further or higher education will have a period of time in which preparations, both practical and emotional, can be made. Therefore, leaving home can be seen as a planned process. In contrast, someone leaving home after a family conflict may have a very short time for preparation. This is shown by one young person interviewed in a study of young homeless people in Glasgow quoted in Bannister et al (1993, p 15):

> When I left, I left in a bit of a rush. I didn't have time to plan anything. I did have it in the back of my head to leave, but the situation at that time was such that I just had to go. Because everything happened so fast I didn't even have time to pack anything. I just grabbed a jacket and a couple of shirts, put them in a bag, and I was off.

It is perhaps not a surprise that this young person subsequently experienced homelessness.

In most cases, even where the initial leaving of the parental home is sudden, the whole process may be protracted. A young person may return to the parental home at weekends or during vacations or may not be able or willing to sustain independent living for a period. Jones (1995) notes that a return to the parental home can be difficult to arrange by the young person because it can involve an admission of dependence and a fear of rejection by the parents, which can undermine the young person's self-esteem. To save face, a young person may use an intermediary such as a family member to engineer an invitation from the parents and to negotiate a return. Of course, it must be remembered that not every young person will have the option to return. For example, they may have been in care, or relationships may have deteriorated to the point that a return is unthinkable by one or both parties.

The initial destination of a young person leaving home may be 'intermediate' accommodation such as a student hall of residence, lodgings, barracks, or other accommodation associated with employment or education. The young person may consider these forms of accommodation to be temporary and not develop a strong attachment to them. Kenyon (1999) argues that there are three homes in a student's life. The first is the parental home, which students still identify with in giving them a sense of belonging, a source of memories and a link with their family. However, they do not envisage spending much time there either at present or in the future, and associate it with a lack of independence and personal autonomy. The second home is the term-time home. This is regarded as being transitional and uncertain. There is no sense of belonging in the neighbourhood, where they consider themselves outsiders and feel they are treated as such by others. This home lacks personal autonomy and independence because of the need to share with others for financial reasons, although this is offset by the ability to surround themselves with personal possessions. The accommodation is considered to be of a basic standard, uncomfortable, cold and unsafe. However, it is thought to offer a good social atmosphere and is associated with friends. The third home is the imagined future permanent home. This is associated with stability and comfort and their own family. All three homes are important to students in a particular way and each is considered to have its advantages and disadvantages. This example shows the difficulty of deciding whether someone has 'left home'.

Heath (1999) shows that shared living, which often has its origins in the student experience, is becoming increasingly popular for young people. Approximately 15% of non-students in their early to mid-twenties were living in shared households in 1991 (Heath and Miret, 1996). Some of this can be explained by a lack of financial resources, which makes sharing necessary to gain access to housing. However, Kenyon and Heath (2001) argue that young professional people are increasingly choosing to share even though they can afford not to. In 1991, 48% of sharers aged 20-29 were in social classes I and II. Kenyon and Heath (2001) point to the strong career orientation of many young sharers and their expectation of geographical mobility in pursuit of their future career goals. Many are in couple relationships, but this does not extend to living together, either through choice or because of geographical constraints often related to the desire to pursue two careers. In their study of sharers, Kenyon and Heath (2001) found that many were happy with their accommodation, which they considered to be of a good standard and much better than in their student days. The presence of other household members was both the greatest weakness and the greatest strength of this form of living. It can provide a ready-made social life for busy, career-oriented people and these networks can "represent surrogate families for those involved, complete with strong emotional, social and economic attachments more usually associated with 'blood' ties" (Heath, 1999, p 557). At the same time, shared living can place added stresses on distance couple relationships through the need to negotiate the place of the non-resident partner within the household.

Giddens (1991) argues that relationships are increasingly 'pure' relationships that exist solely for the rewards which the relationship can offer rather than being regulated by traditional social norms. Heath (1999) argues that young people currently place high value on emotional intimacy, mutual affection and sexual fulfilment within their sexual relationships, but that these qualities are increasingly seen as not necessarily being dependent on living in a couple household. In a culture that increasingly places emphasis on personal autonomy and self-development, an independent living arrangement is an attractive base from which to participate in relationships, offering 'intimacy at a distance' (Heath, 1999). Therefore, shared living arrangements are not necessarily 'transitional' household forms between the parental home and a traditional family of destination. Rather, they may be a desired form of household structure that may be sustained for a considerable proportion of a person's housing pathway.

The move into independent accommodation may be more difficult for some young people than others. Speak (1999) shows that young single mothers find it particularly difficult. She found that many of them were already having problems within the parental home before their pregnancy, which they tried to ease by 'staying out of the way'. The reaction of parents to the pregnancy, which was usually unplanned, sometimes caused added strains, and a young baby made life in the parental home more difficult to negotiate because it was not possible to 'hide'. Some young mothers had already made plans or taken steps towards independent living, but their pregnancy made independence more urgent while also making it more difficult in many ways. The most obvious difficulty was a lack of income with many young mothers dependent on welfare benefits because of their limited work experience, young age and the need to care for children. They also had to cope with the responsibility of balancing a household budget with the added costs of bringing up a child. Not surprisingly, many young mothers need support from their family and this can constrain the suitable housing options available. With limited mobility because of low income, it may be necessary to live close to parents.

Having a young child also changes the social expectations of home life. Whereas many young people experience a number of 'transitional' or temporary housing situations before creating a family home, there is substantial pressure on young mothers to create this environment immediately because of the perceived need to give the child a permanent and stable home. As Speak (1999, p 130) observes, "she [a young single mother] needs more permanent accommodation in which to develop a secure long-term home, and from which she and her child will put down roots and establish themselves as a household within a community".

Speak argues that the material comforts needed to turn a house into a home suitable for a baby or young child are greater than those needed for a single person, and certain standards need to be met quickly. The examples she gives are a refrigerator for food hygiene, carpets for the comfort of a crawling child and a washing machine for the large amount of washing and drying needed. Despite this, she argues that many young mothers live extremely impoverished lives and have to go without even the basics of furnishings and comforts for many years. Support is often needed in creating this home environment; some housing agencies have reacted by the provision of furnished tenancies and some voluntary organisations have established projects to help provide furniture and other items.

With high expectations and a lack of experience and resources, it is not surprising that some young mothers find it difficult to maintain independent living. They have to juggle many different areas of their lives with little room for failure. They do not have the scope to experiment and make mistakes without long-term repercussions, which young people generally enjoy in their pathway to independence.

Ford et al (2002) used the concept of a housing pathway to explore the different experiences of young people. They identified pathways on the basis of three criteria. The first was the ability of young people to plan for and control their leaving home process. An important element of this was whether leaving home was intentional, unexpected or forced. The second criterion was the extent of constraints on the young person, such as income and the state of the local housing market. The third was the degree of family support available. Based around these three dimensions, each of which was seen as a continuum, Ford et al (2002) identified five different pathways. The first was termed a 'chaotic pathway' and consisted of a lack of planning, substantial constraints and an absence of family support. Young people on this pathway were likely to move frequently and to experience episodes of homelessness. The second was termed an 'unplanned pathway', which differed from the previous category largely in the presence of family support that enabled the young people to overcome to some extent the constraints and to work towards a desirable housing destination. The third pathway was termed 'constrained'. Here young people voluntarily left home and received substantial family support, but the constraints they experienced in terms of income and difficulty of access to owner-occupation and public renting meant that their housing situation could be marginal and insecure. The fourth was a 'planned (non student)' pathway where planning was associated with few constraints and family support. Here young people either spent some time in private renting as a prelude to owner-occupation or moved directly into ownership. The final pathway was the 'student' pathway where constraints were managed through the provision of support from educational institutions and family. Ford et al (2002) argue that there are cultural expectations of shared or communal living and an identifiable lifestyle that includes serial returns to the family home. The pathway almost always leads to owner-occupation.

The incidence of different pathways varied according to the constraints in particular localities. Also, young people could move from one pathway to another, but moves were usually to an adjacent and similar pathway rather than reflecting substantial changes in circumstances. The Ford et al (2002) study is an important step forward in taking a dynamic and differentiated view of the housing pathways of young people, and should be used as a stepping stone for further development through the widening of the factors considered and the timescale used.

In summary, this section has focused on the process of leaving home. It has shown that it is a complex process with many different facets. It is difficult to decide when it begins and ends. The reasons for leaving home vary considerably and the process can be short or long, peaceful or conflictual. It results in very different destinations for young people, some of which may be considered transitional and others more permanent. The ability of young people to successfully undertake the process varies considerably because of their different situations, resources and abilities. They are engaged in a process of negotiation with parents or gatekeepers of housing in which their ability to achieve their objectives will vary. Some will encounter severe problems and in a few cases they will experience homelessness. It is to this that we now turn.

Young people and homelessness

It was argued earlier that some younger people find the transition to independent living difficult and may have problems sustaining it even when it is achieved. Homelessness among young people has been viewed as a major problem in recent years. The reasons for the incidence of homelessness are complex and illustrate the importance of taking a holistic view of the circumstances of young people.

Homelessness is a contested concept that can mean many things. At its narrowest it can mean being 'roofless', that is, not having a physical shelter, but at its broadest it can mean lacking all the elements of what is considered to make up a home. Discourses surrounding homelessness also vary and include implicit assumptions about the causes of homelessness and appropriate ways for public policy to deal with it. Jacobs et al (1999) differentiate between a minimalist and a maximalist conception. They argue that the minimalist conception was dominant in Britain before the 1977 Homeless Persons Act, and constructed homelessness as being rooted in individual pathologies. Homelessness was held to be a private trouble that was primarily the responsibility of individuals and their families to deal with. The role of the state was to provide support and correction through social work intervention with individuals and families.

The 1977 legislation encapsulated a maximalist construction with the underlying assumption that there are systemic influences, such as the shortage of accessible housing, that result in homelessness. Therefore, it is constructed as the result of defects in public policy that it is the duty of the state to put right. In the passing of the 1977 legislation, these competing constructions of homelessness were put forward and, although the maximalist definition could be said to be dominant in the legislation, supporters of a minimalist approach succeeded in attaching conditions that restricted the scope of the legislation and ensured that some elements of the minimalist approach were retained. The key conditions related to the concepts of vulnerability, intentionality and local connection, which were designed to ensure that there were procedures to exclude the 'undeserving' from help and to perpetuate concepts of individual pathology in homelessness policy and discourse.

Evans (1999) shows that these concepts have achieved exactly that. She argues that the statutory homeless procedures are complicated and cumbersome, with only 20% of applicants being housed through this route. Many homeless people view the process as alienating and hostile. Evans (1999) found there was no difference between the housing need of those accepted and those excluded. The difference was whether they were considered to be deserving or undeserving. In general, the deserving group consisted of women with dependent children, mostly in single-parent families. Their status as deserving was challenged in legislation in 1996 that sought to restrict their rights to housing. The undeserving group has largely been young single people who are constructed as work-shy and as leaving home unnecessarily. As we shall see later, this has influenced the way that government intervention towards this group has been framed, with an emphasis on control as much as support.

The likelihood of young people experiencing homelessness is influenced by factors in their family lives and leaving-home experience.

In general those leaving home at a young age, with little preparation, for negative 'push' rather than 'pull' reasons, and with little support from family and friends, are more likely to experience periods of homelessness in their housing pathways. In her sample of young homeless people in Glasgow, Fitzpatrick (1999) found some very difficult family circumstances including the violent behaviour of parents towards their children or each other, as well as challenging behaviour from the children themselves, such as inability or unwillingness to find work, drug or alcohol misuse, and criminal behaviour. This pattern of behaviour often started early in life and was linked to difficulties at school, including truanting. It was turned into homelessness by the inability to access or to sustain independent living.

Family breakdown plays a key role in the homelessness of the young people interviewed by Fitzpatrick. At first glance, this may lend weight to the minimalist conception of homelessness, but the key issue is why this breakdown occurred. Maximalist conceptions point to the other social and economic forces and government policies that frame this family breakdown.

> Examples are policies of education which leave some schoolchildren with an alienated experience which leads to poor motivation and achievement and to uncontrolled truancy; social security policies which do not provide for some younger people and create stresses within the family; as well as housing policies which make it difficult for young people to afford or to access good quality housing; as well as economic policies which do not provide opportunities for work to large numbers of young people. To these can be added de-institutionalisation and community care policies which result in some people living without appropriate shelter and support. (Clapham, 1999, p 229)

A common thread in the biographies of young homeless people is the material poverty of their families and their communities. In Fitzpatrick's (1999) research, many families were put under strain by the difficulty of supporting a young person who brought no income into a household that was dependent on state benefits. This created not only material hardship but also emotional tensions and difficulties in the maintenance of a sense of identity and self-worth for the young person.

The experience of homelessness can vary substantially. For some young people it may involve sleeping rough for a short period of time interspersed with periods in a hostel, staying with friends, or living at home. Fitzpatrick (1999) shows that some homeless young people stay in the area in which they were brought up because they feel safe there or they want to remain close to family and friends who may offer some support. This group of people may often not come to the attention of statutory or voluntary services. For others, living on the streets may become a more long-term situation and may be tied in with a particular way of life. This group may have left their home area and gravitated to the centre of major cities where they meet others sleeping rough. In this situation they are likely to become noticed by homelessness agencies and to be given access to the various forms of services available.

There are a number of key aspects of homelessness that need to be borne in mind in any analysis of the phenomenon. The first is the variation in circumstances and experience between young people. It is difficult to generalise in this situation, and the analytical framework must be able to cope with this. Second, the causes of homelessness are complex and varied. They usually include both personal and family factors as well as wider issues of social structure and public policy. The form of public policy is shaped by discourses of youth that contain explanations for homelessness and values to underpin public policy intervention. Third, time is an important variable. The shelter situation of some young people can change quickly and frequently. Any framework for the analysis of homelessness needs to be able to cope with the flows of people in and out of homelessness situations. Fourth, homeless people interpret their own situation and perceive interventions aimed at helping them in different ways. This can lead them to choose to live in what may be thought to be 'objectively' worse housing circumstances, such as sleeping rough, rather than accept certain forms of help, such as hostel provision, because of their own interpretation of 'home'.

Homelessness pathways

The concept of a homelessness pathway has been used by Fitzpatrick (1999) in her study of homeless young people in Glasgow. She criticised the static nature of much research on homelessness and sought to shed light on the dynamic nature of the experience of homelessness of many people. She also sought to provide a holistic framework by placing the housing pathways of young people in relation to other pathways such as the transition from education to employment. Another focus was the relationships between family members and the young person that could influence the process of leaving home and the help received when he or she attempted to live independently. The research technique used was the biographical interview, in which subjects were asked to recount their biography. This was coupled with an (only partially successful) attempt to trace the subjects a year later and to undertake follow-up interviews to shed light on the changes in their position over time. From this research, Fitzpatrick was able to criticise the prevailing view of a downward spiral of homelessness and to identify six particular types of homelessness pathway. These varied according to geographical location (whether in the city centre or in the local area studied), degree of entry to 'official' homelessness agency facilities (such as hostels), and the stability of the young person's housing situation.

Another use of a pathways framework was undertaken by Anderson and Tulloch (2000). They defined a homelessness pathway as a description of "the route of an individual or household into homelessness, their experience of homelessness and their route out of homelessness into secure housing" (Anderson and Tulloch, 2000, p 11). From their review of the research evidence, Anderson and Tulloch identified 23 general pathways, differentiated according to the stage in the life course. Five were associated with young people, 11 with adults and seven with people in later life. The descriptions of these generalised pathways included the trigger factors and the experience of homelessness in terms of the physical location of the individual (for example, a hostel or sleeping rough). Some pathways included a route out of homelessness, but many did not. A limited account was taken of the interaction between homeless people and the policy mechanisms they encountered. Examples include outcomes from dealings with the mechanisms of statutory homelessness procedures, and barriers to accessing housing because of a record of rent arrears.

Both research studies are valuable starting points in using the pathways framework. The strengths of Fitzpatrick's work are the focus on the voices and perceptions of the young people themselves as they constructed their own situation, and the dynamic and holistic nature of the framework used. Both studies use the concept of a pathway in homelessness research to overcome drawbacks of other approaches. For example, they emphasise the dynamic nature of homelessness, showing that homeless people move in and out of homelessness, in some cases a number of times. The diversity of the experiences of homelessness has also been stressed.

However, the research could have been developed further to make the most of the pathways framework. The pathways approach was relatively untheorised and not related to a wider literature. This meant that the large amount of information collected in each case is described rather than analysed. In particular, Fitzpatrick describes the individual biographies and identifies the wider structural factors involved, but does not relate the two. The analysis follows the usual method of describing structural factors as constraints and treating them independently from the biographical factors. Therefore, little light is shed on the interactions between agency and structure. When confronted with the individual biographies and the pathways identified, the focus is on the behaviour of the individual and not on the structural factors that may have influenced this. Although it is clearly not the intention of the authors, the effect is to reinforce the minimalist conception of homelessness.

Homelessness can be seen as an episode or episodes in a person's housing pathway. The pathways framework can shed light on the factors that lead to homelessness, influence the nature of the experience, and enable some people to move out of it. The output of research using the pathways framework has been in the form of biographies that have been used to construct ideal-type pathways. This useful start needs to be supplemented in two major directions to draw most benefit from the framework. These are the incorporation of structural elements into the biography and the analysis of public policy interventions. Each of these will now be considered in turn.

The construction of personal biographies of homeless people that document their experiences in housing and related areas of their lives is a valuable and illuminating tool. At its best it can provide insight into the 'perceptive world' of individuals which influences the construction of their identities and their behaviour. What has been lacking so far is an analysis of the relationship between these perceptive worlds and the discourses that influence and shape them. Homeless people do not construct their lives in a vacuum, but are influenced by the way they are treated by their families and others they come into contact with, as well as their projection in the media and their treatment by professionals and public services they interact with. Of course, homeless people themselves reinforce or challenge these discourses through their individual words and actions as well as collectively through organisations lobbying on their behalf.

A number of related discourses may be relevant here. For example, the discourse of 'the family' will frame expected norms of behaviour between young people and their parents. Where these are breached there may be conflict, which may lead to homelessness. It is important to stress that in this, as in other areas, there may be a number of discourses vying for influence. These may be generally held or may be associated with particular social groups. For example, there may be a different discourse of family held by different generations that may frame conflict between parents and their children. These discourses are associated with categorical identities. Examples are 'parent', 'teenager', or 'drug abuser'. There may be conflicts over the boundaries of these categories such as what constitutes drug abuse in general and in any individual case. Parents may categorise their children as drug abusers, but the children may dispute this categorisation if they feel they are taking recreational drugs in a way sanctioned by their peer group. Discourses may be constructed that differ in, for example, the expected rules of behaviour for a member of a category, the appropriate response of non-members towards members and the status members should receive. The taking of recreational drugs may confer high status within the 'teenager' discourse held by some young people, but confer low status within the discourse held by parents.

The importance of these discourses in interpreting biographical data is vital to understanding the nature of homelessness. A dispute between parents and their children may seem like an individual phenomenon when seen as part of the individual biography, but may be mirroring similar general conflicts between discourses. In this case, the explanation of homelessness cannot be seen as only a result of individual pathology but also as indicative of wider conflicts in society. This has implications for the acceptance of the 'minimalist' or 'maximalist' discourses of homelessness, and the different explanations of causality and related policy discourses and mechanisms that frame the policy responses to homelessness.

The consequence for research on homelessness is that the identification and elucidation of appropriate discourses is a vital part of the research task. It is then necessary to relate them to the 'perceptive world' of key actors in a personal biography in order to relate the personal and the structural.

The second area in which recent pathways research can be developed is in the treatment of public policy. King (1996) argues that public policy can be seen at two levels. The first level is that of action whereby policy can influence behaviour by creating (or changing or destroying) mechanisms that allow (or prevent) households from acting in particular ways. The second level is that of discourse. Policy mechanisms are usually framed by, and sometimes are meant to influence, discourses. For example, employment and training policy towards young people is associated with a discourse that includes a view of the appropriate role of young people, their behaviour and their obligations. At present it is assumed that all young people over 16 should be in work or in full-time education and that any help given to them is conditional on certain norms of behaviour such as attending training every day, not being under the influence of drink or drugs or behaving in a 'proper' manner towards trainers and other trainees. Usually, policy interventions have more or less explicit assumptions about the causes and nature of the problems they are meant to deal with. These assumptions may derive from professional or political definitions of 'the problem' and may serve to challenge or reinforce dominant discourses. Policy interventions will differ in the mix of discourse and action elements. For example, some will be primarily aimed at the level of discourse by providing mechanisms that are mainly symbolic in their reinforcement of particular discourses rather than being meant to be directly used through action.

Many homeless people in the pathways identified by Fitzpatrick (1999) came into contact with public or voluntary agencies designed to 'deal with' them. Agencies differed in their definitions of 'the problem' and the appropriate way to deal with it. For example, some, such as the police, had explicitly emphasised social control, with appropriate behaviour being defined through the legal system. Others were more focused on homeless people themselves and attempted to help them in the way that homeless people themselves thought appropriate by adopting their definition of the 'problem'.

Homeless people may be offered different kinds of services, including accommodation and support. Each package has a particular discourse associated with it that may influence the way that homeless people react to it. Fitzpatrick (1999) probed the meaning that homeless people associated with the idea of 'home'. For many, traditional forms of accommodation for homeless people, such as hostels or shared living arrangements, did not come within the bounds of their definition. Hutson (1999) argues that many forms of accommodation and support for homeless people are based on professional definitions of 'need' that conform with the interests of the professionals in claiming special expertise rather than with the 'needs' as defined by the homeless people themselves. Some homeless people viewed hostels as frightening and hostile places where they felt threatened. Fitzpatrick (1999) identifies many people who would not avail themselves of services in the centre of the city because they felt unsafe venturing outside what they defined as their own area. An interesting phenomenon is emerging in Britain whereby some homeless people are choosing to sleep rough on the streets rather than accept the accommodation and support that is available. For them the streets provide more elements of 'home' than the hostel accommodation they are offered.

The key point is that discourses influence the shape of the interventions designed to 'deal with' the problem of homelessness and that consuming the services can mean accepting the implicit discourse. In consequence, homeless people may judge the services on the basis of the meaning it has for them and their willingness to ascribe to or accept the discourse. Therefore, a key element of research on homelessness should be the elucidation of these discourses and the reaction to them by homeless people.

Homeless people will be confronted with the discourse as they interact with service providers and professionals in seeking to consume the services. These interactions are important in restructuring or destructuring social practices (see Chapter One) and have a structural element based on the dominant discourse that frames the 'rules of the game' within which interaction takes place. They also have an agency element in the way that specific interactions may have the potential to reinforce or challenge these norms. If a large number of interactions destructure in a particular way, this may lead to change in the 'rules of the game'. The outcome of the interaction may well hinge on the power that the parties can bring to bear. Here power is seen as existing and being manifest in the relationships between different actors (Clegg, 1989) and consists of the resources available to the parties and their ability to utilise them effectively. In the situation of a service provider and a homeless person, it is likely that the homeless person will have little potential to destructure where there is an urgent need for access. The ability to walk away from the interaction is probably the only resource the homeless person has. This may be effective where an agency has to meet utilisation targets in order to justify public funding. Destructuring can also be pursued through collective endeavour by pressure groups working on behalf of homeless people to challenge the dominant discourse through media and political channels. This can reinforce the actions of individual homeless people in their interactions with service providers and give them information to facilitate destructuring.

The nature of the services provided to homeless people is determined by the interaction between staff and prospective users. Staff are given a framework for this interaction through the policy and procedures of their organisation, which will be based on and be part of the discourse that underpins the provision and provides its justification and rationale. The interaction with prospective and actual users is where this discourse is put into practice and may confront the discourse of homeless people, which may be different. A process of negotiation may then take place that will determine access to the services, but may also have the effect of restructuring or destructuring (that is, changing) either discourse. The face-to-face interaction between provider and user is where important structural processes are played out and possibly changed. Therefore, a key element of research on homelessness should be the analysis of these interactions. This calls for a research method that can capture this through, for example, participant observation when the interactions are taking place.

Much research on homelessness has followed and reinforced the traditional dichotomy in the social sciences between structural and personal approaches. This has been mirrored by political discourses of minimalist or maximalist definitions of homelessness and its causes. This section outlines an approach to research based on the concept of a housing pathway that enables structural and personal factors to be considered together. The concept of a homelessness pathway has been used in previous research, but the chapter has sought to show that this has been under-conceptualised and has failed to bridge the structure-agency divide. Nevertheless, existing research has shown some of the strengths of the approach through its dynamic and holistic nature and its foregrounding of the voices of homeless people themselves. A clearer specification of the theoretical underpinning of the pathways approach enables existing work to be extended, largely by linking the agency and structural dimensions through analysis of discourses and their use in the interaction between service providers and homeless people. It also gives a way of evaluating public policy interventions in terms of both their action and discourse elements.

Conclusion

This chapter has focused on the early stages of a housing pathway, describing the discourses that have structured public policy and the perceptions and actions of young people and their families. The process of leaving home was considered and viewed as a process of negotiation within the family and between the young person and gatekeepers to housing. With this background the chapter finished with an examination of homelessness among young people, describing the discourses that have framed public policy. However, the main focus has been on using homelessness as an example of the operationalisation of the pathways approach. The chapter has critically reviewed existing research using the pathways framework and shown how it can be used as the basis for a holistic and dynamic research framework. There has been a considerable amount of research on homelessness in Britain, but much of it has been partial in the sense that it has concentrated either on structural factors or on giving emphasis to the voices of homeless people. Further research is needed that pursues a more holistic approach and attempts to bring together these elements. The pathways framework offers such an approach.

EIGHT

Housing pathways in later life

This chapter further examines the pathways approach by concentrating on the later stages of a housing pathway. The chapter adds to analysis of pathways by focusing on the policy discourses that structure the opportunities open to older people in meeting their housing, support and care needs. The central argument of the chapter is that the policy discourse of community care, which has been dominant since at least the 1960s, is ill-suited to the needs, demands and aspirations of many older people today. The discourse has been negative in tone in that it has been overly-concerned with the cost and location of care and support. This emphasis stems from the importance attached to the move away from institutional care and is coupled with a corresponding lack of emphasis on the nature of the care and support provided outside an institution and the power relations that surround it. The theme of the chapter is that the social and economic changes often given the name of postmodernity, and outlined earlier in the book, have changed the context within which older people make housing, support and care choices, and have challenged the relevance of the dominant policy discourse. In particular, following the argument articulated in Chapter One, it is argued that these social changes have resulted in an increased ability of people to 'make their own lives' by choosing their own identity and lifestyle. As a result, the general attitude to housing is changing, with people increasingly seeing it as a means to an end rather than an end in itself. An alternative discourse is described, which builds on the community care discourse while placing more emphasis on the quality of public policy provision through individual choice and empowerment.

The chapter adds to the analysis of housing pathways by showing the importance of discourses in shaping public policy and, therefore, the forms of provision open to households. But discourses are open to change, and it is argued here that the present discourse does not fit well with the social trends of postmodernity emphasised here and is consequently open to challenge. Application of the pathways approach shows the impact that policy discourses can have on household opportunities through its focus on the meaning of housing and household attitudes and perceptions. This orientation can also lead to a way of thinking about policy that is focused less on specific policy outcomes, such as particular housing destinations, and more on the ability of households to achieve self-fulfilment and a desired identity and lifestyle through choice.

The chapter begins with a description of the discourse of 'community care' that has structured public policy and, therefore, the housing, support and care options open to older people. This 'official' discourse is argued to be one that encapsulates a negative image of old age, focusing on problems associated with a failing body. It is argued that policy has been dominated by the perceived need to restrain public expenditure because of the power and impact of the globalisation discourse. Policy has been based on the premise that state aid should be limited to those assessed by professionals as being in most need, and that the form of provision is dictated by professional definitions of need based on the special needs of older people. Also, it is based on the assumption that the quality of care and support delivered in a home or homely setting is inherently superior to care within an institution. The chapter argues that the increasing importance of identity and lifestyle choice undermines this discourse. Older people do not all have the same needs, and they react to the circumstances in which they find themselves in different ways. This means that policy and provision should be sensitive to the needs as defined by older people themselves. An alternative 'positive' discourse is outlined that places more emphasis on the control that older people can exercise over their housing pathways, and the help they may consider themselves to need.

The negative community care discourse

Public policy towards old age has been dominated by the discourse of community care, which has emphasised the undesirability of care in institutions and the virtues of care at home (for a review see Means and Smith, 1988). It is argued here that this official discourse has been negative in tone and has been based on negative views of ageing. In a much-quoted passage, Tyne (1982, p 150) argued that "community care has always suffered from being negatively defined – it was to be all that 'institutional' care in the past was not". The two main drawbacks of institutional care were held to be the cost and the quality of care.

Community care (defined as care outside the institution) was initially said to be cheaper than trying to maintain old and dilapidated buildings or paying for increasing numbers of older people to live in residential or nursing homes. The belief in cheapness was partly based on the idea that community care was to mean care *by* the community as well as care *in* the community (Walker, 1982). This chimed with the discourse of the 'traditional family', which emphasised the primary role of family members in caring for their older relatives (see Chapter Two). The discourse was accepted and developed by writers of the 'new right' associated with the governments of Margaret Thatcher in Britain and Ronald Reagan in the US. For example, Mount (1982) has argued that the traditional family was something natural, universal and enduring, which was an essential bulwark against the encroachment of the state into the private domain. It follows from this that the family is the natural place for all matters of care for the aged, the sick and for children.

When it became evident that the scope for family care was small and that statutory social services at home were not necessarily cheaper than care in institutions, the emphasis changed to the control of cost through cash-limited policy mechanisms. The 1990 NHS and Community Care Act, which formed the basis of the current community care mechanisms, substituted open-ended 'as of right' funding of residential care with a cash-limited and rationed provision of community care. The more recent policy of *Supporting People* (DETR, 2001) has also substituted a cash-limited mechanism of funding for support in place of an open-ended funding of supported housing through Housing Benefit.

The emphasis on restraining costs reflects the increasing pressures on state finances from the 1960s onwards, which, it can be argued, have been brought on by the advance of globalisation (see Chapters One and Three). Globalisation has many dimensions (for a review, see Waters, 1995). An important one to be considered here is the impact of changes in the global financial markets on public finances. Globalisation has been viewed by recent British governments as a desirable and inevitable trend that policy should support or ameliorate but never challenge. The discourse can be argued to be one of the factors that has shaped policies towards public expenditure and the labour market. The rapid movement of capital across the world has contributed to government reluctance to levy income and business taxes at rates that would be seen as a disincentive for investment. This has helped to underpin and rationalise the perceived political need to keep tight control over the amount of public spending and to ensure value for money. In this context it is easy to see why the growing number of economically inactive older people can be seen as a burden on the economically active population, or a rising tide about to swamp the public purse (Phillipson, 1998).

One of the key responses of government to financial pressures has been to distance itself from the universality of the welfare state. For example, in the area of pensions, the value of the state pension has been undermined and people encouraged to provide for their own old age in cooperation with their employers through occupational pension schemes (for a review, see Phillipson, 1998). In the area of care and support for older people, social services resources have been increasingly rationed and concentrated on those with the greatest problems and the fewest resources. Targeted and means-tested support has become the predominant model, as we shall see later.

The negative emphasis in the community care discourse meant that, at least initially, the form of housing, support and care provided as the alternative to institutional care did not receive much attention (Henwood, 1986). The assumption was that the quality of provision was ensured by it being at home or in a homely setting rather than in an institution. As we shall see later, there were positive discourses that could have helped to shape policy and provision, but these were not integrated into policy in any meaningful way.

Heywood et al (2002) illustrate the nature of the negative discourse of community care by focusing on the meaning held by policy makers of the term 'independence'. At first sight this would seem to be a positive term, but the authors argue that what was meant was independence from the state and living independently – that is, outside an institution. The assumption seems to be that the very fact of living outside an institution, either at home or in a homely setting, is enough by itself to establish 'independence'. It was considered that the quality of care was ensured by the fact that it was being provided in the home or a homely setting. Dalley (2002) argues that policy makers and professionals have long subscribed to the view that 'staying put' at home is the best way of ensuring independence. This emphasis is consonant with a whole stream of policy documents, going back to the 1970s, supporting the development of community care. It is also reflected in more recent policy documents such as the White Paper *Modernising social services* (DH, 1998), the NHS plan (DH, 2000) and the housing strategy for older people *Quality and choice for older people's housing* (DETR/DH, 2001). Heywood et al (2002) argue that older people themselves had a different conception of what independence meant to them, which was focused around ideas of control. They point to situations where some older people feel more independent in institutional care because they do not have to rely on family. At the same time some older people can feel a lack of independence at home if they are isolated and lonely and have to rely on their family to provide care. Older people were more likely to define independence as not having to rely on family or friends, and services from the state could enable this to happen.

The choices that older people can make regarding their housing situation clearly depend on the options available. For many older people the options considered are those that have been available in earlier parts of the life course – what may be termed mainstream housing. But there is a range of options that are specifically aimed at older people by either private developers or public agencies. The rationale for the provision of specific accommodation – sometimes linked with support – is the discourse of 'special needs'. Clapham and Smith (1990) argue that the 'special needs' discourse was associated with the growing targeting of housing policy in the 1980s with the increasing political pressure to reduce public expenditure. The acceptance of the neo-liberal paradigm among policy makers meant that the market was seen as the provider of housing for the vast majority of people. State 'intervention' was reserved for those who were deemed to have a legitimate case and had to be justified on the basis of the possession of 'special needs' that the market could not be expected to meet. These 'special needs' were categorised not on the basis of specific attributes but through membership of certain socially constructed groups. These groups tended to be of people deemed to be deserving of state help because of their distance from the labour market. Such groups were those associated with statutory community care policies, that is, people with physical disabilities, learning difficulties, mental health problems, and older people. State help could be provided to these people safe in the knowledge that it did not undermine the work incentive.

The social construction of the groups went together with the construction of a stereotypical set of needs associated with the group. For example, the problems faced by older people were held to be low income, loneliness, and physical disability. Clearly, many older people do suffer from these problems, but many do not suffer from all or any of them, and the problems can vary in nature and degree for each individual. Socially constructed stereotypes of need were coupled with specifically designed forms of intervention to meet those needs. For older people this mainly involved the provision of sheltered housing where the perceived needs for company, social support and help with physical disability could be met by a distinctive mix of accommodation and communal facilities such as a resident warden and common rooms for social events. Since the 1960s, the cornerstone of housing and care for older people had been sheltered housing, and this continued to be the case until the 1990s. The very term 'sheltered' housing betrays the underlying 'disengagement' discourse of old age that stressed the need to support older people to prepare for death by sheltering them and helping them to disengage from the wider society (Cumming and Henry, 1961). The link between membership of the category and the needs that were perceived as flowing from it, on the one hand, and a specific form of provision on the other, could be strong. For example, one local authority in Scotland studied by Clapham and Munro (1990) automatically treated any application for housing by anyone over retirement age as being an application for sheltered housing whether or not this had been asked for by the applicant.

As Clapham and Smith (1990) argue, the adoption of the 'special needs' discourse held advantages for many 'group' members because it unlocked resources at a time when state support for housing was being reduced. Also, the resultant forms of provision were popular with some people whose needs were effectively met. For example, a high proportion of sheltered housing tenants have expressed satisfaction with this form of provision (see Clapham and Munro, 1990). However, the price of receiving support has been the individual and collective acceptance of membership of the socially constructed category of older people, that is socially stigmatising because of its link with negative images of the ageing process. The 'special needs' discourse has reinforced images of old age based on perceived individual failure leading to dependence and physical deterioration – the medical rather than the social model of old age (as in the medical and social models of disability). Not all older people are poor or lonely and in need of special help. The difficulty of living in some houses may be attributable not to the 'special needs' of older people but to particular housing design conventions. The categorisation process leads to a uniformity of perceived needs and an inflexibility of services designed to meet them.

The emphasis on categories as the basis for dealing with need also masks the similarities between the needs of some older people and others. Clapham and Smith (1990) use the example of the absence of outside stairs leading to a flat being perceived as a particular problem for older people whereas it can also be problematic for young people with small children. Many of the 'special adaptations' associated with sheltered housing would be of benefit to a large proportion of the population. However, categorisation according to type of need rather than membership of a particular group would open the door for resources to groups labelled as undeserving. As Clapham and Smith (1990, p 200) observe, "This again illustrates that devising 'special' policies which tend to implicate individual or group characteristics as the cause of housing problems can divert attention away from the need for more comprehensive interventions through mainstream housing policy".

Clapham and Munro (1990) argue that the fundamental flaw in the sheltered housing model is the linking together of accommodation with a fixed form of support, which was expensive since the care was not specifically targeted on those who needed it. This was reinforced by allocation policies of many public providers that sought to achieve a 'balance' between fit and frail older people in a scheme to prevent the overburdening of the warden or the loss of the perceived 'homely' qualities of the scheme. This meant, in practice, that many residents of sheltered housing did not need or use the services of the warden or the other expensive communal services (Clapham and Munro, 1990).

Since the 1980s the policy emphasis has been on separating the funding for accommodation from that for support, on the grounds that appropriate care and support should be provided to people wherever they live. The services of sheltered housing should be available without having to move from one's own home with the resultant danger of cutting ties with family and friends and losing 'independence'. This approach has been institutionalised through the *Supporting People* framework that has reiterated long-standing community care aims. "Helping older people to remain living independently at home can prevent them from having to move to much more expensive and unsatisfactory institutional care, and often help them move back home after a period in hospital" (DETR, 2001, p 11). Sheltered housing is a 'key element' of *Supporting People* as it is intended to provide financial support for the costs of the warden and other support provision. However, there is also an emphasis on funding the wide range of home-based services becoming available. These have become more flexible and comprehensive over time as the drawbacks of previous forms of provision have been highlighted. Services such as Care and Repair or Home Improvement Agencies, emergency alarm systems and aids and adaptations can allow many older people to stay successfully in their own homes. The *Supporting People* regime has been aimed at making available to older people more flexible and practical services that can enable them to live in their own homes.

The recent move towards more flexible policies could be viewed as an extension of the previous community care policies. For example, the changes partly result from a long-standing concern to cap expenditure on rising Housing Benefit costs for care (Heywood et al, 2002). Another stimulus behind current policies is the perceived need to reduce so-called bed blocking in hospitals by older people who cannot be discharged because of a lack of appropriate shelter and care and are therefore using scarce beds and resources. At the same time the recent changes could be seen as a partial breakdown of the original model because of the promotion of flexibility of provision. However, we shall argue that there are strong continuities in the assumption that the quality of care and support is assured by the setting of the home and the continuing emphasis on the professional determination of need.

Therefore, the dominant public policy discourse of community care has been negative in tone and has not focused either on the quality of care in non-institutional settings or on meeting needs as defined by older people themselves. Instead, it has been based on stereotypical views of the needs of older people based on medical and disengagement models of old age. Also, it has been overly-concerned with avoiding residential care and with reducing state expenditure through increased targeting of support.

Need and lifestyle

The shortage of resources combined with targeting has resulted in a lack of help for those defined as having less need. Allen (2002) shows that the average number of contact hours from home care and home helps increased by 12% between 1996 and 2001, but the number of people receiving help fell by 23%. The average number of contact hours per household increased by 45% over the same period as home carers were spending more time with fewer people. In practice, the emphasis has been on providing care for those in danger of being in need of residential care. This means the potential role of care in preventing future more acute need is ignored. Also, the situations where only a small amount of help could enable an older person to continue a valued lifestyle are neglected.

The concept of need, which has been one of the cornerstones of the welfare state, is a problematic one. It has never been a clear concept receiving universal support or even consistency in its definition and operationalisation. Allen (2002) argues that need has assumed a large influence in community care for older people despite the rhetoric of choice. It is clear that the concept of need used in the targeting of care for older people is that of professionally defined need rather than felt need. In other words, the idea is that need is defined by professionals in a supposed 'objective' way that can be applied in a neutral and standardised fashion to the different situations of a number of people. Need has assumed its pre-eminent position because rationing decisions have to be made to ensure equitable distribution of limited resources. On this basis, judgements can be made about who is most deserving of the small amount of help available. This way of treating need gives professionals the central role of definers and arbiters of need and so is promoted and defended by the various professional groups involved.

Heywood et al (2002) argue that the usual way of measuring need is by the use of what are called activity of daily living (ADL) scales. These measure the competence of older people in performing certain household tasks, which are held to be essential for independent living. Most importantly, the definition of need is vested in the assessor rather than the older person being assessed. In these so-called objective tests, the emphasis is on the ageing body, and there is little room for the assessment of different attitudes and lifestyles.

Heywood et al (2002, p 57) say that what older people want is not care but help. "The word help implies that the older person remains the prime mover, remains in control and actually wants the minimum possible, covering only the things they cannot do for themselves or cannot do easily, or the times when they cannot do things." They argue that the concern older people have with control is philosophically and practically in direct conflict with the idea of external assessment based on the idea of need. The concept of need also sits badly with concerns about lifestyle as a means of achieving identity and fulfilment.

An important feature of writing on postmodern society is said to be the increased capacity of people to 'make their own lives' through choosing their own identities and lifestyles (Giddens, 1990). It was argued in Chapter One that lifestyle choice has become an important component of the growing search for meaning and identity. The ownership and consumption of housing is an important element in this, as shown by the force and popularity of the discourse of 'home' (see Chapter Five). A house has become a means to an end rather than an end in itself. The end is a preferred and chosen lifestyle. Giddens argues that households undertake what he terms 'life planning' in a search for identity and self-fulfilment. It was argued in Chapter One that housing is a key element in this. Housing can also be an important source of identity. Earlier reference was made to Taylor's (1998) concept of categorical identity. Categorical identity is concerned with the labels that are ascribed to us by ourselves and society. An example would be the categories of owner–occupier or older person, which bring with them a set of discourses that ascribe their relation to the wider society. This is in addition to categories of social class, gender, ethnicity, sexuality, disability and so on. Ontological identity is how these are forged by individuals into a coherent sense of self-identity. Categorical identity is a key concept because of its mediating position between society and the individual. The categorical identity of old age will structure the experiences of older people and the opportunities open to them.

The discourse of community care was associated with an identity of old age that made assumptions about perceived dependence and need in a stereotypical way that stressed the similarities between individuals. These ideas were based on a traditional view of the nature of the life course that Phillipson (1998) argues has been undermined by the current considerable uncertainty over identity in later life. For example, Laslett (1989) argued that the traditional life course involved the three ages of childhood, maturity and adulthood, and old age. These were largely defined around the centrality of paid employment. Old age was negatively defined around retirement and dependency on the welfare state. The rise of what Laslett (1989) termed the 'third age' of active retirement did not fit into any pre-existing category of life stage. 'Third agers' are distant from paid work and employment but are fit and active and are not dependent on the welfare state.

However, it is not clear that all third agers are distant from the labour market. One of the responses to globalisation has been the move towards a flexible labour market that can respond quickly and efficiently to economic circumstances and changes in technology (see Chapter Three). People have been forced to adapt to the changing economic and social situation brought about by technological change. This has increased the general perception of uncertainty and job insecurity with the risk of unemployment and skills redundancy being felt across the income spectrum. At the same time it has undermined traditional work and career patterns. More people are self-employed, work flexible hours or part-time and are on fixed-term contracts. This means that the concept of a general and relatively fixed life course is breaking down with the increased fluidity of the break from the labour market through retirement. Bernard and Phillips (2000, p 43) argue:

> The pressures producing an increased fragmentation of the contemporary lifecourse will not go away: the concept of a lifelong career in one occupation is fast vanishing, along with earlier certainties about such things as a fixed time for retirement. This calls for much greater flexibility in how we view the lifecourse.

Some older people may retain their link with employment well beyond the statutory retirement age, while others will choose or be forced to leave work well before this. Gilleard and Higgs (2000) refer to the 'blurred transition' that retirement has become. The key element here is the variety in individual circumstances.

Phillipson (1998) argues that many older people have forged an identity as consumers, which has made up for their traditional lack of status as producers in the economic system. This has been made possible by the increasing affluence of many older people with the rise of occupational pensions for more people. The result has been a growth in products and services aimed primarily at older people, whether holidays, other leisure activities or stairlifts.

Some older people have developed lifestyles that are different from those of their parents and show a strong link to contemporary youth culture. As Scase (1999, p 14) notes:

> Perceptions of what constitutes 'old age' will need to change. Today's over 50's – clad in their jeans, trainers and baseball caps – no longer view themselves as old. This age group welcomes retirement as a means of gaining control over their lives. Middle age is no longer the beginning of the end but the beginning of a thirty-year period of personal enjoyment and self-indulgence.

Gilleard (1996, p 495) notes:

> .... more and more older people are joining in this shopping trip searching for reasonably priced identities and personal self care plan to follow through the dangerous territory of infinite desire. Modernity had structured the identities of old people, exchanging their role in the productive processes for a guaranteed but limited security in old age. Late or post-modernity, whilst dislocating and diffusing these earlier collective social identities offers older people the opportunity to engage more comprehensively with the project of identity.

Older people can have difficulty in developing and sustaining a positive identity in a culture that is dominated by youth and the 'cult' of the young body. Featherstone and Hepworth (1990) use the analogy of a mask to describe the way many older people think about themselves and their bodies. The mask of the ageing body hides the identity of the young self within. The relationship between the body and self-identity and the management of any dissonance between them are interesting and important issues. Older people may accept the image of the old body and change their self-perception accordingly. Others may use exercise or cosmetic surgery to change the body by hiding or amending the physical signs of the ageing process. Tulle-Winton (1999) points to the importance attached in contemporary culture to being a 'successful ager', which may involve self-management and the adoption of a proactive relationship to one's body and to one's social circumstances. Two important points follow from this. The first is that older people are active agents in their own ageing. The social construction of a person's self-image and the image that they project to the world are lifetime occupations. As we shall see, a positive image is important for personal self-esteem. Second, older people will vary in the ways they construct their own old age. Therefore, difference is a key variable.

Taylor and Ford (1981) explored the different ways in which older people coped with ageing. Taylor and Ford (1981, p 339) saw later life as a "constant struggle to maintain cherished lifestyles against the threatening impact of both external events and internal changes". They identified ten lifestyle types: taking life easy; gregarious; solitary; spouse-centred; invalid; altruist; hobbyist; family-centred; work-centred; and full-life. This points to the need to be aware that the meaning and use of home may be very different for people with different lifestyle orientations as may their reaction to experiences such as retirement or physical incapacity.

Gilleard and Higgs (2000, p 1) have pointed to the 'fragmentation of ageing as a social attribute'. In contrast to the emphasis on the stereotyping of needs in the negative discourse, they argue that:

> It is increasingly meaningless to consider 'age' as conferring some common social identity or to treat 'older people' as a distinct social group acting out of shared concerns and common interests. The growing disparities of wealth within the retired population and the concomitant rise of lifestyle consumerism mean that more and more 'sites of distinction' are emerging which fragment and render less possible any common cultural position that can be represented as 'ageing'. (Gilleard and Higgs, 2000, p 8)

Phillipson (1998, p 10) criticises the stereotyping of older people which was associated with the negative community care discourse:

Writing in the 1970s one had a relatively clear sense of who older people were; mainly poor, probably with similar outlooks (and indeed appearance), and with limited aspirations for future lifestyles. This may have been an unsatisfactory stereotype then; it certainly must be considered as such now. Despite the trends and similarities ... there are huge variations among older people and this diversity has undoubtedly been a feature of social change in the 1990s.

In a study of the needs and aspirations of a group of older people, Appleton (2002) found that, for most of the years of old age that will be experienced by the large majority of older people, their needs and wants will be shaped more by lifestyle choices than by their future frailty. Gilleard and Higgs (2000) argue that diversity in old age has grown for a number of reasons. The growing number of older people, increasing affluence and the scope for 'lifestyle' consumption, the different approaches of older people to the growth of the body as a cultural focus, the ageing of youth culture and the diversity of individual life histories all lead to the breakdown of ageing as a fixed and homogeneous process. "Ageing has become more complex, differentiated and ill defined, experienced from a variety of perspectives and expressed in a variety of ways at different moments in people's lives" (Gilleard and Higgs, 2000, p 1). This picture contrasts with the discourse of community care which Gilleard and Higgs (2000, p 113) note "continues to construct categories out of an age grouping".

However, it must be borne in mind that access to consumption lifestyles is dependent on financial resources. In a review of the data on the incomes of older people, Phillipson (1998) concludes that income differentials among the older people in Britain widened during the 1980s and 1990s, as they did for the population as a whole. Despite the growing affluence of some older people, others are living at the official poverty level on means-tested benefits. Phillipson estimates that at least one in four people over the age of 75 and one in three over the age of 85 were living at the poverty level in 1996. The increasing reality seems to be that many older people can use their financial resources to pursue lifestyle choice, while others living in poverty are being confined to the needs sphere of public provision.

Home and the quality of life

In the traditional community care discourse the assumption was made that care provided at home is necessarily superior to care provided in an institution. This proposition rests on the perceived importance of home to older people, and there is substantial evidence to support this. Kellaher (2002, p 57) confirms the point made earlier that the house is a means to fulfilment rather than an end in itself, and illustrates this in relation to older people's housing strategies.

> The aim of their moving or staying strategies is maintenance of self as a social being, central if possible, attached at least to a network of family/friends/acquaintances. The house, its location, internal arrangements and presentation through day to day management is the principle [*sic*] vehicle through which this is accomplished. In this sense the building and the material form of home is secondary, whilst being integral to identity.

A withdrawal from the labour market may mean that more time is spent at home, and this is likely to be especially true for those with mobility problems who have to spend a large part of the day at home. Privacy may also take on a particular importance in old age as body maintenance activities may result in feelings of shame or prurience, given the problematic nature of the ageing body in current culture. The emotional meaning of home may be especially important for some older people, particularly if the home has been the scene of important life events and is a repository of memories of previous stages of life or of family members. Also, home is the setting for the display of personal possessions that can be invested with considerable meaning.

In their study of older owner-occupiers undergoing major repairs to their houses, Gurney and Means (1993, p 124) found that some felt deeply attached to their homes. The house was interwoven with people's lives.

> The house, for some, was still 'the place they had come as a bride', 'their mother's house', 'their husband's family home'. People could recall specific days and dates when important events took place in the house, the day they moved in, the day and circumstances of a partner's death, even though this was many years ago.

They concluded:

> The house was either symbolically, and for some actually, an indication of the effort they had put into a life together with their partners. Some clients talked of the steady way they had kept the house in good repair and in some cases transformed it over the years, adding amenities or shaping the garden. Some expressed pride in what they had achieved, others tolerated the house, like an eccentric relative, not expecting great things from something of such an age. (Gurney and Means, 1993, p 124)

The house was also a window on the neighbourhood: "a fixed spot from which they had observed, with varying degrees of pleasure or anxiety, the changing scene of the street or neighbourhood" (Gurney and Means, 1993, p 124). Gurney and Means were studying people who had chosen to stay in their homes and to undertake substantial repairs rather than move.

However, home may not have a completely positive meaning for all older people. Although older people tend to be more satisfied with their houses than people in other age groups, on average they tend to live in worse accommodation (Heywood et al, 2002). Some older people who are more restricted to the home than others because of physical disabilities and mobility problems may, in Allan and Crow's (1989) terms, consider home to be a cage rather than a castle. It is commonly assumed that older people are less inclined to move than younger people. This may partly be because of the positive attraction of the present home, but it may also partly be because of the stress of moving. Percival (2002) shows the importance of housework to many older women for preserving feelings of self-determination and self-esteem. In addition, the appearance of a clean and tidy home reinforces older people's identity in the community. Therefore, the compromising of control or in standards brought about by physical incapacity can threaten feelings of being 'at home'.

Research on the meaning of home to older people is limited. The main preoccupation has been with exploring all the different dimensions of home, but there has been little attempt to identify differences in the way older people weave together the various elements and how this relates to their lifestyle choices.

Despite the policy emphasis on living 'at home', a significant number of older people live in institutions such as hostels, residential care homes and nursing homes. Sometimes this is out of choice, but it may also be because they have needs that cannot be, or are not, met in a domestic setting. Leaving home in these circumstances can be an upsetting experience. "Individuals frequently lose all that is dear to them, their home, their furniture, their freedom, and most upsetting of all for many of them, their pets" (Higgins, 1989, p 165).

The dominance of the ideal of 'home' has meant that it is almost universal for institutional settings to have as their ideal the re-creation of the lost 'home'. For example, the community care legislation talks about care provided in homes or in 'homely settings'. This is partly in response to sustained criticism in the 1960s and 1970s of institutional settings and regimes that were said to lead to loneliness, loss of privacy, identity and individuality, and the lack of control over one's life (Townsend, 1962). Higgins (1989) draws attention to government guidance to the managers of residential care homes, which is entitled *Home Life* and stresses the achievement of 'homely' environments. The attributes of home life are defined as: fulfilment through meaningful activity; dignity through personal space; autonomy through choice; the expression of individuality through personal taste; self-esteem; the meeting of emotional needs; risk-taking in order to undertake 'normal' activities such as shopping and so forth; and overall quality of experience. The value of personal clothing and possessions is stressed, as is the ability to form voluntary social relationships.

Despite the policy emphasis on the creation of 'home' there is a perceived inability of the ideals of 'home' to be achieved in institutional settings (Willcocks et al, 1987). The basis of home in personal loving relationships was highlighted earlier, and these are difficult to sustain and are sometimes frowned on in residential homes. Even close friendships within institutional settings are rare. People often also suffer a lack of meaningful activity and occupation. The highest proportion of residents in residential homes are women, who see their house-making and caring role taken on by paid care staff. The physical environment often falls short of the domestic ideal. "In contrast with the domestic home, these buildings fail to convey any sense of personal ownership, of territoriality, or of individual influence over external appearance" (Willcocks et al, 1987, p 79).

The perceived importance of 'staying at home' has been one of the cornerstones of public policy towards older people. One of the main aims of community care has been to change the location of the provision of care and support from impersonal institutions to a home or 'homely setting'. The home was seen as a perfect antidote to the impersonality, lack of privacy, and powerlessness often associated with institutional life. The location of care and support in the home was seen by some as reflecting a change in the way that care is provided as well as its location. In their own homes, it was thought that older people would be in more control of the care relationship and more powerful in the face of professional and bureaucratic power.

The provision of care in the home, whether by a care worker or a family member, can result in some spatial and temporal reordering. Homes may have to be adapted to allow a disabled person access to some areas such as a kitchen and bathroom, and these may change the 'feel' and meaning attached to them. The need for support in a bathroom can turn a private space into a more public one where the lock cannot be used to obtain privacy. In extreme cases, a bedroom may become the sole living space of a disabled individual in which all functions have to be undertaken. The sitting room may have to perform a wide range of functions for a person unable to access other rooms in the house.

Twigg (2000) gives examples of different ways in which older people have reacted to the potential reordering brought on by the need for care. She cites one person who sought to change existing routines as little as possible by keeping the previous use of rooms and the daily routine of day-to-day life. In another example the use of rooms and the daily routine was fundamentally changed and dominated by the care provision.

The provision of care by care workers coming into the home can raise issues of the control of space and privacy. Twigg (2000) argues that care workers can feel uncertain and uneasy when entering an older person's home for the first time. They are aware that they are entering someone else's territory and this can be an odd and unsettling experience, one that can make care workers feel vulnerable. Twigg (2000) found that, although they were coming to do a job of work, care workers felt themselves to some extent bound by the norms of being a guest. This meant that they asked permission before entering some parts of the house or doing various tasks such as making tea or fetching towels.

Those receiving care have to accept a care worker into the home. Twigg (2000) found that people varied considerably in their response to this, with women in particular finding it intrusive. This may be because women are more likely to view the home as their domain and therefore to feel the presence of a care worker as an intrusion on their control and ordering of space. Some older people also felt a sense of being under public scrutiny and comment with a stranger in their home, thinking that their local reputation would be under threat. Twigg argues, "The ideology of home plays an important part in the power dynamics of care, endowing older and disabled people with an element of control, and making it possible in some degree to resist the dominance of care workers and professionals" (2000, pp 81-2).

Home is a space that belongs to the occupant, and this social norm enables older people to exclude professionals if they want to. Twigg (2000) also argues that home is an embodiment of identity that can offset the depersonalisation of the care process. At home, she argues, surrounded by one's own possessions, it is not possible to be wholly reduced to anonymity. It prevents the professional from establishing control over territory that they have in an institutional setting. Also, the power of home gives the capacity to say 'no' to professional interventions. In an institutional setting the regime is ordered by staff. As one care worker interviewed by Twigg put it:

> [In a residential home] if you've got a bath day then you have your bath whether you want it or not. Whereas in your own home, as I said to you, you can't – you can try and persuade them to do that, but if they don't wanna bath, they don't wanna bath, and there's nothing you can do except try to persuade them – it's their home, their territory. (Twigg, 2000, p 85)

However, it cannot be assumed that older people will choose to or be able to retain their independence when receiving care at home. Aronson (2002) identified three kinds of reaction by older people to receiving home care. The first she names 'taking charge', when older people made active efforts to control their situation and govern the terms under which care workers entered their homes and became involved in intimate aspects of their lives. They strove to ensure that care was tailored to their situations and needs, and minimally compromised their sense of themselves. In contrast, Aronson names the second group 'pushed over the edge', reflecting the lack of ability to influence their situation and the distress they felt in not being in command of their lives. Their powerless position was reflected in a feeling of not being in control of their appearances and their surroundings, which engendered shame and self-criticism. The third category was 'restraining expectations' in which older people adapted to the expectations of carers and to the practical situation in which they found themselves. They resigned themselves to their inability to take charge and to the inevitability of letting go of past preferences and wishes.

Therefore, older people actively respond and negotiate to varying degrees in the home care situation. However, Twigg (2000) points out that the balance of power is heavily in favour of the care giver, despite what she calls 'the power of the home'. Oldman and Quilgars (1999) agree that the provision of care at home is not enough by itself to change the dependent status of many older people.

Since February 2000, local authorities have been able to offer direct payments to older people so that they can arrange and purchase their own home care, usually with the assistance of a support agency. Take-up has been low despite the government imposing a duty on local authorities in England to offer direct payments to those eligible for them. Clark et al (2004) found that many older people using direct payments felt that they, rather than the service providers, were in control. Direct payments enhanced older people's choice, continuity and control of their support arrangements and enabled them to meet their own priorities. For some older people this involved arranging support to enable them to pursue social or lifestyle interests, although the scope within the allocated amount of money was small and they often had to pay extra themselves. Clark et al (2004) concluded that direct payments had a positive impact on older people's social, emotional and physical health, leaving them happier, more relaxed, and able to do more for themselves and go out more often. However, budgetary constraints meant that there was usually enough money only for basic needs to be met, and limited scope and flexibility for older people to meet lifestyle needs.

Oldman and Quilgars (1999) point to the poor quality of life experienced by some older people who feel bored, lonely and trapped in their homes. Many older people wanted more time with care staff, more opportunities to get out of the house, and more things to happen to enliven their day-to-day existence. They conclude that the social isolation that some older people experience in their own homes depersonalises and dehumanises them. They argue that for some older people life at home can be bleak. Oldman and Quilgars (1999) also question the predominant view that older people cannot be happy in institutional care. They criticise research that directly compares the two settings for ignoring the previous life and housing pathway experienced by the residents. They argue for the importance of diversity, stressing that, for some older people, institutional care has been a positive choice that they are happy with. Their previous circumstances influenced the meaning they attached to institutional care and their satisfaction with it. Factors such as the quality of their lives in their previous home and social relationships with family were the important issues for many older people in choosing institutional care. However, a key issue was the extent of choice that older people had and the degree to which others such as family members or professionals, including doctors or carers, made the choice for the older person.

In summary, it is argued that the predominant discourse of community care fits with the attachment felt towards 'home' by many older people, but not all have positive views towards the home. Some older people see the home as a cage, others choose to enter residential care rather than live an isolated existence at home. The provision of care in the home environment is not by itself a guarantee that the older persons feels in control of their situation. When care is provided *to* older people on the basis of professional definitions of need based on physical abilities, it is unlikely to meet the lifestyle and identity needs of older people.

Towards a positive discourse

It was acknowledged earlier that there is a positive aspect to the ideas of community care. In the field of learning disability it has been associated with the discourse of normalisation, or 'social role valorisation', as it later became known (Tyne, 1982). In the field of old age it became associated with notions of a third age as outlined earlier (Laslett, 1989). Laslett argued that the 'third age' of active retirement, which came between working life and a dependent old age, could be extended by health-giving activity and an active engagement with life. Public policy, he argued, should reinforce and encourage this activity rather than stimulate disengagement. It is possible to question the assumption that older people are dependent and are a 'burden' on society. Many older people play a key role in family life and may contribute by looking after grandchildren while their mothers are at work. Dench et al (1999) show the continuing importance of the grandparental relationship, both to older people and to their families. In the British Social Attitudes Survey sample, 91% of grandparents said that being a grandparent was a very rewarding aspect of their lives. Over three quarters said that they feel very close to their grandchildren and 43% saw them at least several times a week. Levels of activity varied considerably, but usually grandparents played a supportive role to the parents and were reluctant to 'interfere too much'. Generally, grandparents were happy with their role, but satisfaction declined where grandparents felt under pressure to adopt a very active role, as when, for example, their child was a lone parent. There was also dissatisfaction where relationship breakdown resulted in lack of contact with a grandchild. Greatest satisfaction seemed to be where grandparents shared caring responsibilities with other family members and could negotiate the nature and extent of their involvement.

It is also possible to point to the contribution made by many older people to charities and to voluntary organisations and local government. In the National Survey of Volunteering it was found that there was an increase from 34% to 45% in formal volunteering of people aged 65 to 74 in the period 1991 to 1997. The proportion aged 75 and over had increased from 25% to 35% (ONS, 1999). This positive view of ageing fits well with the growing importance of the search for personal fulfilment that is such a feature of postmodern society. Like people of other ages, older people are 'making their lives' by making choices about lifestyle with a view to forging a strong ontological identity.

The dominant community care discourse has focused on the achievement of particular destinations on the housing pathway. In other words, the main aim of policy has been to achieve the outcome of living 'at home'. Care and support has been available only to those able to pay for it or those deemed to need it by professionals in the context of increasing targeting. The same is the case for residential or nursing home care. In these circumstances, only those with appropriate financial resources are in control of their situations and able to exercise choice in terms of their destinations. The issue of control is a key one for a positive policy discourse. It has been argued that control is important to many older people who receive care and support. Heywood et al (2002) argue that the positive choice of residential care brings satisfaction as does control over the form of domiciliary services. There is an interesting parallel here with research on the impact of housing on health (see Chapter Five). For example, the importance of factors such as mastery and self-esteem in influencing health was stressed by Macintyre et al (2000). They found that the most important factors in predicting health and psychological outcomes were age, self-esteem and income.

Coleman (1990) argues that self-esteem – what people feel about themselves – is the linchpin of quality of life in old age. He argues that the challenge in later life often is to maintain a strong sense of self-identity if many of the social relationships that underpinned it are lost. An important element of self-esteem is the feeling of being in control, and the perceived loss of control is damaging to both morale and physical health.

Identity and self-esteem stem from the ability to be able to actively choose a socially valued lifestyle. Gilleard and Higgs (2000) contrast the ability of most older people to sustain their self-esteem through lifestyle choice with the situation of older people who are deemed to need state support through community care. They argue that the latter are cut off from the active lifestyle choice of the active third age and excluded from mainstream society because of their situation as needy recipients of state welfare with its concomitant membership of the frail 'fourth age'. They are strongly critical of attempts to improve the position of welfare recipients through what they consider to be only bogus consumer rights through being offered choice in the process of care assessment. It is easy to agree that the consumer rights offered to older welfare recipients are only partial because, as the earlier discussion makes clear, they have not challenged the imbalance of power by enabling older people to exercise control over their circumstances and to pursue a favoured lifestyle.

There is a massive potential for direct payments to increase older people's self-esteem by enabling them to exercise control over their support services and arrange them to suit their preferred lifestyle. For this potential to be realised, older people need to be able to draw on support agencies to help them with the organisation of their support. There also needs to be a recognition of the importance of lifestyle needs in the assessment of the amount of money allocated to individuals if the full benefits of increased health and well-being are to be achieved.

The importance of control in the health and well-being of older people means that the aim of public policy should not be to achieve particular outcomes on the housing pathway but to enable people to take control of their pathway through the ability to make choices. Households are actively and reflexively assessing their housing circumstances and making choices and decisions that they hope will lead to housing circumstances that meet their needs and desires and reflect their identity and lifestyle. Housing policy helps to shape the attitudes and perceptions of individuals and households through discourse and provides policy mechanisms that shape the opportunities and constraints that they will experience.

In these circumstances, the scope of housing policy is reduced when compared with the modern era. It has already been remarked that the state cannot hope to understand the meanings that housing will have to individual households. As King (1996, p 185) argues, the job of the state is "… to equalise opportunities for self-creation and then leave people alone to use or neglect their opportunities". Clearly, current public policies do not lead to an equality of opportunities, and the pursuit of this goal needs to be at the forefront of policy if older people are to be able to join in the search for identity and escape the social exclusion inherent in the needs-based 'ghetto' of public provision.

The pathways approach emphasises the importance of time (Clapham et al, 1993). It has already been argued that the reasons people enter residential care can be found much earlier in their housing pathway. The ability to take control of one's housing pathway in old age may relate back to inequality or risk much earlier in the pathway. Households actively shaping their own housing pathways are inevitably exposed to risk. Households may vary in their willingness to embrace or to avoid risk and so their exposure may vary. There will also be differences in the ability of households to survive risk by mustering emotional and material resources. The politics of risk could emerge as one of the major themes of housing policy and challenge the dominance of the 'special needs' view of housing policy for older people. Emphasis should be placed on mainstream housing policy issues at all stages of the pathway, and the impact of particular housing policies on the ability of older people to make choices should be a major criterion for evaluation of any housing intervention.

Any support that households receive, for example during periods of unemployment, needs to avoid creating disincentives for households to act creatively and accept responsibility for their housing circumstances. Many current housing policy mechanisms fail this test. Housing provision based on the stereotypical needs of older people, and not geared to the achievement of individuals' desired lifestyles, is not likely to lead to self-fulfilment and high self-esteem. Nor is care and support that is based on the physical assessment of needs and does not put the older person in control. The success of the so-far limited provision of direct payments for older people to purchase and organise their own support points to the need for the availability of flexible and responsive forms of housing and support that are based on the different lifestyle preferences of older people. This will be achieved only if older people are able to exercise control and access is on the basis of choice rather than professional assessment of needs. Older people should be seen not as passive recipients of care but as active agents in the social construction of their own lives through the consumption of housing and support.

Giddens (1994) has stressed the need for what he has termed 'regenerative welfare'. This is a form of state intervention that aims to reinforce people's self-esteem and identity, and enables them to exercise choice in pursuing their own lifestyles. The concept of a housing pathway gives a framework for judging the success or otherwise of this intervention. It was argued earlier that it is difficult to define a successful outcome in terms of specific housing destinations because identity and self-esteem may be reinforced in many different housing circumstances depending on the meanings held and lifestyle adopted by different households. It is more in keeping with the idea of regenerative welfare for the appropriate criterion to be the extent to which intervention enables households to take charge of their own housing pathways by exercising choice, independence and control.

Conclusion

The central argument of this chapter is that older people, in common with others at different stages of the life course, are looking to achieve self-fulfilment through forging a positive identity. At present, the dominant policy discourse of community care hinders this for many people, for a number of reasons. The overriding emphasis on keeping people out of residential care and in their own homes has ignored the needs of those people who would actively choose to live in this way. The emphasis on targeting according to professionally defined need ignores issues of identity and lifestyle and overlooks the needs of those who need only a limited amount of help to achieve or maintain a valued lifestyle. Also, it treats older people as passive recipients of care rather than as active agents in the construction of their own lives. The result has been a form of provision that reinforces the social exclusion of those who do not have the financial resources to escape from the 'ghetto' of professionally defined need. Poorer older people are unable to sustain their identity and self-esteem by exercising control through lifestyle choice.

A more positive discourse exists that emphasises the ability of older people to control their own housing pathways and the help they need. This approach is more in keeping with the growing importance in society of self-fulfilment through lifestyle planning, which threatens traditional modes of access to housing and care based on professionally defined need. Elements of this positive discourse can be found in current policy and practice. But if it is to be implemented in full, there will need to be a fundamental change in the balance of power between older people and those providing housing and care. Direct payments for care and support are one way of achieving this change. For those older people unable or unwilling to take advantage of direct payments, there needs to be an increased awareness of the importance of lifestyle choice in the allocation of resources and in the way that services are delivered.

In housing policy, there needs to be a decisive break from the 'special needs' discourse and a realisation that the aim of policy is to enable individuals and households to exercise control over their housing pathways. The factors that influence the ability of individuals and households to control their housing circumstances in later life often occur much earlier in their housing pathways. This realisation offers an appropriate criterion for evaluating any form of housing intervention.

The chapter adds to the analysis of housing pathways by showing the links between discourses, public policy and the meaning of housing. The pathways approach, with its focus on meaning, identity and lifestyle, highlights the inadequacy of public policies that are based on professional assessments of need or specific housing destinations. The approach offers a way of assessing the success of policy based on the control that households are able to achieve over their own situation.

NINE

Researching housing pathways

A major theme of this book has been the espousal of the pathways approach to housing, which is dynamic and which examines the interaction between households and the structures that influence the opportunities and constraints they face. The pathways approach is particularly appropriate in postmodern society where housing is predominantly a means of personal fulfilment and the meaning households attach to their housing, and its relationship to identity and lifestyle in housing decisions, are vital issues. This approach has implications for the kind of housing research needed, as traditional forms of positivist research in housing are ill-adapted to the context of postmodern society.

This chapter starts with an analysis of the research which is needed in the current context to further explore the pathways approach. The pathways approach demands a different research emphasis from much traditional housing research in terms of both the focus of study and the research methods used. Therefore, the general principles of the necessary approach are outlined, and the implications of the pathways approach for the research methods employed, are explored. This is followed by a discussion of the gaps in knowledge of housing that research needs to fill. This brief discussion draws on the analysis in the previous chapters, which have examined particular aspects of pathways. Finally, the chapter focuses on research for policy making. Much housing research is commissioned by government bodies or is designed to influence housing policy. This is one reason why most research is based on a positivist paradigm, as it is designed to influence a policy-making process that gives primacy to the forms of knowledge that such research produces. It is argued that the current form of policy-making process is ill-suited to postmodern society and needs to be replaced with a process that is more open to the kinds of knowledge that the pathways approach produces.

Analysing pathways

Sarre (1986) has laid out a useful framework for applying the concept of structuration to empirical research, which is relevant to the task of elucidating housing pathways. He breaks the research task into four elements:

1. the elucidation of frameworks of meaning with the use of ethnographic or biographical methods to clarify individuals' knowledge of the social structure and their reasons for action;
2. investigation of the context and form of practical consciousness;
3. identification of the bounds of knowledgeability to discover the unacknowledged or unconscious meanings held by individuals and the unintended consequences of actions; and
4. the specification of structural orders, that is, the structural factors that impinge on actions.

In other words, the research needs to employ ethnographic or biographic methods to understand the meaning of individuals and households and the conscious aspects of behaviour. However, we need to explore the unconscious meanings and actions, bearing in mind the constraints and opportunities that structure them and are reproduced by them. Also, the structures themselves need to be analysed.

Not all the elements of an analysis of pathways need to be included in any one empirical research study. Indeed it would be difficult to design and implement research that did include all elements simultaneously. Therefore, concentration on some aspects of the whole is usually necessary, although it must be stressed that all of the elements need to be in place for a full understanding of pathways. One of the strengths of the approach is that it draws attention to the importance of a comprehensive analysis. The emphasis on meaning and the wide-ranging nature of many discourses mean that the pathways approach tends towards holistic forms of understanding. Many positivist research studies look for partial explanations of phenomena by examining the influence of one variable or a small number of variables in what is called a nomothetic explanation. In contrast, an idiographic approach attempts to develop as complete an explanation as possible. Therefore, concepts need to be derived that are holistic, enabling all the factors that influence meaning and behaviour to be related. Where research constraints mean that only a nomothetic analysis is possible, a framework needs to be in place whereby partial pieces of the jigsaw can be related to the rest of the picture.

Research on housing pathways needs to be able to capture the meanings held by households and others while incorporating an awareness of the importance of interaction and the dimension of time.

It is a difficult task to choose research tools that meet all of these criteria. Many of the current widely-used research tools in housing analysis are positivist, thus not being "adequate at the level of meaning" (de Vaus, 2001, p 11) and are cross-sectional rather than longitudinal in design, thus limited in their approach to the time dimension. In addition, the distance of most research tools from interaction means that this aspect has been relatively neglected.

As de Vaus (2001, p 235) argues, "actions have meanings to people performing those actions and this must form part of our understanding of the causes and meaning of any behaviour. To simply look at behaviour and *give* it a meaning rather than *take* the meaning of actors is to miss out on an important source of understanding of human behaviour" (emphasis in original).

Some of the elements of the pathways approach build on traditional modes of research. For example, the meanings and perceptions of households can be elucidated with the use of biographical or other forms of in-depth interviewing. Structures can be examined through discourse analysis. There has been an upsurge in the use of discourse analysis in the field of housing in recent years (for a review see Hastings, 2000) and it has proved useful in elucidating meaning at the societal level. However, there has been little research on meaning at the level of the individual household and its relationship to wider discourses. Where such research has been undertaken, as for example in the literature on the meaning of home, the primary research technique employed has been the semi-structured interview. In this research tool, households are encouraged to relate 'the story' of their lives, or at least the part of it of interest to the researcher. The semi-structured interview has a long pedigree in social science research and its strengths and weaknesses are well rehearsed. It can be an effective way of entering the assumptive world of subjects and thus capturing the meaning they attach to their situation.

It is a mistake to equate one particular research design, such as the pathways approach, with particular research methods. As Marsh (1982) argues, survey research has not traditionally been good at tapping into subjective meaning as meaning was usually imposed from the outside by the researchers. Nevertheless, this does not mean that subjective meaning cannot be incorporated into survey research. Structured surveys can be designed in a way that allows respondents to project their meaning. Surveys can be useful in allowing the generalisation of data because one of the problems of in-depth qualitative interviews is that it can be difficult to generalise reliably beyond the individual case. However, if qualitative surveys can be effectively linked with more quantitative survey approaches, the level of meaning can be effectively considered and appropriate generalisations made.

A comprehensive way of examining the structural, conscious and unconscious elements of meanings and actions is through the analysis of interactions. These may be of one household with other households living in the neighbourhood or with professionals such as housing officers or building society staff. These interactions could involve different sets of meanings and involve the kind of power games highlighted earlier. The example was given in Chapter One of the interactions between housing officers and tenants (Clapham et al, 2000). These often involved a battle over meanings associated with the category of tenant or the rules of the game that framed interactions. Tenants would put forward their situation as they saw it and the housing officer would interpret this in the light of predetermined categories based on organisational policies and procedures. Implicit in these policies and procedures, and the way they were implemented, were conceptions of appropriate behaviour by 'good' tenants. Behaviour that accorded with this norm was rewarded and inappropriate behaviour punished by, for example, refusing to use discretion to favour the tenant. In these interactions, the housing officer was in a powerful position, with the tenant being a supplicant and not always possessing the knowledge or the skills to be able to challenge the judgement of the housing officer. Such interactions structured the nature of the landlord–tenant relationship.

Implicit in the social construction of the 'good' tenant, that is, the categorical identity of tenant, were wider structures. These included the concept of social exclusion, which defined the nature of poverty and framed the way poor tenants were seen. Conceptions of the appropriate role of council housing as a tenure and its role were also important. Implicit in the actions of some housing officers were also ideas of appropriate lifestyles and behaviour as a neighbour, which had a social class dimension. Housing officers usually came from a different social class from that of the tenants. Therefore, an understanding of a housing pathway is dependent on analysis of the more structural discourses that framed interactions and the meanings held by households and others. In turn these wider structures were partly reproduced through housing interactions. Research needs to be able to understand processes of interaction. This can be done by attempting to reconstruct interactions from interviews with participants or observers. However, a more direct and effective technique is to observe the interaction itself through forms of participant or non-participant observation.

Government housing policy is often important in mediating between wider social structures and household pathways. The analysis of policy should involve both levels of action and discourse: that is, not just the description of policy mechanisms and the way they are implemented, but also the language and meanings of policy documents. The language of policy influences the meanings held by actors and therefore frames interactions.

Research needs to incorporate the important dimension of time. However, most empirical research is cross-sectional in design because of the practical constraints of research funding and administration that tend to militate against long-lasting research projects. As de Vaus (2001) points out, cross-sectional designs are unable to unambiguously establish the time sequence in which events occur. Because of this, they face the problem of identifying causal factors and causal direction. Much housing research is content to examine differences between groups at one point in time. This approach neglects the flows of households between different situations over time. For example, the number of homeless people sleeping rough at one point in time is a fraction of those who sleep rough at some time over a period. An understanding of homelessness needs to embrace the dynamics of this movement into and out of different situations.

The semi-structured interview, which is used in much research attempting to elucidate meaning, is essentially a cross-sectional research tool. However, it can be given a time dimension in a number of ways. One way is to encourage interviewees to talk about their past lives. This biographical interviewing has been criticised because interviewees may tell the stories of their lives by reconstructing their past through a mixture of selective memory and hindsight. Therefore, it is argued that it provides little insight into how they felt at the time as past events, attitudes and perceptions are filtered through the lens of current understanding. The very act of recounting the past in a story gives order to a diverse set of experiences. "Thus a coherent and explanatory narrative is carved out of a set of diverse experiences and a set of past identities are assembled to account for a present identity" (Hockey and James, 2003, p 210).

Hockey and James (2003, pp 85-6) ask important questions of the biographical method:

> ... we might ask to what extent can life histories, enlisted by a researcher for a particular purpose, be regarded as unmediated and unambiguous accounts of the complexities through which social life has taken place in another

geographical setting or epoch? How far does the translation from verbal account to written transform the meaning of a life recalled and what roles do memory and forgetfulness play?

Despite these problems, biographical interviewing can be a useful tool that provides insight into the way that people construct their lives over time (Gearing and Dant, 1990).

A way of avoiding the pitfalls of retrospective interviewing is to interview the same households at different points in time. This can be done in the form of a panel survey whereby the same households are tracked over time. Panel surveys such as the British Social Attitudes Survey or the Child Development Study provide valuable information about change over time. However, in the field of housing they have not been used primarily to elucidate meaning as they have usually been based on structured questionnaire surveys. A panel survey that took the exploration of the meaning of housing as its primary focus, and used semi-structured interviews, would be extremely valuable.

In Chapter One it was argued that generalisation of individual pathways was necessary in order to design national housing policy or to characterise the housing system in comparison with other countries. Generalised pathways could be deduced from empirical study, but as we have seen there is very limited appropriate knowledge at present. Alternatively they could be inductive, that is, constructed as ideal types based on theorising, which could then be used as hypotheses for empirical research. Typologies are of use in categorising households in a way that can be useful for understanding and policy making. Policy making needs typologies if it is to be based on an understanding of the reactions that different kinds of households will have to policy mechanisms. Coolen (2003) argues that data on meaning (what he calls less structured data) can be analysed in the same way as structured data with the use of statistical techniques. The only difference is that the important function of categorisation is undertaken during the data collection, data processing and data analysis phases rather than being undertaken before the collection of data, which is the common approach in much survey research. The challenge is to find ways of categorisation that retain the richness and holism of the original data. In generalising from individual pathways, a number of elements must be retained in any generalisation. The first is the focus on meanings. Although the precise meaning of its housing held by a household will vary because of its own particular situation, some features may be held in common by a number of households. Existing work on the meaning of home has succeeded in achieving the balance between making generalisations and retaining the importance of subjectivity. The second element is the characterisation of households as creative agents acting upon, negotiating and developing their own housing experience through life planning and lifestyle choice.

The third crucial element is the dynamic nature of pathways. The importance of change over time must be retained if the insights generated by the approach are not to be lost. The fourth element is the importance of social practices and the factors that frame them. Particularly important here is what has been called the politics of identity and the resultant categories and their associated discourses, which frame public policy and the expectation and attitudes of households.

Gaps in knowledge

The preceding chapters have highlighted many areas where knowledge of the housing sector is limited. In general there is much more information on the structural discourses and their influence on policy. Examples are the discourses of old age and community care that have influenced housing and public policy towards older people. There has been substantial analysis of the appropriate policies and their links to general, societal discourses. The areas of knowledge that are considerably less developed are the perceptions of households and their reactions to the discourses and the policy mechanisms based on them.

At numerous points in the book it has been argued that there are large gaps in our knowledge of the meaning, attitudes and behaviour of households as well as only rudimentary knowledge of their internal dynamics. How do households reconcile different views of their members on housing issues such as layout and use of the home or moving house? How are societal discourses on gender or age perceived, and how do they influence the social practices of households in the home? Are mobility decisions determined by the employment circumstances of the male adult or are other issues considered to be equally or more important? How and why do households in similar financial situations decide to spend substantially different proportions of their income on housing?

The concern with household dynamics is important because of its role in furthering understanding of their outcome in terms of housing decisions. The relationship between the internal dynamics and the outcome is shown by the above examples of housing expenditure and mobility. It is not sufficient to focus solely on the outcome because this does not allow the understanding of the processes involved, which is necessary for understanding and prediction. For example, the outcome of government policy intended to increase geographical mobility will not be known unless the way that households will perceive and react to it is understood. The outcome of any policy will depend on its interaction with the practices of households.

It was shown in a number of places that many households react positively to the circumstances in which they find themselves. This will not always be the case, as the example of young lone parents shows in Chapter Two. Many felt that their situation was out of their control and so lacked a belief that any action of theirs could improve their lot. However, in the discussion of household's reaction to mortgage arrears in Chapter Four it was shown that some households pursue complex strategies to cope with and improve their circumstances. Households are not passive ciphers of structural forces, whether societal discourses or public policies, but actively construct and react to their situation.

In some areas the meanings that households hold, and their related perceptions and attitudes, have been well explored. For example, there is a large literature on the meaning of home, which was reviewed in Chapter Five. However, this work has a number of limitations. It has mainly been concerned with exploring the range of factors that make up 'home' without reaching judgements about the links between them and their relative weight. There have been one or two attempts to construct typologies of households, as for example in different 'types' of owner-occupiers. However, attitudes towards 'home' have not been linked with other housing dimensions (such as attitudes towards housing expenditure) or with non-housing issues. The links between the meaning of housing and lifestyle and identity are unexplored.

The major task in developing an understanding of housing is to explore the different meaning of housing for households in all of its manifestations. For example, how do attitudes towards home link with decisions on housing expenditure, attitudes towards geographical mobility, attitudes towards and identity with neighbourhood and locality, and work orientation? How do all of these link to lifestyle choice and the identity of households and their individual members? The analysis of existing knowledge in the preceding chapters has revealed evidence that households differ substantially on each of these dimensions. When the dimensions are related, the extent of variation is likely to be substantially greater. The aim is to establish categories or typologies of households that hold similar meanings towards housing and, therefore, can be expected to act in similar ways. An understanding of this action is crucial to the ability to understand and predict the outcomes of public policy.

Research for policy making

It has been argued throughout the book that it is increasingly difficult for the state to act as a central intelligence, defining and meeting need because of the emphasis on individualisation and lifestyle choices. Giddens (1994) argues that current government is built on the idea of a 'cybernetic model' of social life in which society can best be organised by being subordinated to a directive intelligence (the state). Housing has been described as the 'wobbly pillar' of the welfare state as direct state provision has not been a major feature as it has been in, for example, health or education. Nevertheless, the state has made assessments of housing need and has assumed the responsibility to ensure these needs are met. It is doing this increasingly by making land available through the planning system to enable private sector development to take place, as was described in Chapters Three and Five.

The role of assessing and planning to meet need is made more difficult in a number of ways. First, as argued in a number of places in the book, it is difficult to define need in any objective sense. This is seen in attempts to define housing quality or to assess need for community care services for older people where the primacy of political or professional definitions of need is under threat. Second, devolution has meant that the assessment of need is now undertaken at national, regional and local levels. Therefore, there is not a 'centralising intelligence', but a number of different agencies with different functions. Planning has become a matter of reconciling different views. Third, plans depend for their implementation on private sector agencies that cannot be relied on to act as hoped or expected. In other words, need for housing may exist, but private developers may not meet it if to do so does not fit their business objectives. Fourth, the impact of policy depends on the way that it is perceived by households and their reactions to it. As argued in Chapter One, households help constitute the outcomes of policy through their behaviour.

Despite these criticisms, the current, dominant models of the policy-making process are based on the cybernetic model of rational planning that underpins most models of policy planning and policy analysis (for a review, see Hogwood and Gunn, 1984). The essence of rational planning is the adoption of a policy-making process that follows a number of defined steps. The first is analysis of the environment of the decision-making organisation (here, the state) in order to define and quantify problems and needs. The second stage is the identification of goals or objectives in order to meet these needs. Different ways of meeting these objectives are then derived and the most cost-effective ones chosen with the use of techniques such as cost–benefit analysis. The policies are implemented and finally the impact of the policy is assessed with the use of cost-effectiveness techniques such as performance indicators. This is said to be a circular and continuous process, with the results of the impact analysis feeding back into the assessment of need.

This model was first implemented in the private sector and underpinned management thought in the 1960s and growing areas such as marketing. It was introduced into British government in the late 1960s following the lead from the US. Although rational decision-making is rarely talked about today in these terms, it underlies much recent public sector thinking. For example, in Britain the most recent introduction is the concept of Best Value, which has succeeded Compulsory Competitive Tendering for public services. Best Value is based firmly on rational decision making, as Boyne et al (1999) have pointed out. The widespread use of performance indicators in public services also shows the universality of the idea. The current Labour government has adopted rational planning as the cornerstone of its ideas for ensuring the effectiveness of public services. It has also used the idea to underpin a public policy discourse that stresses the end of ideology and the application of good management in designing and delivering services. The emphasis is on 'doing what works' and on basing policy on an examination of the 'facts' through what has been termed 'evidence-based policy'.

There have been many criticisms of the rational decision-making approach. The main criticism that concerns us here is its positivist nature. Which facts are to be examined? Who defines what works? Which or whose evidence shapes policy? The assumption is that social facts exist that can be uncovered through research and that objective analysis can be used to ascertain 'what works best'. The place of values in this scheme is difficult to see. If society is seen as consisting of many people with different attitudes, values and perceptions, then it is difficult to accept this approach. Why is the perception of a policy analyst superior to that of any other person? How does one cope with a situation where perceptions of appropriate objectives and means to achieve them differ?

Rational planning is often contrasted with Lindblom's model of 'muddling through' (Lindblom, 1959). This views decision making as an incremental process that is the outcome of bargaining between concerned groups, each with its own perceptions of 'fact' and its own interests. A good policy is not one that meets any test of cost-effectiveness but rather is one that everyone can agree on. Lindblom's approach is essentially a political view of policy making, although it has been criticised for its acceptance of a pluralist view of a wide dispersion of power. In practice, the outcome of the bargaining process would depend on the distribution of power between the groups.

However, the importance of incorporating perceptions into policy making is a key issue that has been grasped by many politicians. Focus groups are now commonly used to help politicians gauge whether they are in touch with 'public opinion' and what the perceptions of different policies will be. The result has been a discrepancy between a 'perceptually aware' political approach and an 'objective' analytical one, which has led in the past to difficulty in getting politicians to accept a 'rational' approach (see for example Clapham, 1984). A number of authors associated with ideas of collaborative planning have stressed the importance of perceptions in policy making (Fischer and Forester, 1993; Healey, 1997). They accept the socially constructed nature of reality and the consequent inadequacy of the rational approach with its search for 'objective' facts. Healey (1997) argues that planning is about turning the different perceptions and attitudes of social groups into a consensus through discussion. There are a number of problems with this approach. It assumes that consensus is both possible and desirable, and tends to mask issues of differential power. Nevertheless, the approach does recognise the centrality of meaning in policy making.

It was argued earlier that the meaning attached to housing and its relationship to the perceptions and attitudes of households has become important. Any positivist approach to policy making is not going to capture this and is more suited to the cybernetic state outlined earlier. What is needed for the postmodern state is a policy process that is attuned to the importance of subjective perception and to multiple definitions of reality.

Another criticism of the rational approach is that it is a 'top-down' form of policy making. This has led to concern about the difficulty of implementing policy. For example, housing management policies devised by top managers may be ignored or reinterpreted or misunderstood by front-line housing officers in their interactions with tenants. The outcome of housing management policies is determined by this interaction, in which the official organisational policy is only one of many variables involved (see Clapham et al, 2000). Policy-making circles tend to assume that the 'right' policy will always achieve its desired outcome. For example, if the aim is to get more young people into council housing, it is merely necessary to change the allocation scheme to give them more priority. However, the success of this change will depend on how young people interpret the change and react to it. Research has shown that access to council housing is the result of a complex interaction between the housing organisation and the applicant (Clapham and Kintrea, 1986). Different allocation policies may result in the same outcome because of the nature of this interaction. With the growing importance of consumer choice in the delivery of public services, there is a need to understand these interactions in designing policy.

The cybernetic approach to policy can also lead to difficulties in implementation in a situation where responsibility for policy is split between different government agencies operating at different spatial scales. It was argued earlier that responsibility for some aspects of housing policy is being devolved to the regional level, but many aspects are still controlled at the level of the nation state and some are coming within the auspices of the European Union. If the continuing importance of local authorities is added along with the rising importance of private agencies in delivering housing, then it can be seen that the policy-making process is diffuse and involves many agencies, each with its own interests and perspective.

Finally, the pathways approach draws attention to the dynamic nature of people's housing experiences. In times of fast change and increasing risk, households may be continually remaking their lives. One extreme example is the young homeless person who may sleep in a different place every night. Perhaps a more general example is the impact of the accumulated housing experience in the housing pathway on housing outcomes in old age. Particular choices and experiences shape others and can both open new opportunities and close off others.

The pathways approach highlights different ways of evaluating public policy. Following King (1996), housing policy can be seen to operate at two levels. The first is the level of discourse. Policy instruments can serve to support particular discourses that may contain 'world views' delimiting definitions and causes of problems and solutions. These discourses may be of varying power, but they have the potential to influence the attitudes and perceptions of households and other agents in the housing field and perhaps to change behaviour. The second level is that of action. Housing policy can influence behaviour by creating (or changing or destroying) mechanisms that allow (or prevent) households from acting in particular ways.

If the 'right to buy' given to council tenants is taken as an example, this policy reinforced the desirability and superiority of owner-occupation while giving council tenants the opportunity to change tenure. Another policy such as the 'right to manage' given to council tenants to enable them to change their landlord was not taken up by large numbers of tenants, but it reinforced the ideas of choice and tenant participation, and so could be considered successful at the level of discourse. Policies can contain different mixes of discourse and action elements and can be evaluated at both levels.

At the level of action, the pathways approach also raises questions about the appropriate evaluative criteria. Success of a policy could be judged on the basis of the impact it makes on housing outcomes. The pathways approach emphasises the key element of time. At what stage is the outcome to be measured? For example, intervention may enable a homeless person to move from rough sleeping to a hostel. This may be considered a success in the short term, but may only be a transitional stage with the person either moving on to permanent accommodation or perhaps reverting back to living on the streets. Particular outcomes have to be seen in this dynamic way. Changes can be characterised as key junctions in a housing pathway where housing circumstances alter markedly. Policy may be judged on its impact at particular key junctions. The outcomes may be easy to measure and be widely acceptable if they involve changing tenure or perhaps moving from rough sleeping to secure accommodation. A problem arises when one is concerned with changes in housing quality above this basic level, where it is more difficult to define 'objective' and generally agreed measures. The importance of seeing housing as a means to an end rather than an end in itself has been stressed in the pathways approach. The importance of 'lifestyle' was also outlined earlier. How does one evaluate the impact that housing policy mechanisms have on lifestyle? The answer must lie in developing evaluation criteria that are based on the attitudes and perceptions of the individual households concerned.

An alternative way of evaluating policy would be not to focus on housing outcomes but to concentrate on the control that households have in their housing pathway. Giddens (1994) has stressed the increasing capacity that people have to make their own lives, but households clearly differ in their capacity to do this. For example, some homeless young people have to live from hour to hour, not knowing where they are to spend the next night. An important criterion of success for housing policy could be the change in the capacity of households to control their situation and exercise choice, whatever choices they actually make and the resultant housing outcomes.

The role of research in the policy process will vary according to the model adopted. The current vogue for 'evidence-based policy' fits with a rational process in which evaluation research can provide answers as to 'what works'. It is argued here that the policy process has a diverse number of participants all with their own perceptions and attitudes, and the outcomes are difficult to measure and sometimes disputed. In this case 'what works' may not be an uncontested concept. The role of research in this context is to work within the different world views of the participants to describe discourses and to evaluate policy with the use of different sets of subjective criteria. The pathways approach emphasises the centrality of the perceptions and attitudes of households; and much research needs to be geared to understanding these, in particular their interaction with policy mechanisms and discourses. The major challenge is to devise research techniques that can focus on the question of control of a housing pathway and can engage with issues such as people's identity and self-esteem.

Conclusion

The pathways approach places the meanings of a household at the forefront of the analysis of its housing experience, but places this within the structural discourses which frame perceptions and attitudes. It focuses on the interactions between households and other actors in housing that embody both agency and structural dimensions and serve to restructure or to change structural discourses.

In this chapter, the implications of the adoption of the pathways approach for research methods in housing has been outlined. A research focus on interaction has been advocated as a way of conducting holistic research that captures both agency and structural dimensions. The pathways approach promises a fresh look at housing by building on the strengths of the social constructionist tradition of research that has concentrated on issues of meaning by incorporating this work within a coherent and holistic analytical framework. There is clearly much further work to do in elucidating key concepts in this framework and applying them to the study of housing. For example, the concepts of identity and lifestyle have been used loosely here without being precisely defined or related in a rigorous way. These are key concepts if we are to understand the role of housing in furthering personal fulfilment. As well as conceptual development, innovation is needed in techniques of data collection and analysis. In particular, the ability to generalise by constructing useful categorisations from unstructured data is crucial to the successful application of the pathways approach.

This brief review has also drawn attention to the many gaps in our current empirical knowledge of housing that the pathways approach throws into sharp relief. In particular, the lack of understanding of the dynamics of household planning and decision making on key aspects of housing as part of the making of lifestyle choices is an important gap to fill. This task will demand a different approach to housing research, with more emphasis on understanding the interactions that shape the housing experience of households.

A postmodern society restricts the scope of housing policy and demands an alternative approach to policy making. Rather than research designed to produce 'evidence-based policy' or 'Best Value', a form of research needs to be introduced that supports a policy-making process which places the meaning that households hold of their own circumstances at the centre of analysis. Policy should be judged on the basis of the impact that it has on households' pathways. This could be expressed in terms of the achievement of particular housing destinations. However, the importance to self-esteem of the 'project of identity' and the feeling of being in control of one's situation mean that a more valuable evaluative criterion is the degree to which households are in control of their housing pathway.

References

Abbott, P. and Wallace, C. (1992) *The family and the new right*, London: Pluto.

Allan, G. (1985) *Family life*, Oxford: Blackwell.

Allan, G. and Crow, G. (eds) (1989) *Home and family: Creating the domestic sphere*, Basingstoke: Macmillan.

Allan, G. and Crow, G. (1989) 'Introduction', in G. Allan and G. Crow (eds) *Home and family: Creating the domestic sphere*, Basingstoke: Macmillan, pp 1-13.

Allan, G. and Crow, G. (2001) *Families, households and society*, Basingstoke: Palgrave.

Allen, I. (2002) 'The relationship between current policies on long term care and the expectations of older people', in K. Sumner (ed) *Our homes, our lives: Choice in later life living arrangements*, London: Centre for Policy on Ageing, pp 118-29.

Allen, I. and Bourke Dowling, S. (1999) 'Teenage mothers: decisions and outcomes', in S. McRae (ed) *Changing Britain: Families and households in the 1990s*, Oxford: Oxford University Press, pp 334-53.

Altman, I. and Werner, C.M. (eds) (1985) *Home environments: Human behavior and environment*, New York, NY: Plenum Press.

Anderson, I. (1999) 'Social housing or social exclusion', in S. Hutson and D. Clapham (eds) *Homelessness: Public policies and private troubles*, London: Continuum, pp 155-72.

Anderson, I. and Tulloch, D. (2000) *Pathways through homelessness: A review of the research evidence*, Edinburgh: Scottish Homes.

Anderson, M., Bechhofer, F. and Gershuny, J. (1994) 'Introduction', in M. Anderson, F. Bechhofer and J. Gershuny (eds) *The social and political economy of the household*, Oxford: Oxford University Press, pp 1-18.

Anderson, M., Bechhofer, F. and Kendrick, S. (1994) 'Individual and household strategies', in M. Anderson, F. Bechhofer and J. Gershuny (eds) *The social and political economy of the household*, Oxford: Oxford University Press, pp 19-67.

Anyadike-Danes, M., Fothergill, S., Glyn, A., Grieve Smith, J., Kitson, M., Martin, R., Rowthorn, R., Turok, I., Tyler, P. and Webster, D. (2001) *Labour's new regional policy: An assessment*, Seaford: Regional Studies Association.

Appleton, N. (2002) *The needs and aspirations of older people living in general housing. Findings*, York: Joseph Rowntree Foundation.

Archer, M. (2000) *Being human: The problem of agency*, Cambridge: Cambridge University Press.

Arias, E. (1993) 'Introduction', in E. Arias (ed) *The meaning and use of housing*, Aldershot: Avebury, pp 1-25.

Aronson, J. (2002) 'Elderly people's account of home care rationing: missing voices in long-term care policy debates', *Ageing and Society*, vol 22, pp 399-418.

Atkinson, R. and Kintrea, K. (1998) *Reconnecting excluded communities: The neighbourhood impacts of owner occupation*, Edinburgh: Scottish Homes.

Atkinson, R. and Kintrea, K. (2002) 'Area effects: what do they mean for British housing and regeneration policy?', *European Journal of Housing Policy*, vol 2, no 2, pp 147-66.

Audit Commission (2003) *Local authority housing rent income: Rent collection and arrears management by local authorities in England and Wales*, London: Audit Commission.

Ball, D. (1974) 'The family as a sociological problem', in A. Skolnick and J. Skolnick (eds) *Intimacy, family and society*, Boston, MA: Little, Brown, pp 25-40.

Ball, M. (1983) *Housing policy and economic power: The political economy of home ownership*, London: Methuen.

Bannister, J., Dell, M., Donnison, D., Fitzpatrick, S. and Taylor, R. (1993) *Homeless young people in Scotland: The role of social work services*, Edinburgh: HMSO.

Barker, K. (2003) *Review of housing supply*, London: The Stationery Office.

Bauman, Z. (1992) *Intimations of post modernity*, London: Routledge.

Beck, U. (1992) *Risk society: Towards a new modernity*, London: Sage Publications.

Beck, U. (2000) *The brave new world of work*, Cambridge: Polity Press.

Beck-Gernsheim, E. (2002) *Reinventing the family*, London: Routledge.

Bengtsson, B. (2002) 'Promising but not post modern. A comment on David Clapham's concept of housing pathways', *Housing, Theory and Society*, vol 19, no 2, pp 69-70.

Berger, P. and Luckmann, T. (1967) *The social construction of reality*, Harmondsworth: Penguin Press.

Bernard, M. and Phillips, J. (2000) 'The challenge of ageing in tomorrow's Britain', *Ageing and Society*, vol 20, no 1, pp 33-54.

Berrington, A. and Murphy, M. (1994) 'Changes in the living arrangements of young adults in Britain during the 1980s', *European Sociological Review*, vol 10, no 3, pp 235-57.

Berthoud, R. (1997) 'Income and standards of living', in T. Modood and R. Berthoud with J. Lakey, J. Nazroo, P. Smith, S. Virdee and S. Beishon, *Ethnic minorities in Britain: Diversity and disadvantage*, London: Policy Studies Institute, pp 150-83.

Berthoud, R., McKay, S. and Rowlingson, K. (1999) 'Becoming a single mother', in S. McRae (ed) *Changing Britain: Families and households in the 1990s*, Oxford: Oxford University Press, pp 354-74.

Biddulph, M. (2001) *Home Zones: A planning and design handbook*, Bristol/York: The Policy Press/Joseph Rowntree Foundation.

Bines, W., Kemp, P., Pleace, N. and Radley, C. (1993) *Managing social housing*, London: HMSO.

Boddy, M. (1980) *The building societies*, Basingstoke: Macmillan.

Bohl, C. (2000) 'New urbanism and the city: potential applications and implications for distressed inner-city neighbourhoods', *Housing Policy Debate*, vol 11, no 4, pp 761-802.

Bornat, J., Dimmock, B., Jones, D. and Peace, S. (1999) 'The impact of family change on older people: the case of stepfamilies', in S. McRae (ed) *Changing Britain: Families and households in the 1990s*, Oxford: Oxford University Press, pp 248-62.

Bourdieu, P. (1984) *Distinction: A social critique of the judgement of taste*, London: Routledge and Kegan Paul.

Bovaird, E., Harloe, M. and Whitehead, C. (1985) 'Private rented housing: its current role', *Journal of Social Policy*, vol 14, no 1, pp 1-23.

Boyne, G., Gould-Williams, G., Law, J. and Walker, R. (1999) 'Best value in Welsh local government: progress and prospects', *Local Government Studies*, vol 7, pp 299-308.

Bradshaw, J. and Millar, J. (1991) *Lone parent families in the UK*, London: HMSO.

Bramley, G. and Pawson, H. (2002) 'Low demand for housing: extent, incidence and national policy implications', *Urban Studies*, vol 39, no 3, pp 393-422.

Breugel, I. (1996) 'The trailing wife: a declining breed?', in R. Crompton, D. Gallie and K. Purcell (eds) *Changing forms of employment*, London: Routledge, pp 235-58.

Brindley, T. (1999) 'The modern house in England: an architecture of exclusion', in T. Chapman and J. Hockey (eds) *Ideal homes? Social change and domestic life*, London: Routledge, pp 30-43.

Bristow, G., Munday, M. and Gripaios, P. (2000) 'Call centre growth and location: corporate strategy and the spatial division of labour', *Environment and Planning A*, vol 32, no 3, pp 519-38.

Buck, J. and Ermisch, J. (1995) 'Cohabitation in Britain', *Changing Britain*, vol 3, pp 3-5.

Bulmer, M. (1987) *The social basis of community care*, London: Allen and Unwin.

Bulos, M. and Chaker, W. (1995) 'Sustaining a sense of home and personal identity', in D. Benjamin and D. Stea (eds) *The home: Words, interpretations, meanings and environments*, Aldershot: Avebury, pp 227-42.

Burnett, J. (1986) *A social history of housing 1815-1985* (2nd edn), London: Methuen.

Burrows, R. and Nettleton, S. (2000) 'What role for housing studies in the new paradigm for welfare research? A case study of families experiencing mortgage possession', Paper given to the Housing Studies Association Conference, University of York, April.

Burrows, R. and Rhodes, D. (1998) *Unpopular places? Area disadvantage and the geography of misery*, Bristol: The Policy Press.

Butler, T. and Robson, G. (2001) 'Social capital, gentrification and neighbourhood change in London: a comparison of three south London neighbourhoods', *Urban Studies*, vol 38, no 12, pp 2145-62.

Byrne, D., Harrison, S., Keithley, J. and McCarthy, P. (1986) *Housing and health*, Aldershot: Gower.

Cairncross, L., Clapham, D. and Goodlad, R. (1997) *Housing management, consumers and citizens*, London: Routledge.

Campbell, B. (1993) *Goliath: Britain's dangerous places*, London: Methuen.

Carmona, M., Carmona, S. and Gallent, N. (2003) *Delivering new homes*, London: Routledge.

Centre for Housing Research (1989) *The nature and effectiveness of housing management in England*, London: HMSO.

Champion, A. (1999) 'Migration and British cities in the 1990s', *National Institute Economic Review*, 4/99, pp 60-77.

Chaney, D. (1996) *Lifestyles*, London: Routledge.

Chapman, T. (1999a) 'Stage sets for ideal lives: images of home in contemporary show homes', in T. Chapman and J. Hockey (eds) *Ideal homes? Social change and domestic life*, London: Routledge, pp 44-58.

Chapman, T. (1999b) 'Spoiled identities: the experience of burglary', in T. Chapman and J. Hockey (eds) *Ideal homes? Social change and domestic life*, London: Routledge, pp 133-46.

Chartered Institute of Housing (1998) *Unlocking the future: Tackling social exclusion*, Edinburgh: Chartered Institute of Housing in Scotland.

Cheshire, P., Monastiriotis, V. and Sheppard, S. (2003) 'Income inequality and residential segregation', in R. Martin and P. Morrison (eds) *Geographies of labour market inequality*, London: Routledge, pp 83-109.

Cicourel, A. (1981) 'Notes on the integration of micro and macro levels of analysis', in K. Knorr-Cetina and A. Cicourel (eds) *Advances in social theory and methodology: Towards an integration of micro and macro sociologies*, London: Routledge, pp 51-81.

Clapham, D. (1984) 'Rational planning and politics: the example of local authority corporate planning', *Policy & Politics*, vol 12, no 1, pp 31-52.

Clapham, D. (1996) 'Housing and the economy: broadening comparative housing research', *Urban Studies*, vol 33, pp 631-47.

Clapham, D. (1999) 'Conclusions', in S. Hutson and D. Clapham (eds) *Homelessness: Public policies and private troubles*, London: Routledge, pp 226-34.

Clapham, D. and Kintrea, K. (1986) 'Rationing, choice and constraint: the allocation of public housing in Glasgow', *Journal of Social Policy*, vol 15, no 1, pp 51-67.

Clapham, D. and Kintrea, K. (1995) 'Housing cooperatives and community', in A. Heskin and J. Leavitt (eds) *The hidden history of housing cooperatives*, Los Angeles, CA: University of California, pp 261-80.

Clapham, D. and Munro, M. (1990) 'Ambiguities and contradiction in the provision of sheltered housing for older people', *Journal of Social Policy*, vol 19, no 1, pp 27-45.

Clapham, D. and Smith, S. (1990) 'Housing policy and special needs', *Policy & Politics*, vol 18, no 3, pp 193-206.

Clapham, D., Franklin, B. and Saugeres, L. (2000) 'Housing management: the social construction of an occupational role', *Housing, Theory and Society*, vol 17, no 2, pp 68-82.

Clapham, D., Kintrea, K. and McAdam, G. (1993) 'Individual self-provision and the Scottish housing system', *Urban Studies*, vol 30, no 8, pp 1355-69.

Clapham, D., Means, R. and Munro, M. (1993) 'Housing, the life course and older people', in S. Arber and M. Evandrou (eds) *Ageing, independence and the life course*, London: Jessica Kingsley, pp 132-48.

Clapham, D., Walker, R., Meen, G. and Wilcox, S. (1995) *Building homes building jobs*, London: National Housing Forum.

Clark, H., Gough, H. and Macfarlane, A. (2004) *'It pays dividends': Direct payments and older people*, Bristol: The Policy Press.

Clark, W. and Dieleman, F. (1996) *Households and housing: Choice and outcomes in the housing market*, New Jersey, NJ: Rutgers.

Clegg, S. (1989) *Frameworks of power*, London: Sage Publications.

Cole, I. and Furbey, C. (1994) *The eclipse of council housing*, London: Routledge.

Coleman, A. (1985) *Utopia on trial: Vision and reality in planned housing*, London: Hilary Shipman.

Coleman, P. (1990) 'Adjustment in later life', in J. Bond and P. Coleman (eds) *Ageing in society: An introduction to social gerontology*, London: Sage Publications, pp 89-122.

Coles, B. (1995) *Youth and social policy: Youth citizenship and young careers*, London: UCL Press.

Commission on Social Justice (1994) *Social justice: Strategies for national renewal*, London: Vintage.

Coolen, H. (2003) 'The measurement and analysis of less structured data', Paper to the international conference on Methodologies in Housing Research, Stockholm, Sweden, 22-24 September.

Craib, I. (1992) *Anthony Giddens*, London: Routledge.

Craib, I. (1998) *Experiencing identity*, London: Sage Publications.

Craik, J. (1989) 'The making of mother: the role of the kitchen in the home', in G. Allan and G. Crow (eds) *Home and family*, Basingstoke: Macmillan, pp 48-65.

Croft, J. (2004) 'Transitions from the ephemeral: curtailing exclusionary reverberations within risk-imbued housing careers', Paper given to the ENHR Conference, Cambridge, July.

Crook, A. (1992) 'Private rented housing and the impact of deregulation', in J. Birchall (ed) *Housing policy in the 1990s*, London: Routledge, pp 91-112.

Crook, A. and Kemp, P. (1996) 'The revival of private rented housing in Britain', *Housing Studies*, vol 11, no 1, pp 51-68.

Crook, A. and Kemp, P. (2002) 'Housing Investment Trust: a new structure of rental housing provision', *Housing Studies*, vol 17, no 5, pp 741-54.

Crow, G. (1989) 'The use of the concept of strategy in recent sociological literature', *Sociology*, vol 23, no 1, pp 1-24.

Csikszentmihalyi, M. and Rochberg-Halton, E. (1981) *The meaning of things: Domestic symbols and the self*, Cambridge: Cambridge University Press.

Cumming, E. and Henry, W. (1961) *Growing old*, New York, NY: Basic Books.

Dalley, G. (2002) 'Independence and autonomy – the twin peaks of ideology', in K. Sumner (ed) *Our homes, our lives: Choice in later life living arrangements*, London: Centre for Policy on Ageing, pp 10-25.

Dallos, R. (1997) 'Constructing family life: family belief systems', in J. Muncie, M. Wetherell, M. Langan, R. Dallos and A. Cochrane (eds) *Understanding the family* (2nd edn), London: Sage Publications, pp 173-212.

Dallos, R. and Sapsford, R. (1997) 'Patterns of diversity and lived realities', in J. Muncie, M. Wetherell, M. Langan, R. Dallos and A. Cochrane (eds) *Understanding the family* (2nd edn), London: Sage Publications, pp 125-70.

Dean, J. and Hastings, A. (2000) *Challenging images: Housing estates, stigma and regeneration*, Bristol: The Policy Press.

Denby, E. (1941) 'Plan the home', *Picture Post*, 4 January, pp 21-3.

Dench, G., Ogg, J. and Thomson, K. (1999) 'The role of grandparents', in National Centre for Social Research, *British Social Attitudes Survey – the 16th Report*, Aldershot: Ashgate, pp 135-56.

Dennis, N. and Erdos, G. (1993) *Families without fatherhood*, London: Institute of Economic Affairs.

DETR (Department of the Environment, Transport and the Regions) (1999) *Projections of households in England to 2021*, London: The Stationery Office.

DETR (2000) *Housing quality indicators: Live piloting* (Housing Research summary number 131), London: DETR.

DETR (2001) *Supporting People: Policy into practice*, London: DETR.

DETR/DH (Department of Health) (2001) *Quality and choice for older people's housing: A strategy framework*, London: The Stationery Office.

DH (1998) *Modernising social services: Promoting independence, improving protection, raising standards*, London: The Stationery Office.

DH (2000) *The NHS plan: A plan for investment, a plan for reform*, London: The Stationery Office.

DTI (Department of Trade and Industry) (2001) *Opportunity for all in a world of change* (www.dti.gov.uk/opportunityforall).

de Vaus, D. (2001) *Research designs in social research*, London: Sage Publications.

Diamond, D. and Lea, M. (1992) 'Housing finance in developed countries: an international comparison of efficiency', *Journal of Housing Research*, vol 3, pp 115-44.

Dickens, P., Duncan, S., Goodwin, M. and Gray, F. (1985) *Housing, states and localities*, London: Methuen.

Dobash, R. and Dobash, R. (1979) *Violence against wives*, Wells: Open Books.

Doogan, K. (1996) 'Labour mobility and the changing housing market', *Urban Studies*, vol 33, no 2, pp 199-221.

Dorling, D. and Cornford, J. (1995) 'Who has negative equity? How house price falls in Britain have hit different groups of home buyers', *Housing Studies*, vol 10, no 2, pp 151-78.

Dovey, K. (1985) 'Home and homelessness', in I. Altman and C. Werner (eds), *Home environments*, New York, NY: Plenum Press, pp 33-64.

Dunleavy, P. (1981) *The politics of mass housing in Britain 1945-1975*, Oxford: Clarendon Press.

Edgell, S. (1980) *Middle class couples*, London: Allen and Unwin.

Esping-Andersen, G. (1990) *The three worlds of welfare capitalism*, Cambridge: Polity Press.

Etzioni, A. (1995) *The spirit of community*, London: Harper Collins.

Evans, A. (1999) 'Rationing device or passport to social housing? The operation of the homelessness legislation in Britain in the 1990s', in S. Hutson and D. Clapham (eds) *Homelessness: Public policies and private troubles*, London: Continuum, pp 133-54.

Featherstone, M. and Hepworth, M. (1990) 'Images of ageing', in J. Bond and P. Coleman (eds) *Ageing in society: An introduction to social gerontology*, London: Sage Publications, pp 250-75.

Felstead, A., Burchell, B. and Green, F. (1998) 'Insecurity at work: is job insecurity really much worse now than before?', *New Economy*, pp 180-4.

Finch, J. (1989) *Family obligations and social change*, Cambridge: Polity Press.

Fischer, F. and Forester, J. (eds) (1993) *The argumentative turn in policy analysis and planning*, London: UCL Press.

Fitzpatrick, S. (1999) *Young homeless people*, Basingstoke: Macmillan.

Fitzpatrick, S. and Clapham, D. (1999) 'Homelessness and young people', in S. Hutson and D. Clapham (eds) *Homelessness: Public policies and private troubles*, London: Continuum, pp 173-90.

Flowerdew, R., Al-Hamad, A. and Hayes, L. (1999) 'The residential mobility of divorced people', in S. McRae (ed) *Changing Britain: Families and households in the 1990s*, Oxford: Oxford University Press, pp 427-40.

Fog Olwig, K. (1999) 'Travelling makes a home: mobility and identity among West Indians', in T. Chapman and J. Hockey (eds) *Ideal homes? Social change and domestic life,* London: Routledge, pp 73-83.

Ford, J. (1999) 'Young adults and owner occupation: a changing goal?', in J. Rugg (ed) *Young people, housing and social policy*, London: Routledge, pp 17-34.

Ford, J. and Burrows, R. (1999) 'To buy or not to buy? A home of one's own', in National Centre for Social Research, *British Social Attitudes Survey - 16th Report*, Aldershot: Ashgate, pp 97-112.

Ford, J., Kempson, E. and England, J. (1996) *Housing costs, housing benefits and work disincentives*, York: Joseph Rowntree Foundation.

Ford, J., Rugg, J. and Burrows, R. (2002) 'Conceptualising the contemporary role of housing in the transition to adult life in England', *Urban Studies*, vol 39, no 13, pp 2455-67.

Forrest, R. (2000) 'What constitutes a balanced community', in I. Anderson and D. Sim (eds) *Social exclusion and housing: Context and challenges*, Coventry: Chartered Institute of Housing, pp 207-19.

Forrest, R. and Kearns, A. (2001) 'Social cohesion, social capital and the neighbourhood', *Urban Studies*, vol 38, no 12, pp 2125-43.

Forrest, R. and Kemeny, J. (1984) 'Careers and coping strategies: micro and macro aspects of the trend towards owner occupation', University of Bristol: mimeo.

Forrest, R., Kennett, P. and Leather, P. (1999) *Home ownership in crisis*, Aldershot: Ashgate.

Forrest, R., Kennett, P., Leather, P. with Gordon, G. (1994) *Home owners in negative equity*, Bristol: SAUS Publications.

Forrest, R. and Murie, A. (1987) 'The affluent home owner: labour market position and the shaping of housing histories', in N. Thrift and P. Williams (eds) *Class and space*, London: Routledge and Kegan Paul, pp 330-59.

Forrest, R. and Murie, A. (1995) *Housing and family wealth*, London: Routledge.

Forrest, R., Murie, A. and Williams, P. (1991) *Home ownership: Differentiation and fragmentation*, London: Unwin Hyman.

Fothergill, S. (2001) 'The true scale of the regional problem in the UK', *Regional Studies*, vol 35, no 3, pp 241-6.

Furlong, A. and Cartmel, C. (1997) *Young people and social change: Individualization and risk in late modernity*, Philadelphia: Open University Press.

Garfinkel, H. (1967) *Studies in ethnomethodology*, Englewood Cliffs, NJ: Prentice Hall.

Gauldie, E. (1974) *Cruel habitations: A history of working-class housing 1780-1918*, London: George, Allen and Unwin.

Gearing, B. and Dant, T. (1990) 'Doing biographical research', in S. Peace (ed) *Researching social gerontology: Concepts, methods and issues*, London: Sage Publications, pp 143-59.

Gergen, K. (1999) *An invitation to social construction*, London: Sage Publications.

Gibb, K., Munro, M. and Satsangi, M. (1999) *Housing finance in the UK: An introduction* (2nd edn), Basingstoke: Macmillan.

Giddens, A. (1984) *The constitution of society*, Cambridge: Polity Press.

Giddens, A. (1990) *The consequences of modernity*, Cambridge: Polity Press.

Giddens, A. (1991) *Modernity and self identity: Self and society in the late modern age*, Cambridge: Polity Press.

Giddens, A. (1994) *Beyond left and right*, Cambridge: Polity Press.

Giddens, A. (1998) *The third way*, Cambridge: Polity Press.

Gilleard, C. (1996) 'Consumption and identity in later life: toward a cultural gerontology', *Ageing and Society*, vol 16, no 1, pp 27-55.

Gilleard, C. and Higgs, P. (2000) *Cultures of ageing: Self, citizen and the body*, Harlow: Prentice Hall.

Goffman, E. (1971) *The presentation of self in everyday life*, Harmondsworth: Pelican.

Goldsack, L. (1999) 'A haven in a heartless world? Women and domestic violence', in T. Chapman and J. Hockey (eds) *Ideal homes? Social change and domestic life*, London: Routledge, pp 121-32.

Goldthorpe, D., Lockwood, D., Bechhofer, F. and Platt, J. (1969) *The affluent worker in the class structure*, Cambridge: Cambridge University Press.

Goodchild, B. (1997) *Housing and the urban environment*, Oxford: Blackwell.

Gordon, I. (2003) 'Unemployment and spatial labour markets: strong adjustment and persistent concentration', in R. Martin and P. Morrison (eds) *Geographies of labour market inequality*, London: Routledge, pp 55-82.

Gorrell Barnes, G., Thompson, P., Daniel, G. and Burchardt, N. (1998) *Growing up in step-families*, Oxford: Oxford University Press.

Goulborne, H. (1999) 'The transnational character of Caribbean kinship in Britain', in S. McRae (ed) *Changing Britain: Families and households in the 1990s*, Oxford: Oxford University Press, pp 176-98.

Gower Davies, J. (1972) *The evangelistic bureaucrat*, London: Tavistock.

Granovetter, M. (1973) 'The strength of weak ties', *American Journal of Sociology*, vol 78, pp 1360-80.

Gripaios, P. (2002) 'The failure of regeneration policy in Britain', *Regional Studies*, vol 36, pp 568-77.

Guest, A. and Wierzbicki, S. (1999) 'Social ties at the neighbourhood level: two decades of GSS evidence', *Urban Affairs Review*, vol 35, pp 92-111.

Gurney, C. (1996) 'Meanings of home and home ownership: myths histories and experiences', Unpublished PhD thesis, University of Bristol.

Gurney, C. (1999) 'Pride and prejudice: discourses of normalisation in public and private accounts of home ownership', *Housing Studies*, vol 14, no 2, pp 163-83.

Gurney, C. and Means, R. (1993) 'The meaning of home in later life', in S. Arber and M. Evandrou (eds) *Ageing independence and the life course*, London: Jessica Kingsley, pp 119-31.

Hagerstrand, T. (1976) *Innovation as a spatial process*, Chicago, IL: University of Chicago Press.

Hall, R., Ogden, P. and Hill, C. (1999) 'Living alone: evidence from England and Wales and France for the last two decades', in S. McRae (ed) *Changing Britain: Families and households in the 1990s*, Oxford: Oxford University Press, pp 265-96.

Hall, S. (1996) 'Who needs identity?', in S. Hall and P. du Gay (eds) *Questions of cultural identity*, London: Sage Publications, pp 1-17.

Hardey, M. (1989) 'Lone parents and the home', in G. Allan and G. Crow (eds) *Home and family: Creating the domestic sphere*, Basingstoke: Macmillan, pp 122-40.

Harriott, S. and Mattthews, L. (1998) *Social housing: An introduction*, Harlow: Longman.

Harrison, M. (with C. Davis) (2001) *Housing, social policy and difference*. Bristol: The Policy Press.

Haskey, J. (1996) 'Population review (6) Families and households in Great Britain', *Population Trends*, vol 85, pp 7-24.

Hastings, A. (2000) 'Discourse analysis: what does it offer housing studies?', *Housing, Theory and Society*, vol 17, no 3, pp 131-8.

Haugaard, M. (1992) *Structures, restructuration and social power*, Aldershot: Avebury.

Healey, P. (1997) *Collaborative planning: Shaping places in fragmented societies*, London: Macmillan.

Heath, S. (1999) 'Young adults and household formation in the 1990s', *British Journal of Sociology of Education*, vol 20, no 4, pp 545-61.

Heath, S. and Miret, P. (1996) *Living in and out of the parental home in Spain and Great Britain: A comparative approach*, Cambridge Group for the History of Population and Social Structure, Working Paper Series no 2, Cambridge: Cambridge Group.

Henning, C. and Lieberg, M. (1996) 'Strong ties or weak ties? Neighbourhood networks in a new perspective', *Scandinavian Housing and Planning Research*, vol 13, pp 3-26.

Henwood, M. (1986) 'Community care: policy, practice and prognosis', in *Yearbook of Social Policy 1985/6*, London: Routledge and Kegan Paul, pp 147-69.

Hepworth, M. (1999) 'Privacy, security and respectability: the ideal Victorian home', in T. Chapman and J. Hockey (eds) *Ideal homes? Social change and domestic life*, London: Routledge, pp 17-29.

Heywood, F., Means, R. and Oldman, C. (2002) *Housing and home in later life*, Buckingham: Open University Press.

Heywood, F. and Naz, M. (1990) *Clearance: The view from the street*, Birmingham: Community Forum.

Higgins, J. (1989) 'Home and institutions', in G. Allan and G. Crow (eds) *Home and family: Creating the domestic sphere*, Basingstoke: Macmillan, pp 159-73.

Hillier, W., Burdett, R., Peponis, J. and Penn, A. (1987) 'Creating life: or does architecture create anything?', *Architecture and Behaviour*, vol 3, no 3, pp 233-50.

Hills, J. (1991) *Unravelling housing finance: Subsidies, benefits and taxation*, Oxford: Oxford University Press.

Hills, J. (1993) *The future of welfare: A guide to the debate*, York: Joseph Rowntree Foundation.

Hills, J. (1998) *Income and wealth: The latest evidence*, York: Joseph Rowntree Foundation.

Hills, J. (2001) 'Inclusion or exclusion? The role of housing subsidies and benefits', *Urban Studies*, vol 38, no 11, pp 1887-902.

Hinds, K. and Jarvis, L. (2000) 'The gender gap', in National Centre for Social Research, *British Social Attitudes Survey – The 17th Report*, London: Sage Publications, pp 101-18.

Hochschild, A. (1997) *The time bind: When work becomes home and home becomes work*, New York, NY: Metropolitan Books.

Hockey, J. and James, A. (2003) *Social identities across the lifecourse*, Basingstoke: Palgrave Macmillan.

Hogwood, B. and Gunn, L. (1984) *Policy analysis for the real world*, Oxford: Blackwell.

Holme, A. (1985) *Housing and young families in East London*, London: Routledge and Kegan Paul.

Holtermann, S. (1975) 'Areas of urban deprivation in Great Britain: an analysis of 1971 census data', *Social Trends*, vol 6, pp 37-47.

Horrell, S., Rubery, J. and Burchell, B. (1994) 'Working time patterns, constraints and preferences', in M. Anderson, F. Bechhofer and J. Gershuny (eds) *The social and political economy of the household*, Oxford: Oxford University Press, pp 100-32.

Hughes, G. and McCormick, B. (1990) 'Housing and labour market mobility', in J. Ermisch (ed) *Housing and the national economy*, Aldershot: Avebury, pp 94-108.

Hunt, P. (1989) 'Gender and the construction of home life', in G. Allan and G. Crow (eds) *Home and family: Creating the domestic sphere*, Basingstoke: Macmillan, pp 66-81.

Hutson, S. (1999) 'The experience of "homeless" accommodation and support', in S. Hutson and D. Clapham (eds) *Homelessness: Public policies and private troubles*, London: Cassell, pp 208-25.

Hutson, S. and Jenkins, R. (1989) *Taking the strain: Families, unemployment and the transition to adulthood*, Buckingham: Open University Press.

Jacobs, J. (1965) *The death and life of great American cities: The failure of town planning*, Harmondsworth: Penguin.

Jacobs, K. and Manzi, A. (2000) 'Evaluating the social constructionist paradigm in housing research', *Housing, Theory and Society*, vol 17, no 1, pp 35-42.

Jacobs, K., Kemeny, J. and Manzi, A. (1999) 'The struggle to define homelessness: a social constructionist approach', in S. Hutson and D. Clapham (eds) *Homelessness: Public policies and private troubles*, London: Cassell, pp 11-28.

Jacobs, K., Kemeny, J. and Manzi, A. (eds) (2004) *Social constructionism in housing research*, Aldershot: Ashgate.

Jarvis, S. and Jenkins, S. (1998) 'Income and poverty dynamics in Great Britain', in L. Leisering and R. Walker (eds) *The dynamics of modern society: Poverty, policy and welfare*, Bristol: The Policy Press, pp 145-60.

Jenkins, R. (1996) *Social identity*, London: Routledge.

Jephcott, P. (1971) *Homes in high flats*, Edinburgh: Oliver and Boyd.

Jones, G. (1995) *Leaving home*, Buckingham: Open University Press.

Jorgensen, N. (1995) *Investigating families and households*, London: Harper Collins.

Jupp, B. (1999) *Living together: Community life on mixed tenure estates*, London: Demos.

Keenan, P., Lowe, S. and Spencer, S. (1999) 'Housing abandonment in inner cities - the politics of low demand for housing', *Housing Studies*, vol 14, no 5, pp 703-16.

Kellaher, L. (2002) 'Is genuine choice a reality?', in K. Sumner (ed) *Our homes, our lives: Choice in later life living arrangements*, London: Centre for Policy on Ageing, pp 36-58.

Kemeny, J. (1992) *Housing and social theory*, London: Routledge.

Kemp, P. (1993) 'Rebuilding the private rented sector?', in P. Malpass and R. Means (eds) *Implementing housing policy*, Buckingham: Open University Press, pp 59-73.

Kemp, P. (1998) *Housing benefit: Time for reform*, York: Joseph Rowntree Foundation.

Kemp, P. (2000) 'Images of council housing', in National Centre for Social Research, *British Social Attitudes Survey – The 17th Report*, London: Sage Publications, pp 137-54.

Kempson, E. (1993) *Household budgets and housing costs*, London: Policy Studies Institute.

Kenyon, L. (1999) 'A home from home: students' transitional experience of home', in T. Chapman and J. Hockey (eds) *Ideal homes? Social change and domestic life*, London: Routledge, pp 84-95.

Kenyon, E. and Heath, S. (2001) 'Choosing this life: narratives of choice amongst house sharers', *Housing Studies*, vol 16, no 5, pp 619-36.

King, P. (1996) *The limits of housing policy: A philosophical investigation*, London: Middlesex University Press.

King, P. (2002) 'Who needs postmodernism?', *Housing, Theory and Society*, vol 19, pp 76-8.

Kintrea, K. and Scott, S. (1992) *Tenants rent arrears – A problem? Tenants' attitudes*, Edinburgh: Accounts Commission.

Knight, D. (2002) 'The biographical narratives and meanings of home of private tenants', Unpublished PhD thesis, University of Wales.

Lang, J. (1993) 'Methodological issues and approaches: a critical analysis', in E. Arias (ed) *The meaning and use of housing*, Aldershot: Avebury, pp 51-72.

Laslett, P. (1989) *A fresh map of life*, London: Weidenfield and Nicholson.

La Valle, I., Arthur, S., Millward, C., Scott, S. with Clayden, M. (2002) *Happy families? Atypical work and its influence on family life*, Bristol: The Policy Press.

Lawless, P. (1989) *Britain's inner cities*, London: Paul Chapman.

Leather, P. (2000) *Crumbling castles: Helping owners to repair and maintain their homes*, York: Joseph Rowntree Foundation.

Leather, P., Littlewood, A. and Munro, M. (1999) *Make do and mend: Homeowner's attitudes to repair and maintenance*, Bristol: The Policy Press.

Leather, P. and Mackintosh, S. (1997) 'Towards sustainable policies for housing renewal in the private sector', in P. Williams (ed) *Directions in housing policy: Towards sustainable housing policies for the UK*, London: Paul Chapman, pp 138-55.

Le Corbusier (1960) *My work*, London: Architectural Press.

Lee, P. and Murie, A. (1999) 'Spatial and social divisions within British cities: beyond residualisation', *Housing Studies*, vol 14, no 5, pp 625-40.

Le Grand, J. (1982) *The strategy of equality*, London: George Allen and Unwin.

Leisering, L. and Walker, R. (eds) (1998) *The dynamics of modern society: Poverty, policy and welfare*, Bristol: The Policy Press.

Lewis, O. (1966) *La Vida: A Puerto Rican family in the culture of poverty*, York: Random House.

Lindblom, C. (1959) 'The science of muddling through', *Public Administration Review*, vol 19, pp 79-88.

London Research Centre (1994) *Houses in multiple occupation in London*, London: London Planning Advisory Committee.

Lowry, S. (1991) *Housing and health*, London: British Medical Journal.

Macintyre, S., Kearns, A., Ellaway, A. and Hiscock, R. (2000) *The Thaw Report*, Glasgow: University of Glasgow.

MacIver, R. and Page, C. (1961) *Society: An introductory analysis*, London: Macmillan.

MacKay, R. (2003) 'Twenty-five years of regional development', *Regional Studies*, vol 37, no 3, pp 303-17.

Maclennan, D. (1994) *A competitive UK economy: The challenges for housing policy*, York: Joseph Rowntree Foundation.

Madigan, R. and Munro, M. (1999) 'The more we are together: domestic space, gender and privacy', in T. Chapman and J. Hockey (eds) *Ideal homes? Social change and domestic life*, London: Routledge, pp 61-72.

Marsh, A., Gordon, D., Pantazis, C. and Heslop, P. (1999) *Home sweet home: The impact of poor housing on health*, Bristol: The Policy Press.

Marsh, C. (1982) *The survey method: The contribution of surveys to sociological explanation*, London: George Allen and Unwin.

Marshall, T. (1950) *Citizenship and social class*, Cambridge: Cambridge University Press.

Mason, J. (1989) 'Reconstructing the public and the private: the home and marriage in later life', in G. Allan and G. Crow (eds) *Home and family: Creating the domestic sphere*, Basingstoke: Macmillan, pp 102-21.

Mason, J. (1999) 'Living away from relatives: kinship and geographical reasoning', in S. McRae (ed) *Changing Britain: Families and households in the 1990s*, Oxford: Oxford University Press, pp 156-75.

McCrone, D. (1994) 'Getting by and making out in Kirkcaldy', in M. Anderson, F. Bechhofer and J. Gershuny (eds) *The social and political economy of the household*, Oxford: Oxford University Press, pp 68-99.

McGlone, F., Park, A. and Roberts, C. (1999) 'Kinship and friendship: attitudes and behaviour in Britain, 1986-1995', in S. McRae (ed) *Changing Britain: Families and households in the 1990s*, Oxford: Oxford University Press, pp 141-55.

McGregor, A., Munro, M., Healey, M. and Symon, P. (1992) 'Moving job, moving house: the impact of housing on long distance labour mobility', Discussion Paper No 38, Glasgow: Centre for Housing Research, University of Glasgow.

McLaughlin, E., Millar, J. and Cooke, K. (1989) *Work and welfare benefits*, Andover: Avebury.

McRae, S. (1999) 'Introduction: family and household change in Britain', in S. McRae (ed) *Changing Britain: Families and households in the 1990s*, Oxford: Oxford University Press, pp 1-34.

Means, R. and Smith, R. (1988) *Community care: Policy and practice* (2nd edn), London: Macmillan.

Meen, G. (1995) 'Is housing good for the economy?', *Housing Studies*, vol 10, pp 405-24.

Morgan, P. (1998) 'An endangered species', in M. David (ed) *The fragmenting family: Does it matter?*, London: Institute for Economic Affairs, pp 68-99.

Mount, F. (1982) *The subversive family*, London: Cape.

Muncie, J. and Sapsford, R. (1997) 'Issues in the study of the family', in J. Muncie, M. Wetherell, M. Langan, R. Dallos and A. Cochrane (eds) *Understanding the family* (2nd edn), London: Sage Publications, pp 7-38.

Muncie, J. and Wetherell, M. (1997) 'Family policy and political discourse', in J. Muncie, M. Wetherell, M. Langan, R. Dallos and A. Cochrane (eds) *Understanding the family* (2nd edn), London: Sage Publications, pp 39-80.

Munro, M. and Madigan, R. (1989) 'Do you ever think about us?', *Architects' Journal*, vols 25 and 26, p 58, 20 and 27 December.

Murie, A., Leather, P., Phillimore, J. and Revell, K. (2001) *Tenants' views of social rented housing*, Cardiff: National Assembly for Wales.

Murphy, M. (1996) 'Household and family structure among ethnic minority groups', in D. Coleman and J. Salt (eds) *Ethnicity in the 1991 census, Vol 1: Demographic characteristics of the ethnic minority populations*, London: The Stationery Office, pp 213-42.

Murphy, M. (1997) 'Changing in the living arrangements in Britain in the last quarter century: Insights from the General Household Survey', in O. Rowlands, N. Singleton, J. Maher and V. Higgins (eds) *Living in Britain: Results from the 1995 General Household Survey*, London: The Stationery Office, pp 178-89.

Murray, C. (1989) 'Underclass: a disaster in the making', *Sunday Times*, 26 November.

Murray, C. (1994) *Underclass: The crisis deepens*, London: IEA Health and Welfare Unit/*Sunday Times*.

Myers, D., Baer, E. and Seong-Youn Choi (1996) 'The changing problem of overcrowded housing', *American Planning Association Journal*, Winter, pp 66-83.

Nasar, J. (1993) 'Connotative meanings of house styles', in E. Arias (ed) *The meaning and use of home*, Aldershot: Avebury, pp 143-68.

Nettleton, S., Burrows, R., England, J. and Seavers, J. (1999) *Losing the family home: Understanding the social consequences of mortgage repossession*, York: Joseph Rowntree Foundation.

Newman, O. (1972) *Defensible space: Crime prevention through urban design*, New York, NY: Macmillan.

ODPM (Office of the Deputy Prime Minister) (2003a) *Housing and households: 2001 Census and other sources*, Housing Statistics Summary no 16, London: ODPM.

ODPM (2003b) *English house condition survey 2001: Building the picture*, London: ODPM.

ODPM (2003c) *Building sustainable communities: Building for the future*, London: The Stationery Office.

ODPM (2004) *Survey of English housing: Provisional results 2003/4*, Housing Statistics Summary no 23, London: ODPM.

ONS (Office for National Statistics) (1999) *Social focus on older people*, London: The Stationery Office.

ONS (2003) *Labour Force Survey*, London: The Stationery Office.

Oakley, A. (1974) *The sociology of housework*, Oxford: Martin Robertson.

Oakley, A. (1976) *Housewife*, Harmondsworth: Penguin.

Oldman, C. and Quilgars, D. (1999) 'The last resort? Revisiting ideas about older people's living arrangements', *Ageing and Society*, vol 19, pp 363-84.

Pahl, J. (1985) *Marital violence and public policy*, London: Routledge.

Pahl, J. (1989) *Money and marriage*, Basingstoke: Macmillan.

Palmer, G., Rahman, M. and Kenway, P. (2002) *Monitoring poverty and social exclusion 2002*, York: Joseph Rowntree Foundation.

Parsons, T. (1959) 'The social structure of the family', in R. Anshen (ed) *The family: Its functions and destiny*, New York, NY: Harper and Row, pp 241-74.

Percival, J. (2002) 'Domestic spaces: uses and meanings in the daily lives of older people', *Ageing and Society*, vol 22, pp 729-49.

Phelps, N. and Tewdwr-Jones, M. (2001) 'Globalisation, regions and the state: exploring the limitations of economic modernisation through inward investment', *Urban Studies*, vol 38, no 8, pp 1253-72.

Phillipson, C. (1998) *Reconstructing old age*, London: Sage Publications.

Phillipson, C., Bernard, M., Phillips, J. and Ogg, J. (1999) 'Older people in three urban areas: household composition, kinship and social networks', in S. McRae (ed) *Changing Britain: Families and households in the 1990s*, Oxford: Oxford University Press, pp 229-47.

Power, A. (1982) *Priority Estates Project 1982: Improving problem council estates*, London: DoE.

Power, A. (1987) *Property before people: The management of twentieth century council housing*, London: George Allen and Unwin.

Putnam, R. (1998) 'Foreword', *Housing Policy Debate*, vol 9, no 1, pp v-viii.

Randall, G. and Brown, S. (1996) *From street to home: An evaluation of phase 2 of the rough sleepers initiative*, London: The Stationery Office.

Ravetz, A. (2001) *Council housing and culture: The history of a social experiment*, London: Routledge.

Ravetz, A. and Turkington, R. (1995) *The place of home: English domestic environments 1914-2000*, London: Spon.

Revell, K. and Leather, P. (2000) *The state of UK housing: A fact file on housing conditions and housing renewal policies in the UK*, Bristol: The Policy Press.

Rex, J. and Moore, R. (1967) *Race, community and conflict*, Oxford: Oxford University Press.

Roberts, M. (1991) *Living in a man made world*, London: Routledge.

Robinson, R. and O'Sullivan, A. (1983) 'Housing tenure polarisation: some empirical evidence', *Housing Review*, vol 32, pp 116-17.

Rowlands, R. and Gurney, C. (2001) 'Young people's perceptions of housing tenure: a case study in the socialisation of tenure prejudice', *Housing Theory and Society*, vol 17, no 3, pp 121-30.

Rugg, J. (ed) (1999) *Young people, housing and social policy*, London: Routledge.

Rugg, J. and Burrows, R. (1999) 'Setting the context: young people, housing and social policy', in J. Rugg (ed) *Young people, housing and social policy*, London: Routledge, pp 1-16.

Rutter, M. and Madge, N. (1976) *Cycles of disadvantage: A review of research*, London: Heinemann.

Rijpers, B. and Meets, J. (1998) 'Housing challenge: managing neighbourhood image', Paper given at European Network for Housing Research Conference, Cardiff, September.

Sarre, P. (1986) 'Choice and constraint in ethnic minority housing: a structurationist view', *Housing Studies*, vol 1, pp 71-86.

Saunders, P. (1990) *A nation of home owners*, London: Unwin Hyman.

Sayer, A. (2000) *Realism and social science*, London: Sage Publications.

Scase, R. (1999) *Britain towards 2010:The changing business environment*, London: DTI.

Scottish Office Strategy Action Team (1999) *Inclusive communities*, Edinburgh: Scottish Executive.

Shilling, C. (1993) *The body and social theory*, London: Sage Publications.

Skifter Anderson, H. (2002) 'Excluded places: the interaction between segregation, urban decay and deprived neighbourhoods', *Housing Theory and Society*, vol 19, pp 153-69.

Smith, J., Gifford, S. and O'Sullivan, A. (1998) *The family background of homeless young people*, London: Family Policy Studies Centre.

Social Exclusion Unit (2000) *National strategy for neighbourhood renewal: A framework for consultation*, London: Cabinet Office.

Somerville, P. (1992) 'Homelessness and the meaning of home: rooflessness or rootlessness', *International Journal of Urban and Regional Research*, vol 16, no 4, pp 529-39.

Speak, S. (1999) 'Housing and young single parent families', J. Rugg (ed) *Young people, housing and social policy*, London: Routledge, pp 127-44.

Steger, M. (2003) *Globalization*, Oxford: Oxford University Press.

Stephens, M. (1995) 'Monetary policy and house price volatility in western Europe', *Housing Studies*, vol 10, pp 551-64.

Stephens, M. (2001) 'Building society demutualisation in the UK', *Housing Studies*, vol 16, no 3, pp 335-52.

Swenarton, M. (1981) *Homes fit for heroes*, London: Heinemann.

Taylor, D. (1998) 'Social identity and social policy: engagements with post modern theory', *Journal of Social Policy*, vol 27, no 3, pp 329-50.

Taylor, R. and Ford, G. (1981) 'Lifestyle and ageing', *Ageing and Society*, vol 1, pp 329-45.

Todd, J., Bone, M. and Noble, I. (1982) *The privately rented sector in 1978*, London: HMSO.

Townsend, P. (1962) *The last refuge*, London: Routledge and Kegan Paul.

Tulle-Winton, E. (1999) 'Growing old and resistance: towards a new cultural economy of old age?', *Ageing and Society*, vol 19, pp 281-99.

Twigg, J. (2000) *Bathing – the body and community care*, London: Routledge.

Tyne, A. (1982) 'Community care and mentally handicapped people', in A. Walker (ed) *Community care*, Oxford: Blackwell and Robertson, pp 141-58.

Urban Task Force (1999) *Towards an urban renaissance*, London: DETR.

Walker, A. (ed) (1982) *Community care*, Oxford: Blackwell and Robertson.

Walmesley, D. (1988) *Urban living: The individual in the city*, Harlow: Longman.

Waters, M. (1995) *Globalization*, London: Routledge.

Whitehead, C. (1994) 'Markets in the United Kingdom: introduction and update', *Housing Policy Debate*, vol 5, pp 231-40.

Wilcox, S. (2002) *Housing Finance Review 2002/3*, Coventry: Chartered Institute of Housing.

Wilcox, S. (2003) *Housing Finance Review 2003/4*, Coventry: Chartered Institute of Housing.

Willcocks, D., Peace, S. and Kellaher, L. (1987) *The residential life of older people*, London: Polytechnic of North London.

Williams, F. and Popay, J. (1999) 'Balancing polarities: developing a new framework for welfare research', in F. Williams, J. Popay and A. Oakley (eds) *Welfare research: A critical review*, London: UCL Press, pp 156-83.

Willmott, P. (1986) *Social networks, informal care and public policy*, London: Policy Studies Institute.

Wirth, L. (1938) 'Urbanism as a way of life', *American Journal of Sociology*, vol 44, no 1, pp 58-82.

Woodin, S., Delves, C. and Wadhams, C. (1996) *Just what the doctor ordered*, London: London Borough of Hackney.

Yen, M. (1993) 'The meaning and use of neighbourhood: spatial attributes and social dynamics', in E. Arias (ed) *The meaning and use of housing*, Aldershot: Avebury, pp 235-9.

Young, M. and Willmott, P. (1957) *Family and kinship in East London*, London: Routledge and Kegan Paul.

Young, M. and Willmott, P. (1975) *The symmetrical family*, Harmondsworth: Penguin.

Index

time, and social constructionism 23–4, 32,
33–4, 243–4
Townsend, P. 228
traditional nuclear families 40–4, 163–4,
170–1
and care of older people 214–15
demographic data 49
effects of flexible employment 67
and social policy 40–1, 42–3
young people leaving home 187
transitions in life, young people 186–8
travellers 45
Tudor Walters report 128–9
Tulle-Winton, E. 224
Twigg, J. 229–31
Tyne, A. 214, 232

U

underclass 170
and US ghettos 171
unemployment 67
'hidden' statistics 68
and regional variations 67–8
university education *see* higher and
further education; student lifestyles
urban regeneration discourses
job creation schemes 79–81
neighbourhood design issues 179–82
Urban Task Force (1999) 181–2

V

Victorian houses 128–9, 157
voluntary work, older people 233

W

Wales, unemployment rates 68
Walker, A. 215
Walmesley, D. 121
'warm bath theory' of the family
(Jorgensen) 40, 136
Waters, M. 11–12, 215
welfare benefits
and private tenants 77
and teenage mothers 48
as work disincentive 71, 93
Whitehead, C. 101
Wilcox, S. 68, 75, 101, 108, 112
Willcocks, D. et al 228
Williams, F. and Popay, J. 8
Willmott, P. 164–5, 176
Wirth, L. 163

women
employment 65
and relocation decisions 83, 84
and the family discourse 41–3, 54–5
single-person households 48–9
see also lone mothers; teenage pregnancy
Woodin, S. et al 121
working from home 133, 134, 142

Y

Yen, M. 157
young people
and homelessness 151–2, 201–10
support services and assistance 207–10
and leaving home 186–201
family attitudes 194–6
gender and ethnicity 189–90
home ownership aspirations 190,
191–2, 195
parental dependency 188–9
private rented accommodation 191–2
processes 193–201
public sector housing 192, 194
reasons 196–7
support services and assistance 193–4
relationships and housing 198–9
transition periods 186–8
and urban living 180–2
'youth' defined 187
Young, M. and Willmott, P. 43, 54–5, 162–
3, 167
youth, defined 187

Making it work
The keys to success for young people living independently
Jamie Harding

"Harding has made a bold contribution to current debates on routes out of homelessness and the role of structure and agency in shaping the lives of young people living independently. There is plenty of food for thought for those in policy, practice and research, seeking to improve the effectiveness of responses to youth homelessness." *Dr Isobel Anderson, Housing Policy and Practice Unit, University of Stirling*

This book evaluates the extensive and innovative range of housing services that have been developed for 16-17 year olds living in Newcastle. It provides vital indicators to other authorities and nominated RSLs of the approaches that they can take to increase successful tenancies and independent living among this age group.

Paperback £17.99 US$31.00 ISBN 1 86134 532 1
234 x 156mm 144 pages June 2004

Two steps forward
Housing policy into the new millennium
Edited by David Cowan and Alex Marsh

"... a stimulating collection of essays containing both practical observations and theoretical consideration of the basis and direction of New Labour's 'Third Way' in housing." *SCOLAG Legal Journal*

This book makes a distinctive and innovative contribution to the debate on housing policy. Bringing together leading scholars from the fields of housing law and housing policy, it engages with the central concerns of policy and demonstrates that the parallel debates of housing studies and socio-legal studies can be strengthened by a fuller exchange of ideas.

Paperback £19.99 US$32.50 ISBN 1 86134 229 2
Hardback £50.00 US$69.95 ISBN 1 86134 252 7
216 x 148mm 408 pages July 2001

The private rented sector in a new century
Revival or false dawn?
Edited by Stuart Lowe and David Hughes

"I am delighted to welcome a book that focuses on private rented housing and the role it continues to play in the housing market. The issues considered here will be of great interest to policy makers and those thinking about the development of housing law." *Martin Partington, Law Commissioner for England and Wales*

Against a century-long trend of decline, the private rented sector grew significantly during the 1990s. This book explores why and looks at the consequences for tenants and landlords, as well as the wider implications for housing policy.

Paperback £21.99 US$32.50 ISBN 1 86134 348 5
Hardback £50.00 US$69.95 ISBN 1 86134 349 3
234 x 156mm 240 pages September 2002

Immigration and homelessness in Europe
Bill Edgar, Joe Doherty and Henk Meert

This book makes a timely contribution to the current political and policy debate on immigration to Europe. Set within the context of immigrant social exclusion and marginalisation, it examines in detail the problematic relationship between migrants, their access to adequate housing and increasing vulnerability to homelessness.

Paperback £19.99 US$32.95 ISBN 1 86134 647 6
234 x 156mm 208 pages November 2004
Published in association with FEANTSA

Access to housing
Homelessness and vulnerability in Europe
Bill Edgar, Joe Doherty and Henk Meert

This comprehensive book offers the first EU wide examination of housing provision, its changing nature and impact on homelessness. It identifies the institutional changes and policy prescriptions that are necessary to manage the demands of homelessness and inadequate housing among Europe's most vulnerable people.

Paperback £19.99 US$32.50 ISBN 1 86134 482 1
234 x 156mm 176 pages October 2002
Published in association with FEANTSA

Women and homelessness in Europe
Pathways, services and experiences
Edited by Bill Edgar and Joe Doherty
Women have been neglected and marginalised in much contemporary
European housing policy and practice. Nowhere is this more apparent than in
the development of policies on homelessness. This book examines the gender-
specific factors leading to homelessness and the ability of women to access
appropriate services for rehousing and social integration.

Paperback £16.99 US$28.95 ISBN 1 86134 351 5

234 x 156mm 296 pages September 2001

Published in association with FEANTSA

Support and housing in Europe
Tackling social exclusion in the European Union
Bill Edgar, Joe Doherty and Amy Mina-Coull
This comprehensive study explores the development of designated 'supported
accommodation' and other social support mechanisms for vulnerable people in
Europe over the last two decades.

Paperback £16.99 US$28.95 ISBN 1 86134 275 6

234 x 156mm 240 pages September 2000

Published in association with FEANTSA

Services for homeless people
Innovation and change in the European Union
Bill Edgar, Joe Doherty and Amy Mina-Coull
This highly topical book provides a synthesis of developments in innovative service
provision for homeless people in the member countries of the European Union.

Paperback £14.99 US$26.95 ISBN 1 86134 189 X

234 x 156mm 244 pages July 1999

Published in association with FEANTSA

To order further copies of this publication or any other Policy Press titles please
visit **www.policypress.org.uk** or contact:

In the UK and Europe:
Marston Book Services, PO Box 269,
Abingdon, Oxon, OX14 4YN, UK
Tel: +44 (0)1235 465500
Fax: +44 (0)1235 465556
Email: direct.orders@marston.co.uk

In the USA and Canada:
ISBS, 920 NE 58th Street, Suite 300,
Portland, OR 97213-3786, USA
Tel: +1 800 944 6190 (toll free)
Fax: +1 503 280 8832
Email: info@isbs.com

In Australia and New Zealand:
DA Information Services, 648 Whitehorse Road
Mitcham, Victoria 3132, Australia
Tel: +61 (3) 9210 7777
Fax: +61 (3) 9210 7788
E-mail: service@dadirect.com.au

Further information about all of our titles can
be found on our website.